HELLGATE

LONDON

HELLGATE
LONDON

STORY Ian Edginton
ART Steve Pugh

☿

COLORS Dan Jackson
LETTERS Dave Lanphear
COVER Aleksi Briclot

Dark Horse Books®

PUBLISHER Mike Richardson

ART DIRECTOR Lia Ribacchi

DESIGNER Keith Wood

ASSISTANT EDITOR Katie Moody

EDITOR Dave Land

DARK HORSE COMICS, INC.
10956 SE MAIN STREET
MILWAUKIE, OR 97222

DARKHORSE.COM
HELLGATELONDON.COM

TO FIND A COMIC SHOP IN YOUR AREA CALL
THE COMIC SHOP LOCATOR SERVICE TOLL-FREE
AT (888) 266-4226

FIRST EDITION: JUNE 2007
ISBN-10: 1-59307-681-9
ISBN-13: 978-1-59307-681-8

10 9 8 7 6 5 4 3 2 1

PRINTED IN CHINA

HELLGATE LONDON

THIS BOOK COLLECTS ISSUES ZERO THROUGH THREE
OF THE COMIC-BOOK SERIES HELLGATE LONDON.

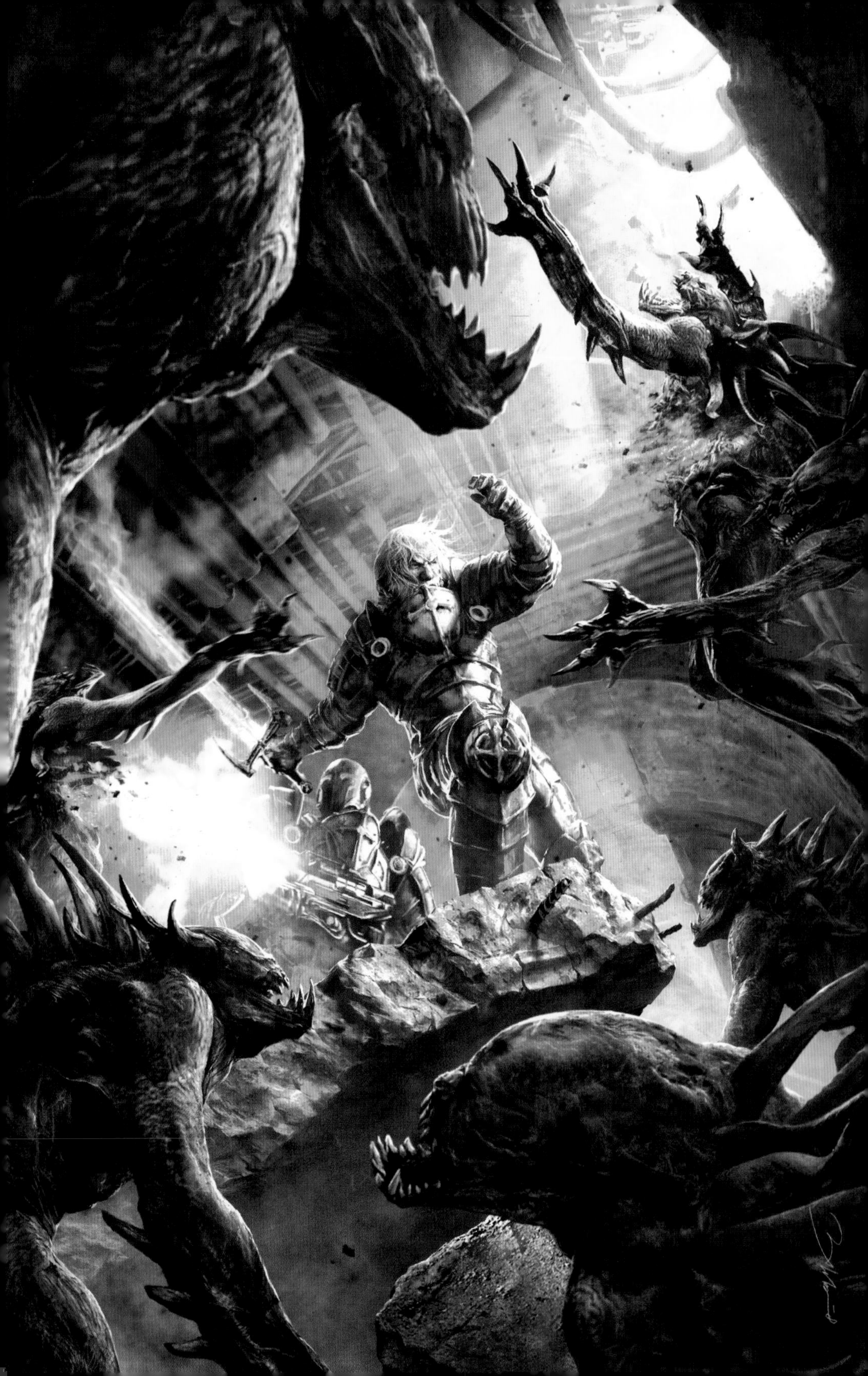

CHAPTER
One

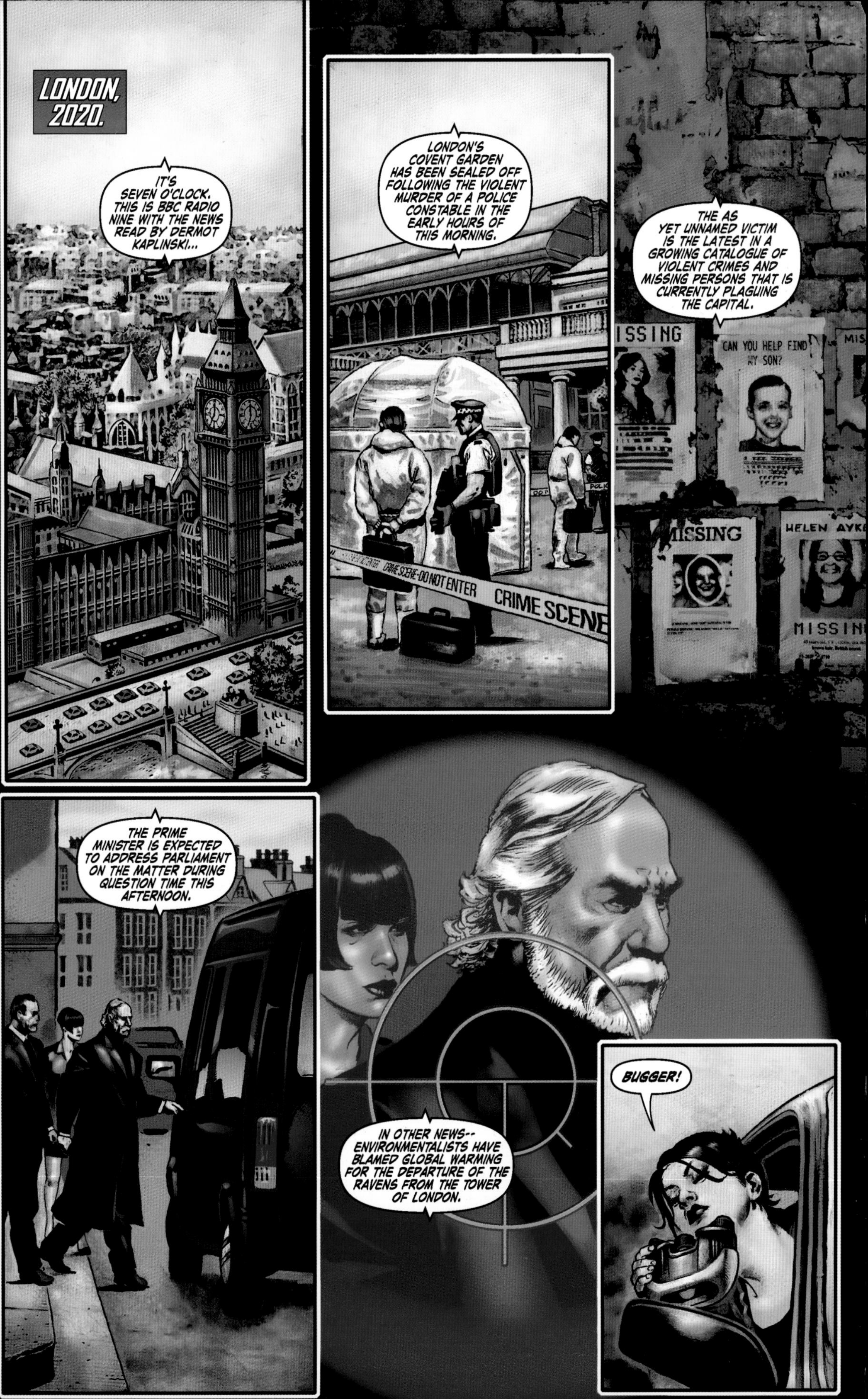
LONDON, 2020.
IT'S SEVEN O'CLOCK. THIS IS BBC RADIO NINE WITH THE NEWS READ BY DERMOT KAPLINSKI...
LONDON'S COVENT GARDEN HAS BEEN SEALED OFF FOLLOWING THE VIOLENT MURDER OF A POLICE CONSTABLE IN THE EARLY HOURS OF THIS MORNING.
CRIME SCENE-DO NOT ENTER
CRIME SCENE
THE AS YET UNNAMED VICTIM IS THE LATEST IN A GROWING CATALOGUE OF VIOLENT CRIMES AND MISSING PERSONS THAT IS CURRENTLY PLAGUING THE CAPITAL.
MISSING
CAN YOU HELP FIND MY SON?
MISSING
THE PRIME MINISTER IS EXPECTED TO ADDRESS PARLIAMENT ON THE MATTER DURING QUESTION TIME THIS AFTERNOON.
IN OTHER NEWS-- ENVIRONMENTALISTS HAVE BLAMED GLOBAL WARMING FOR THE DEPARTURE OF THE RAVENS FROM THE TOWER OF LONDON.
BUGGER!

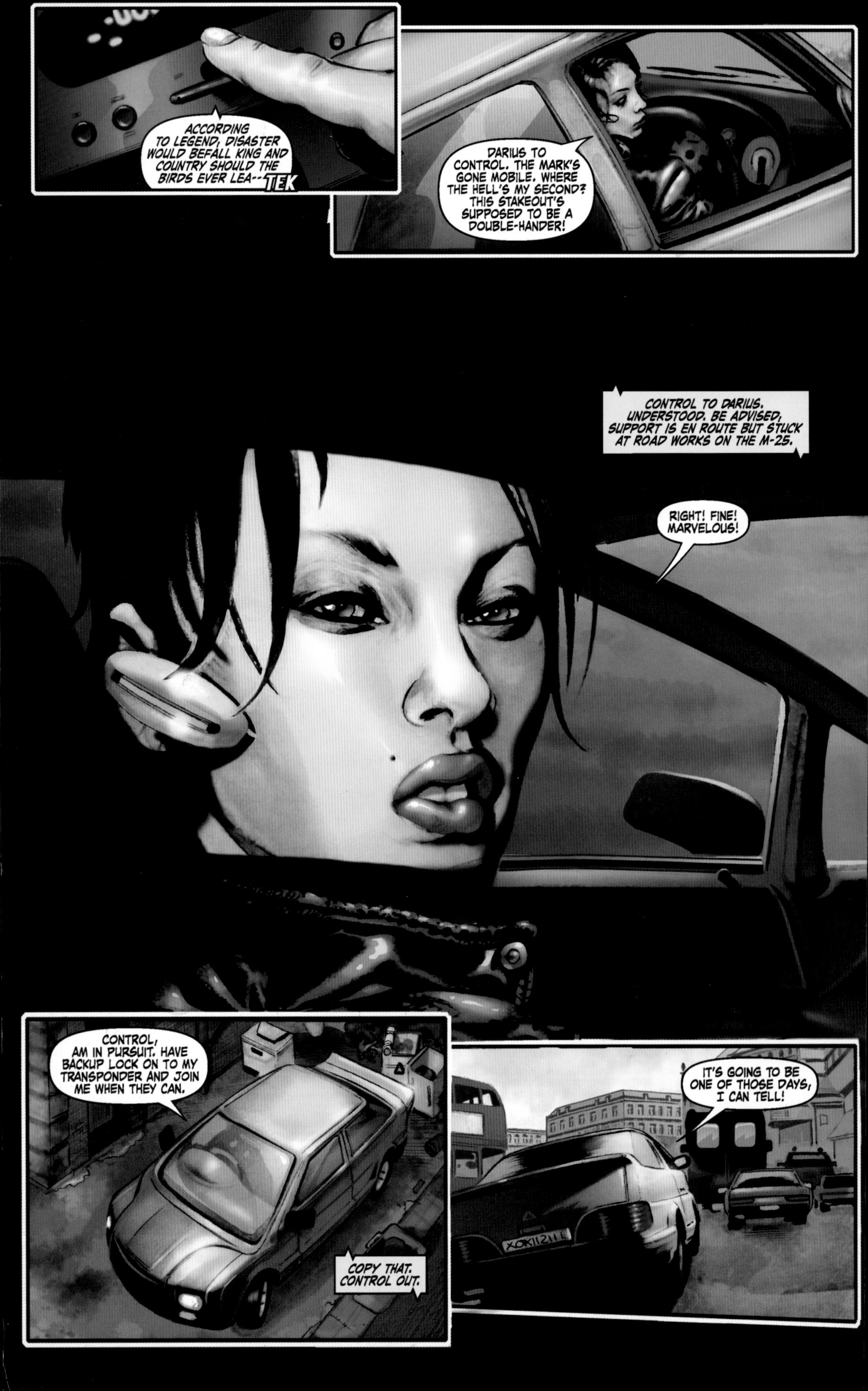
ACCORDING TO LEGEND, DISASTER WOULD BEFALL KING AND COUNTRY SHOULD THE BIRDS EVER LEA--
TEK
DARIUS TO CONTROL. THE MARK'S GONE MOBILE. WHERE THE HELL'S MY SECOND? THIS STAKEOUT'S SUPPOSED TO BE A DOUBLE-HANDER!
CONTROL TO DARIUS. UNDERSTOOD. BE ADVISED, SUPPORT IS EN ROUTE BUT STUCK AT ROAD WORKS ON THE M-25.
RIGHT! FINE! MARVELOUS!
CONTROL, AM IN PURSUIT. HAVE BACKUP LOCK ON TO MY TRANSPONDER AND JOIN ME WHEN THEY CAN.
COPY THAT. CONTROL OUT.
IT'S GOING TO BE ONE OF THOSE DAYS, I CAN TELL!

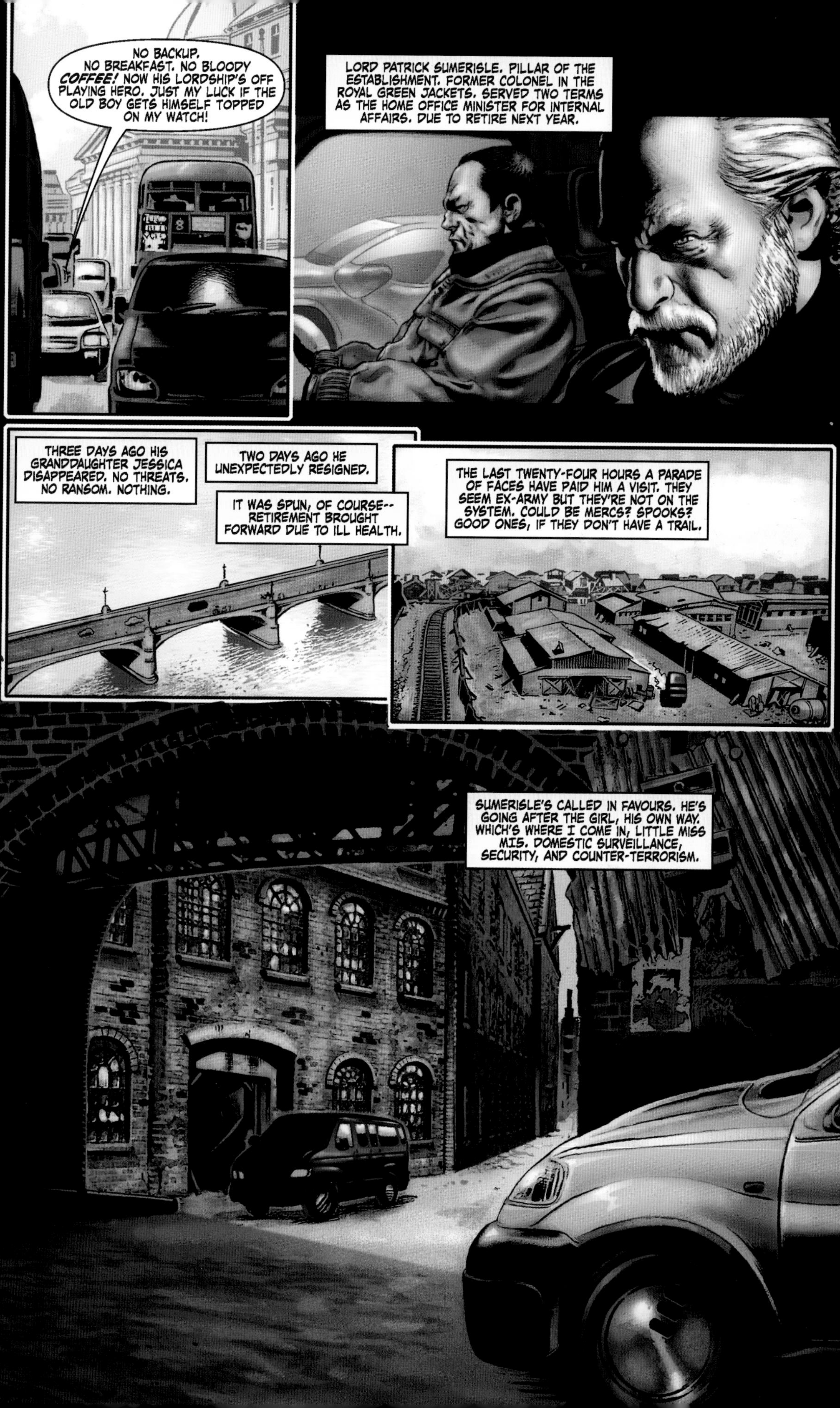
NO BACKUP. NO BREAKFAST. NO BLOODY *COFFEE!* NOW HIS LORDSHIP'S OFF PLAYING HERO. JUST MY LUCK IF THE OLD BOY GETS HIMSELF TOPPED ON MY WATCH!
LORD PATRICK SUMERISLE. PILLAR OF THE ESTABLISHMENT. FORMER COLONEL IN THE ROYAL GREEN JACKETS. SERVED TWO TERMS AS THE HOME OFFICE MINISTER FOR INTERNAL AFFAIRS. DUE TO RETIRE NEXT YEAR.
THREE DAYS AGO HIS GRANDDAUGHTER JESSICA DISAPPEARED. NO THREATS. NO RANSOM. NOTHING.
TWO DAYS AGO HE UNEXPECTEDLY RESIGNED.
IT WAS SPUN, OF COURSE-- RETIREMENT BROUGHT FORWARD DUE TO ILL HEALTH.
THE LAST TWENTY-FOUR HOURS A PARADE OF FACES HAVE PAID HIM A VISIT. THEY SEEM EX-ARMY BUT THEY'RE NOT ON THE SYSTEM. COULD BE MERCS? SPOOKS? GOOD ONES, IF THEY DON'T HAVE A TRAIL.
SUMERISLE'S CALLED IN FAVOURS. HE'S GOING AFTER THE GIRL, HIS OWN WAY. WHICH'S WHERE I COME IN, LITTLE MISS MI5. DOMESTIC SURVEILLANCE, SECURITY, AND COUNTER-TERRORISM.

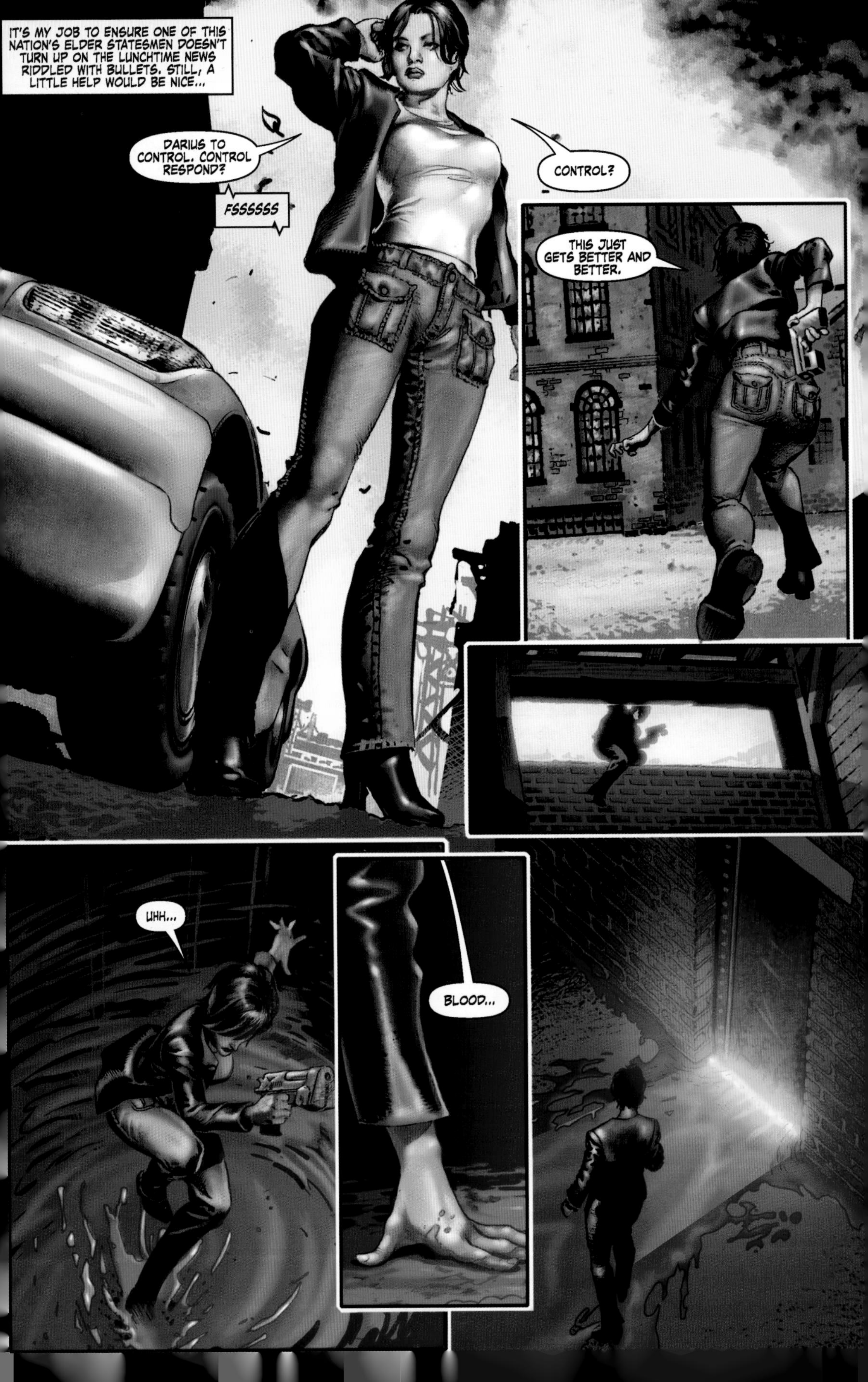
IT'S MY JOB TO ENSURE ONE OF THIS NATION'S ELDER STATESMEN DOESN'T TURN UP ON THE LUNCHTIME NEWS RIDDLED WITH BULLETS. STILL, A LITTLE HELP WOULD BE NICE...
DARIUS TO CONTROL. CONTROL RESPOND?
FSSSSSS
CONTROL?
THIS JUST GETS BETTER AND BETTER.
UHH...
BLOOD...

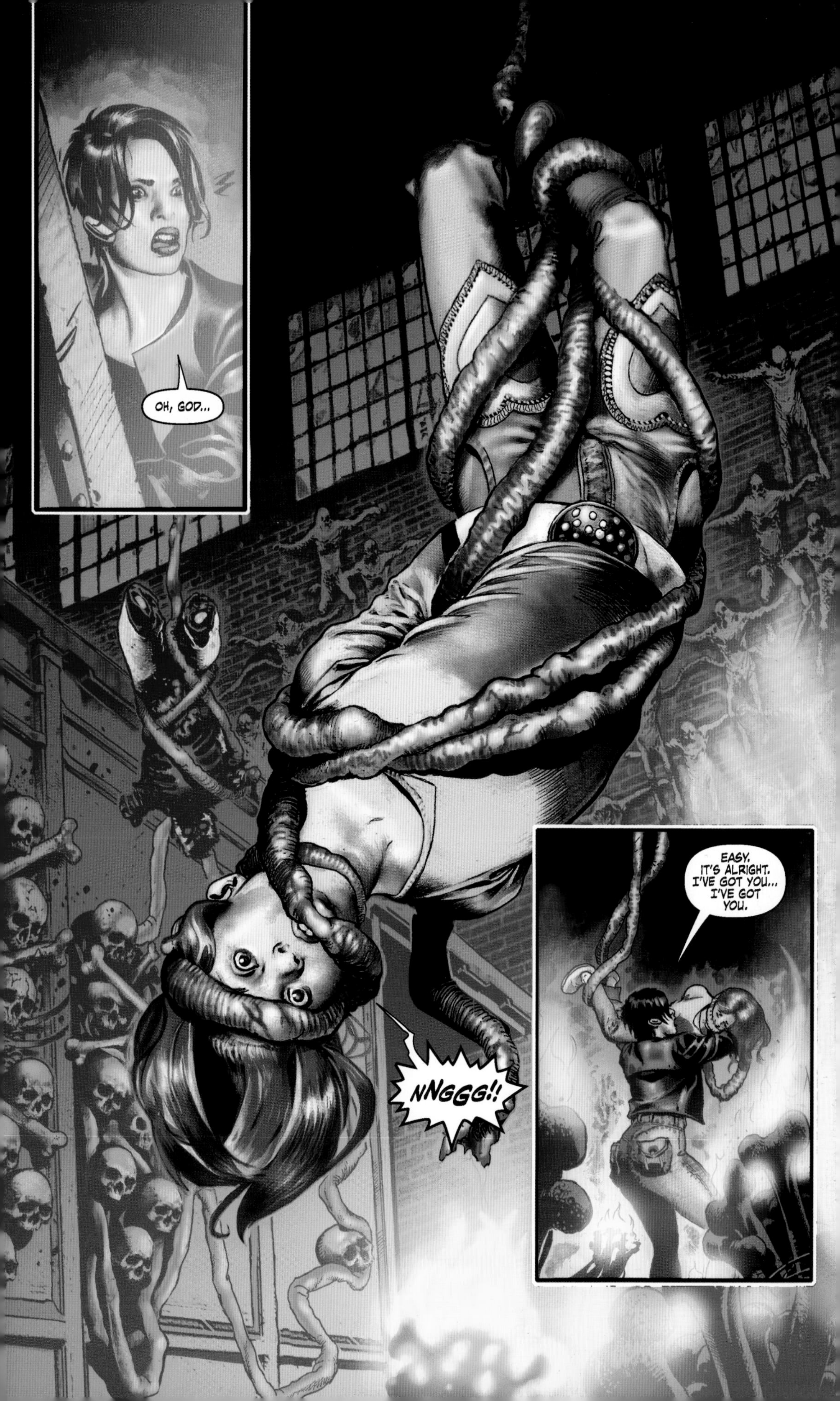
OH, GOD...
NNGGG!!
EASY. IT'S ALRIGHT. I'VE GOT YOU... I'VE GOT YOU.

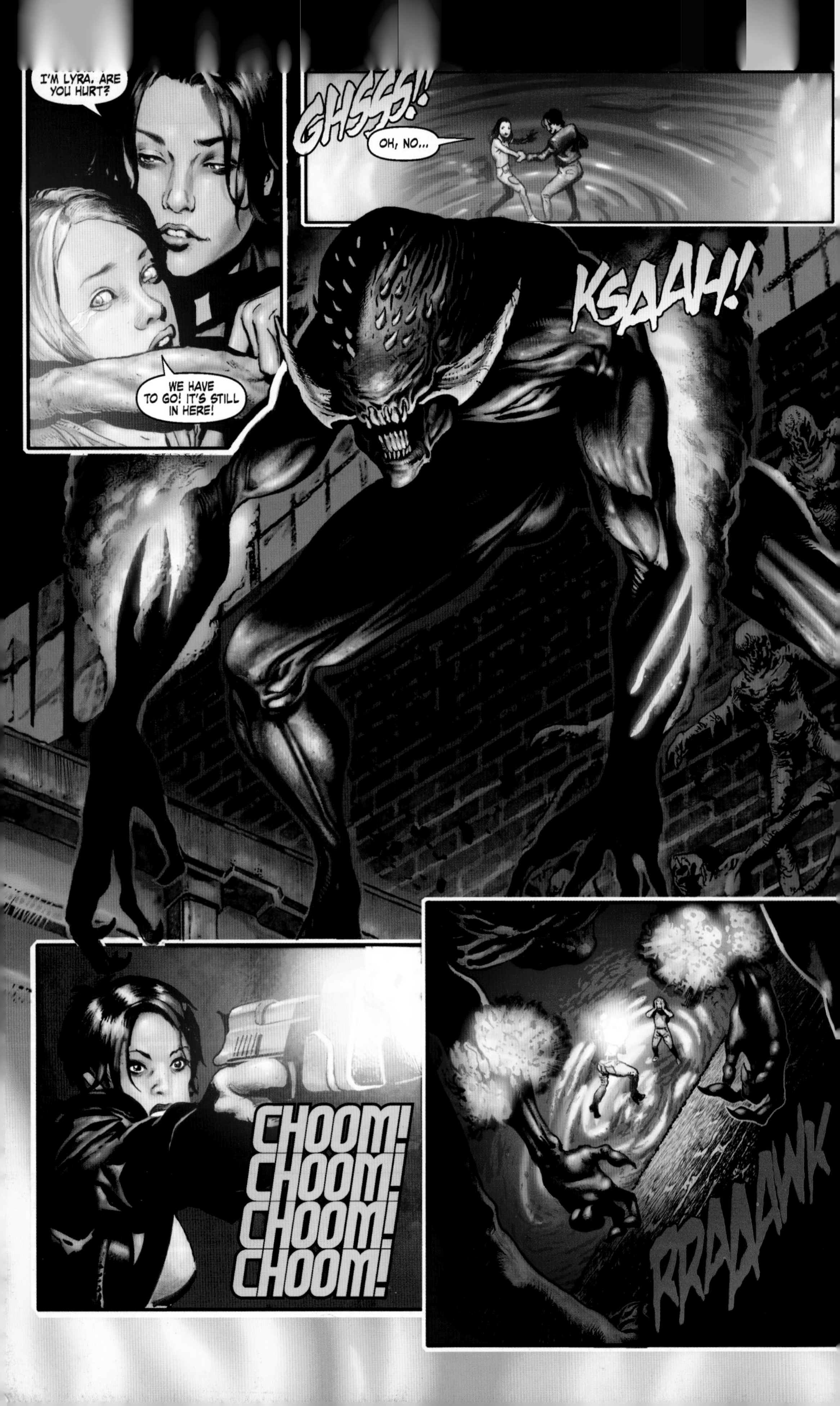

I'M LYRA. ARE YOU HURT?
WE HAVE TO GO! IT'S STILL IN HERE!
GHSSS!
OH, NO...
KSAAH!
CHOOM! CHOOM! CHOOM! CHOOM!
RRAAAWK

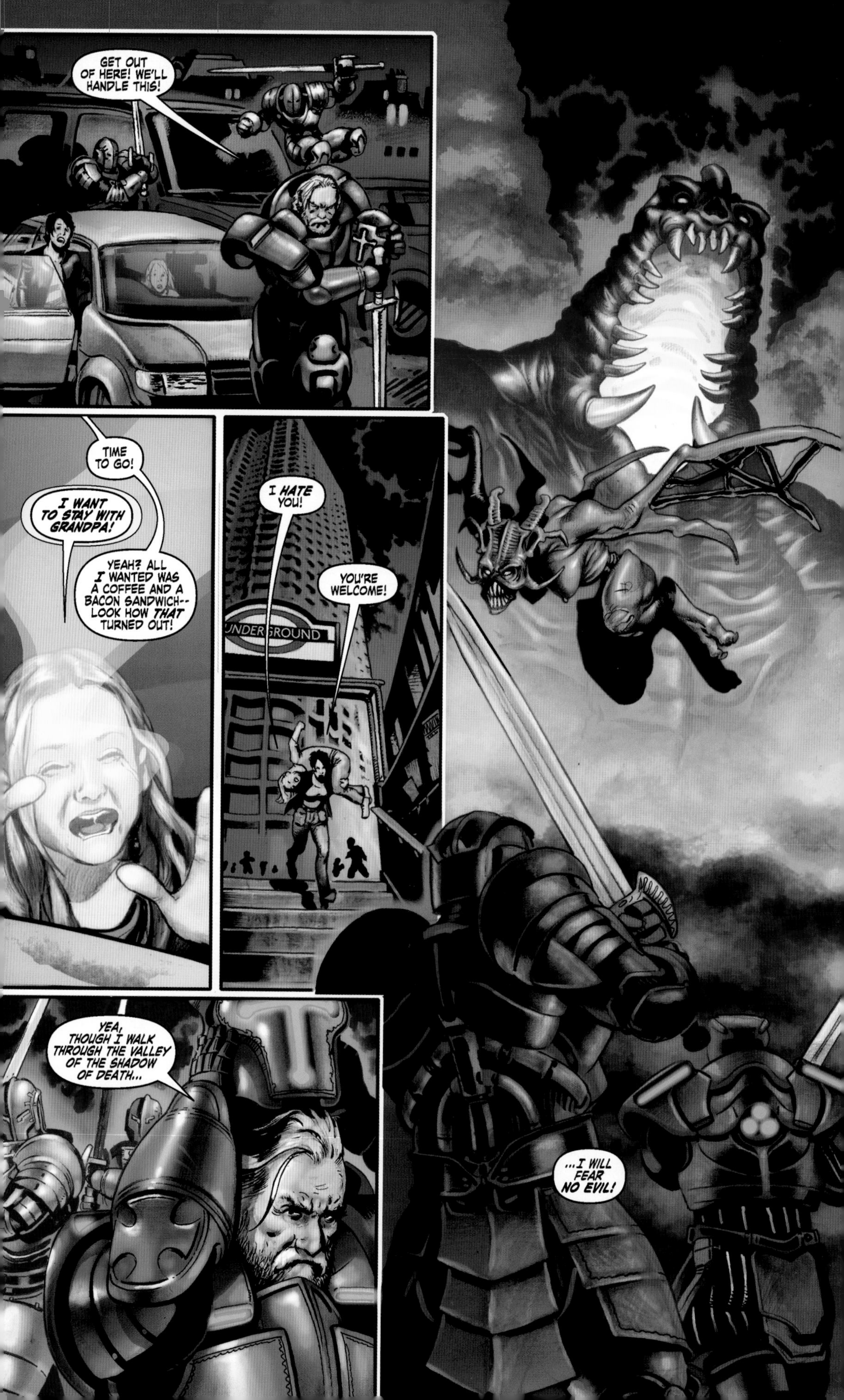

GET OUT OF HERE! WE'LL HANDLE THIS!
TIME TO GO!
I WANT TO STAY WITH GRANDPA!
YEAH? ALL I WANTED WAS A COFFEE AND A BACON SANDWICH-- LOOK HOW THAT TURNED OUT!
I HATE YOU!
YOU'RE WELCOME!
UNDERGROUND
YEA, THOUGH I WALK THROUGH THE VALLEY OF THE SHADOW OF DEATH...
...I WILL FEAR NO EVIL!

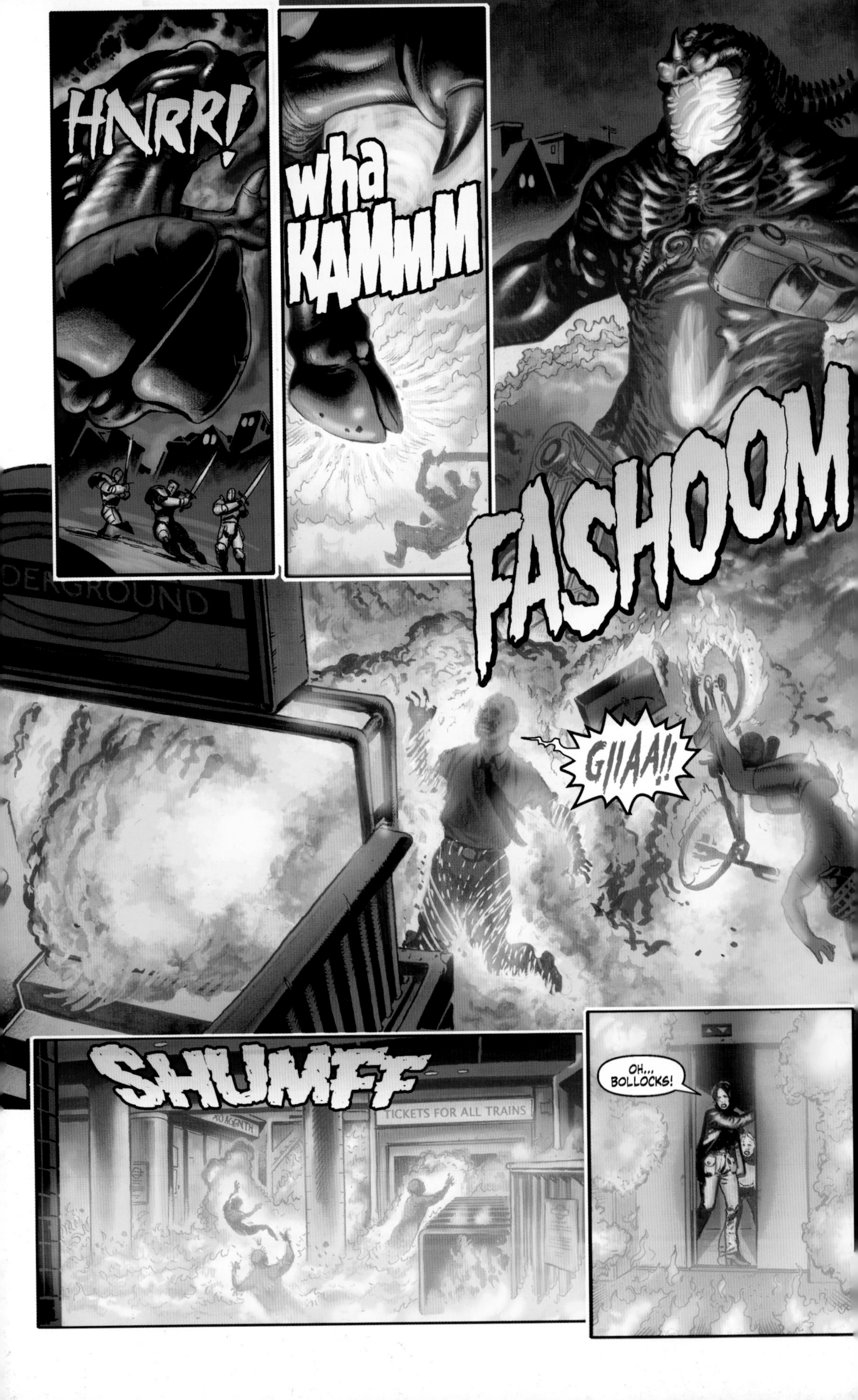
HNRR!
wha KAMMMM
FASHOOM
DERGROUND
G!!AA!!
SHUMFF
TICKETS FOR ALL TRAINS
OH... BOLLOCKS!

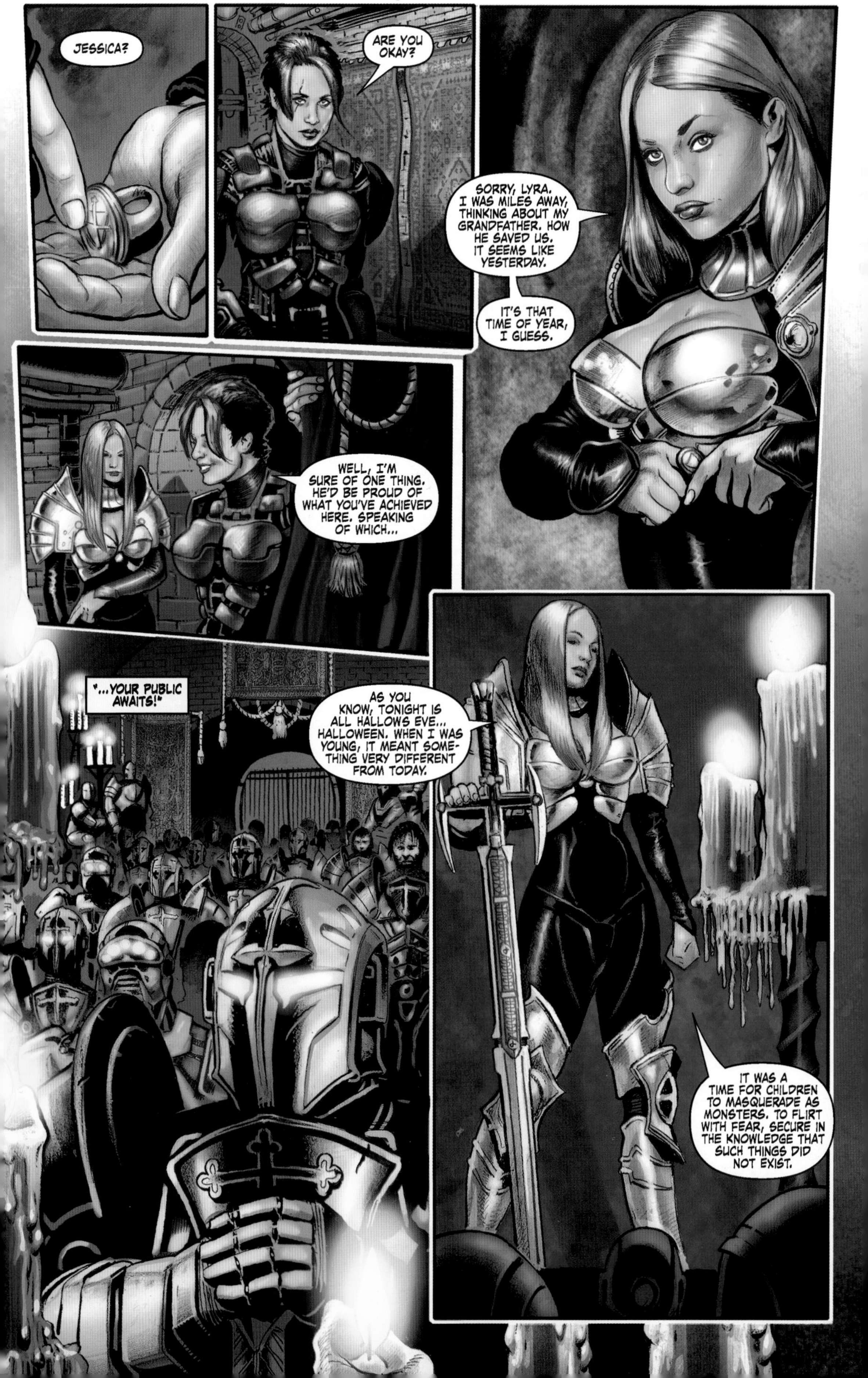
JESSICA?
ARE YOU OKAY?
SORRY, LYRA. I WAS MILES AWAY, THINKING ABOUT MY GRANDFATHER. HOW HE SAVED US. IT SEEMS LIKE YESTERDAY.
IT'S THAT TIME OF YEAR, I GUESS.
WELL, I'M SURE OF ONE THING. HE'D BE PROUD OF WHAT YOU'VE ACHIEVED HERE. SPEAKING OF WHICH...
"...YOUR PUBLIC AWAITS!"
AS YOU KNOW, TONIGHT IS ALL HALLOWS EVE... HALLOWEEN. WHEN I WAS YOUNG, IT MEANT SOME-THING VERY DIFFERENT FROM TODAY.
IT WAS A TIME FOR CHILDREN TO MASQUERADE AS MONSTERS. TO FLIRT WITH FEAR, SECURE IN THE KNOWLEDGE THAT SUCH THINGS DID NOT EXIST.

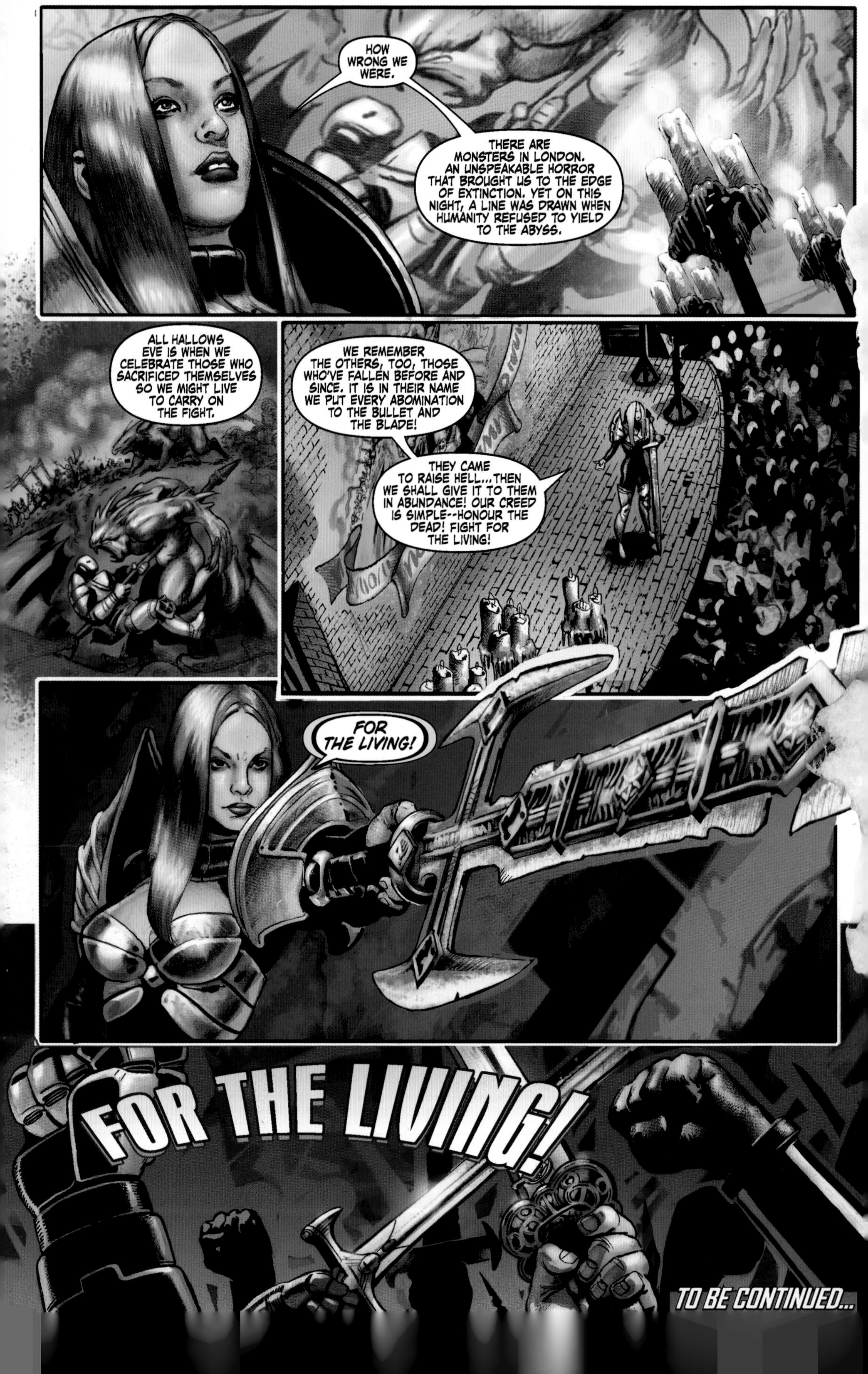
HOW WRONG WE WERE.
THERE ARE MONSTERS IN LONDON. AN UNSPEAKABLE HORROR THAT BROUGHT US TO THE EDGE OF EXTINCTION. YET ON THIS NIGHT, A LINE WAS DRAWN WHEN HUMANITY REFUSED TO YIELD TO THE ABYSS.
ALL HALLOWS EVE IS WHEN WE CELEBRATE THOSE WHO SACRIFICED THEMSELVES SO WE MIGHT LIVE TO CARRY ON THE FIGHT.
WE REMEMBER THE OTHERS, TOO, THOSE WHO'VE FALLEN BEFORE AND SINCE. IT IS IN THEIR NAME WE PUT EVERY ABOMINATION TO THE BULLET AND THE BLADE!
THEY CAME TO RAISE HELL...THEN WE SHALL GIVE IT TO THEM IN ABUNDANCE! OUR CREED IS SIMPLE--HONOUR THE DEAD! FIGHT FOR THE LIVING!
FOR THE LIVING!
FOR THE LIVING!
TO BE CONTINUED...

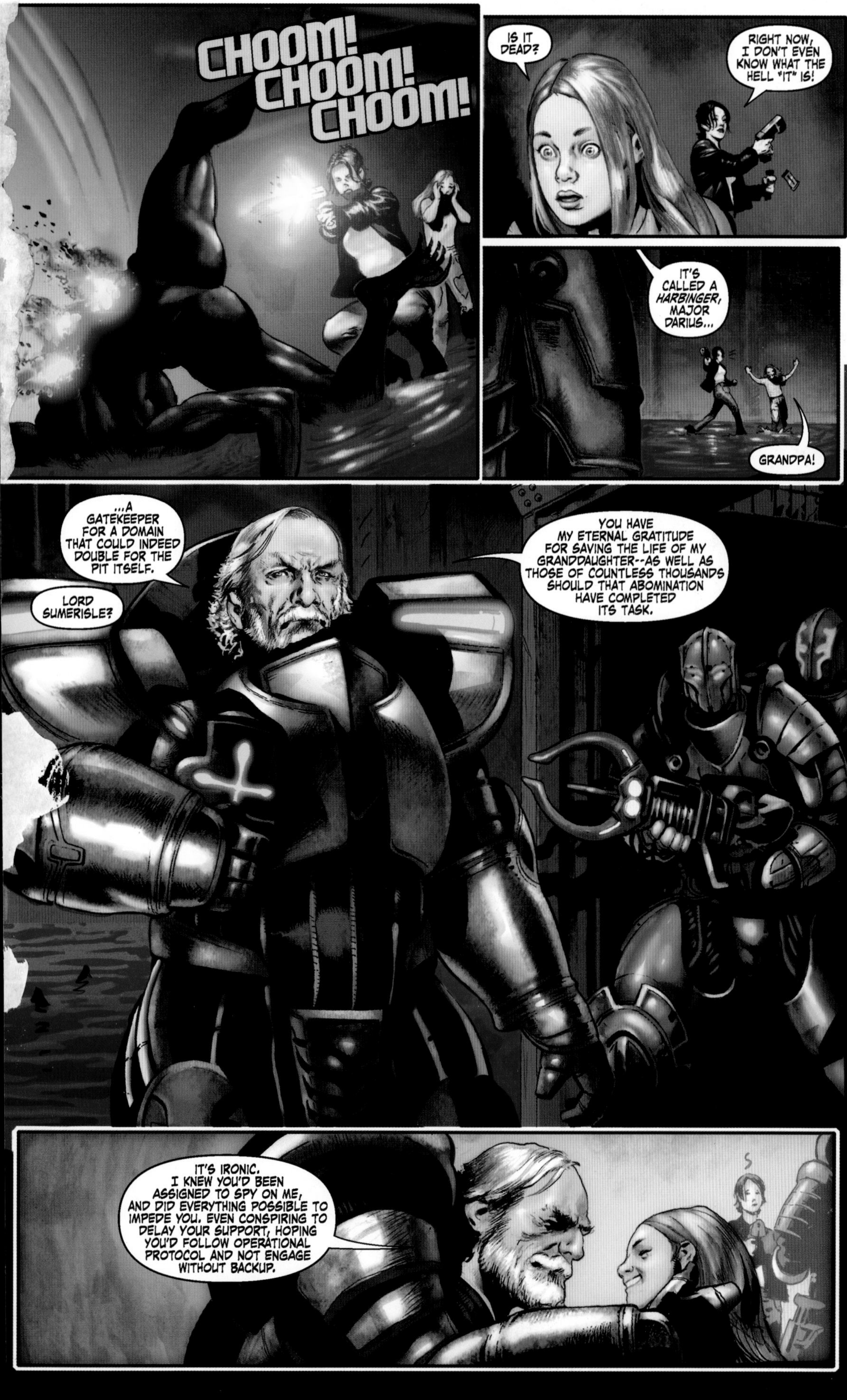
CHOOM! CHOOM! CHOOM!
IS IT DEAD?
RIGHT NOW, I DON'T EVEN KNOW WHAT THE HELL "IT" IS!
IT'S CALLED A *HARBINGER*, MAJOR DARIUS...
GRANDPA!
...A GATEKEEPER FOR A DOMAIN THAT COULD INDEED DOUBLE FOR THE PIT ITSELF.
LORD SUMERISLE?
YOU HAVE MY ETERNAL GRATITUDE FOR SAVING THE LIFE OF MY GRANDDAUGHTER--AS WELL AS THOSE OF COUNTLESS THOUSANDS SHOULD THAT ABOMINATION HAVE COMPLETED ITS TASK.
IT'S IRONIC. I KNEW YOU'D BEEN ASSIGNED TO SPY ON ME, AND DID EVERYTHING POSSIBLE TO IMPEDE YOU. EVEN CONSPIRING TO DELAY YOUR SUPPORT, HOPING YOU'D FOLLOW OPERATIONAL PROTOCOL AND NOT ENGAGE WITHOUT BACKUP.

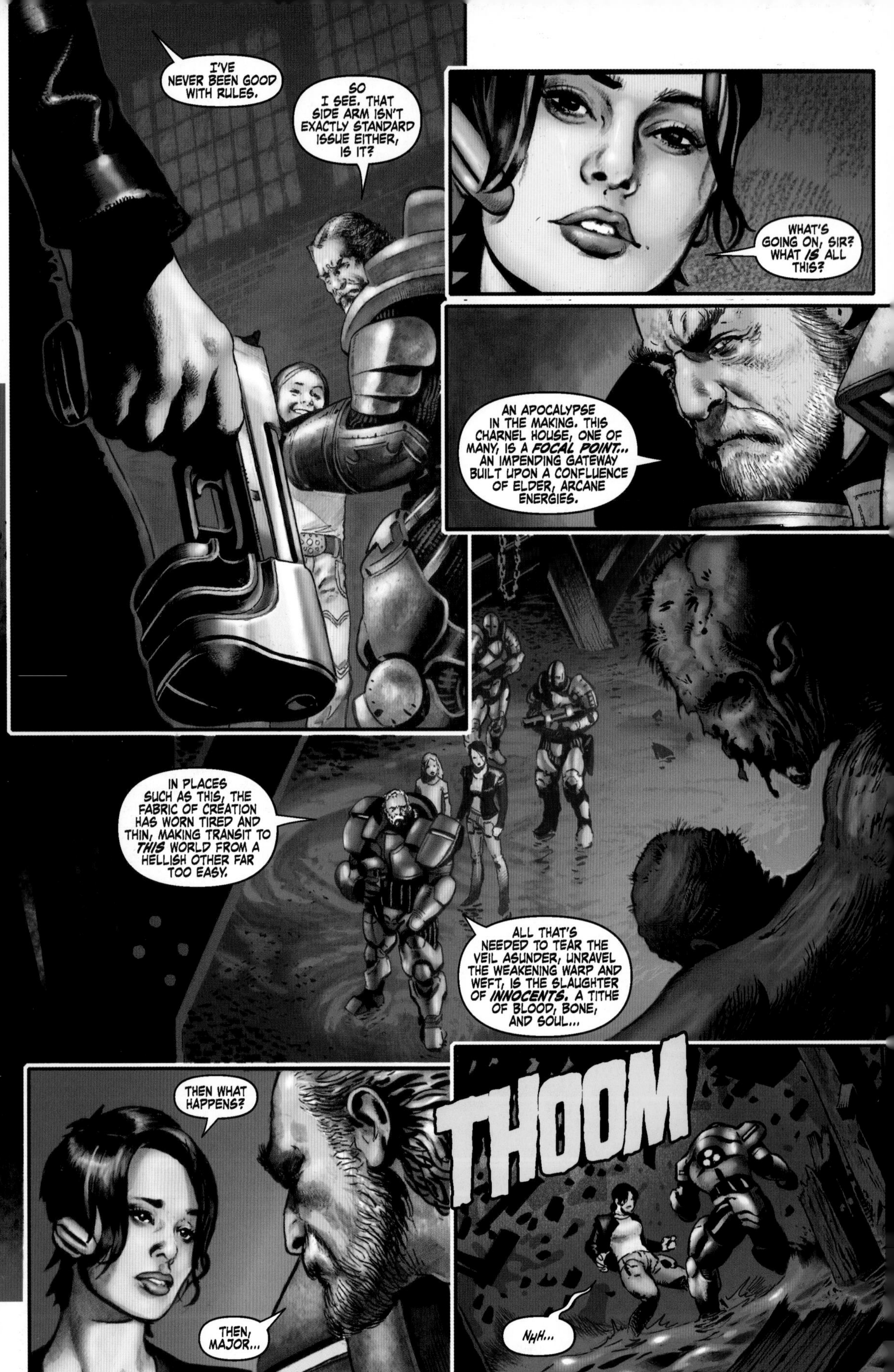

I'VE NEVER BEEN GOOD WITH RULES.
SO I SEE. THAT SIDE ARM ISN'T EXACTLY STANDARD ISSUE EITHER, IS IT?
WHAT'S GOING ON, SIR? WHAT *IS* ALL THIS?
AN APOCALYPSE IN THE MAKING. THIS CHARNEL HOUSE, ONE OF MANY, IS A *FOCAL POINT...* AN IMPENDING GATEWAY BUILT UPON A CONFLUENCE OF ELDER, ARCANE ENERGIES.
IN PLACES SUCH AS THIS, THE FABRIC OF CREATION HAS WORN TIRED AND THIN, MAKING TRANSIT TO *THIS* WORLD FROM A HELLISH OTHER FAR TOO EASY.
ALL THAT'S NEEDED TO TEAR THE VEIL ASUNDER, UNRAVEL THE WEAKENING WARP AND WEFT, IS THE SLAUGHTER OF *INNOCENTS.* A TITHE OF BLOOD, BONE, AND SOUL...
THEN WHAT HAPPENS?
THEN, MAJOR...
THOOM
NHH...

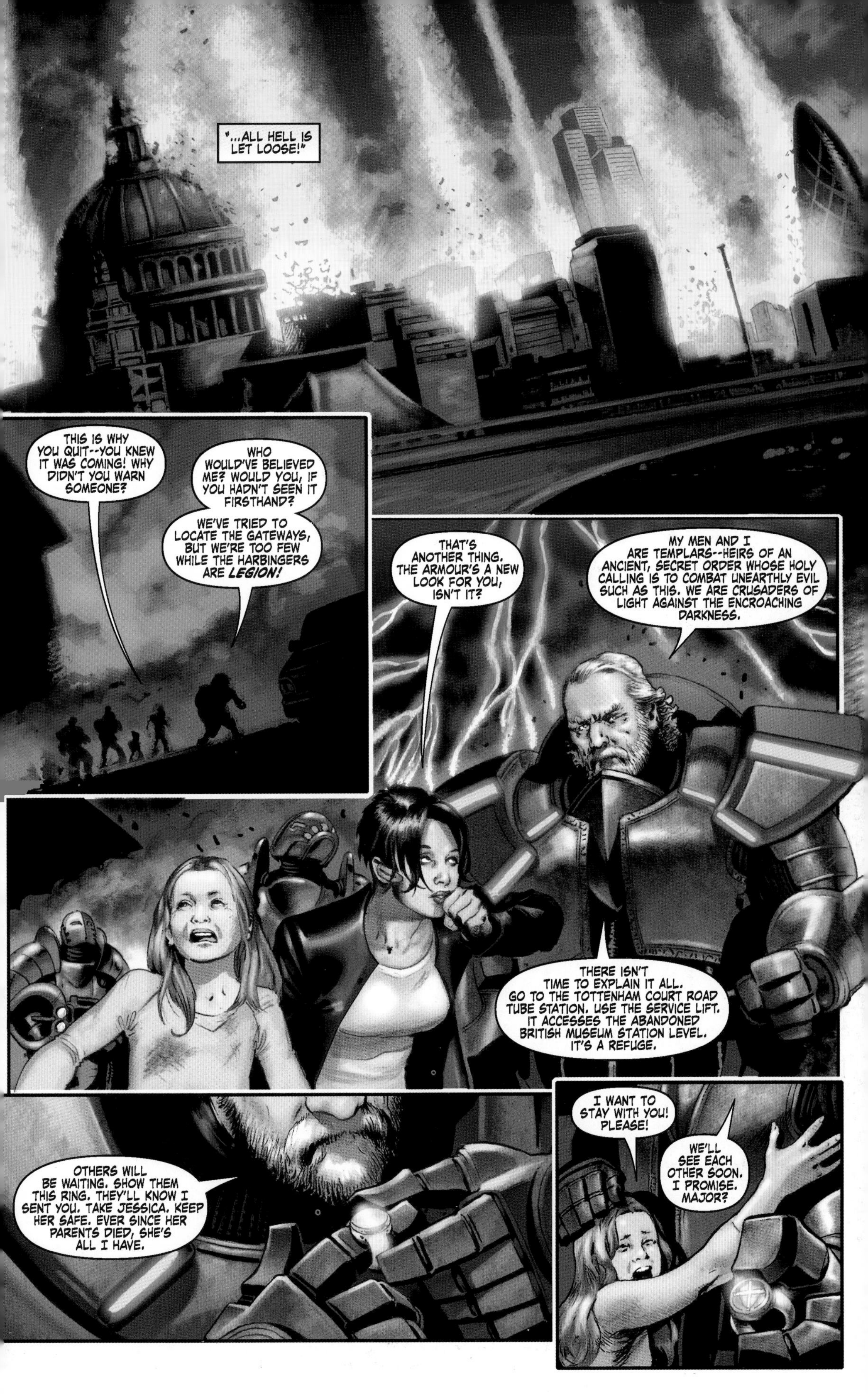
"...ALL HELL IS LET LOOSE!"
THIS IS WHY YOU QUIT--YOU KNEW IT WAS COMING! WHY DIDN'T YOU WARN SOMEONE?
WHO WOULD'VE BELIEVED ME? WOULD YOU, IF YOU HADN'T SEEN IT FIRSTHAND?
WE'VE TRIED TO LOCATE THE GATEWAYS, BUT WE'RE TOO FEW WHILE THE HARBINGERS ARE *LEGION!*
THAT'S ANOTHER THING. THE ARMOUR'S A NEW LOOK FOR YOU, ISN'T IT?
MY MEN AND I ARE TEMPLARS--HEIRS OF AN ANCIENT, SECRET ORDER WHOSE HOLY CALLING IS TO COMBAT UNEARTHLY EVIL SUCH AS THIS. WE ARE CRUSADERS OF LIGHT AGAINST THE ENCROACHING DARKNESS.
THERE ISN'T TIME TO EXPLAIN IT ALL. GO TO THE TOTTENHAM COURT ROAD TUBE STATION. USE THE SERVICE LIFT. IT ACCESSES THE ABANDONED BRITISH MUSEUM STATION LEVEL. IT'S A REFUGE.
OTHERS WILL BE WAITING. SHOW THEM THIS RING. THEY'LL KNOW I SENT YOU. TAKE JESSICA. KEEP HER SAFE. EVER SINCE HER PARENTS DIED, SHE'S ALL I HAVE.
I WANT TO STAY WITH YOU! PLEASE!
WE'LL SEE EACH OTHER SOON. I PROMISE. MAJOR?

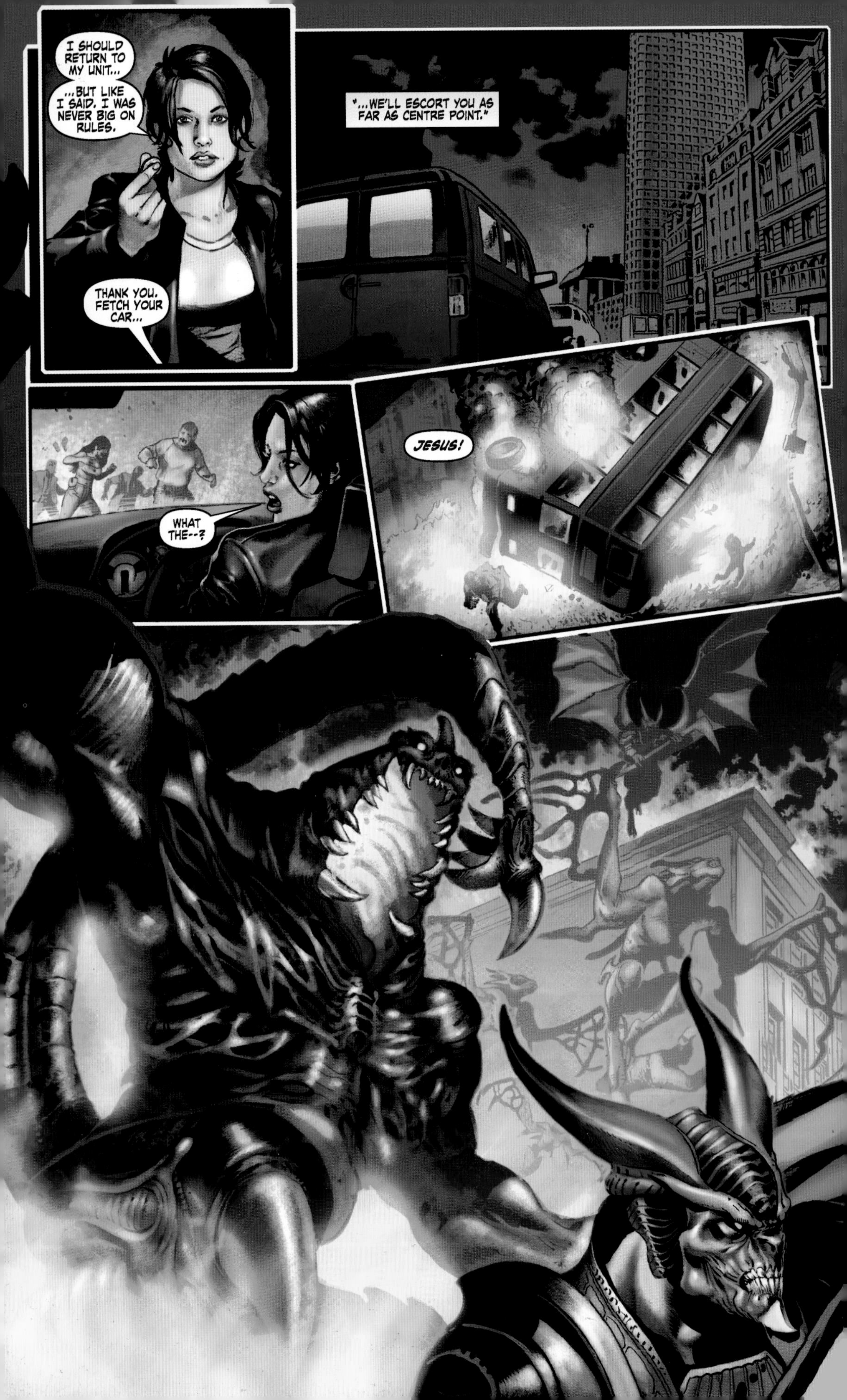
I SHOULD RETURN TO MY UNIT...
...BUT LIKE I SAID, I WAS NEVER BIG ON RULES.
THANK YOU. FETCH YOUR CAR...
"...WE'LL ESCORT YOU AS FAR AS CENTRE POINT."
WHAT THE--?
JESUS!

Chapter Two

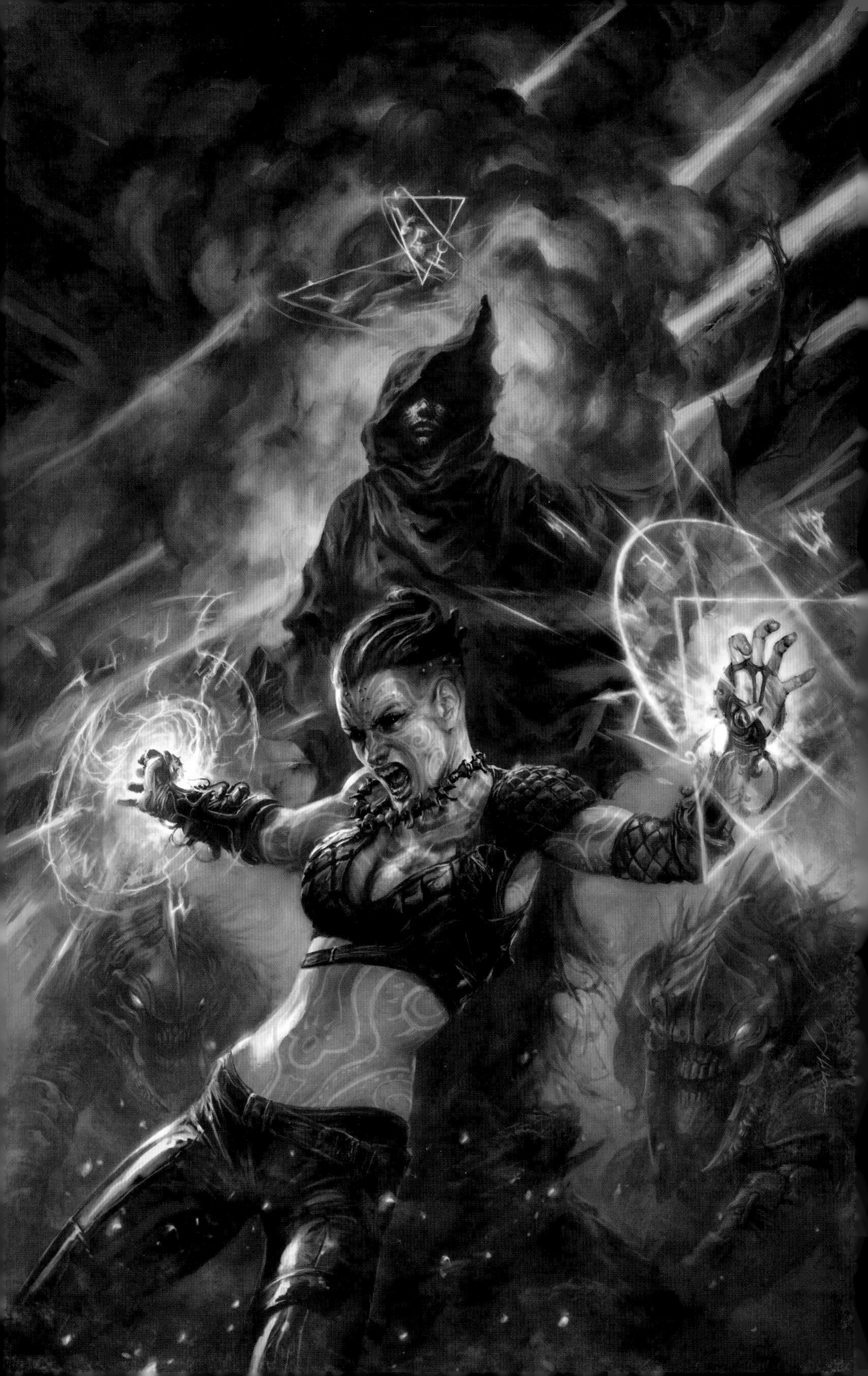

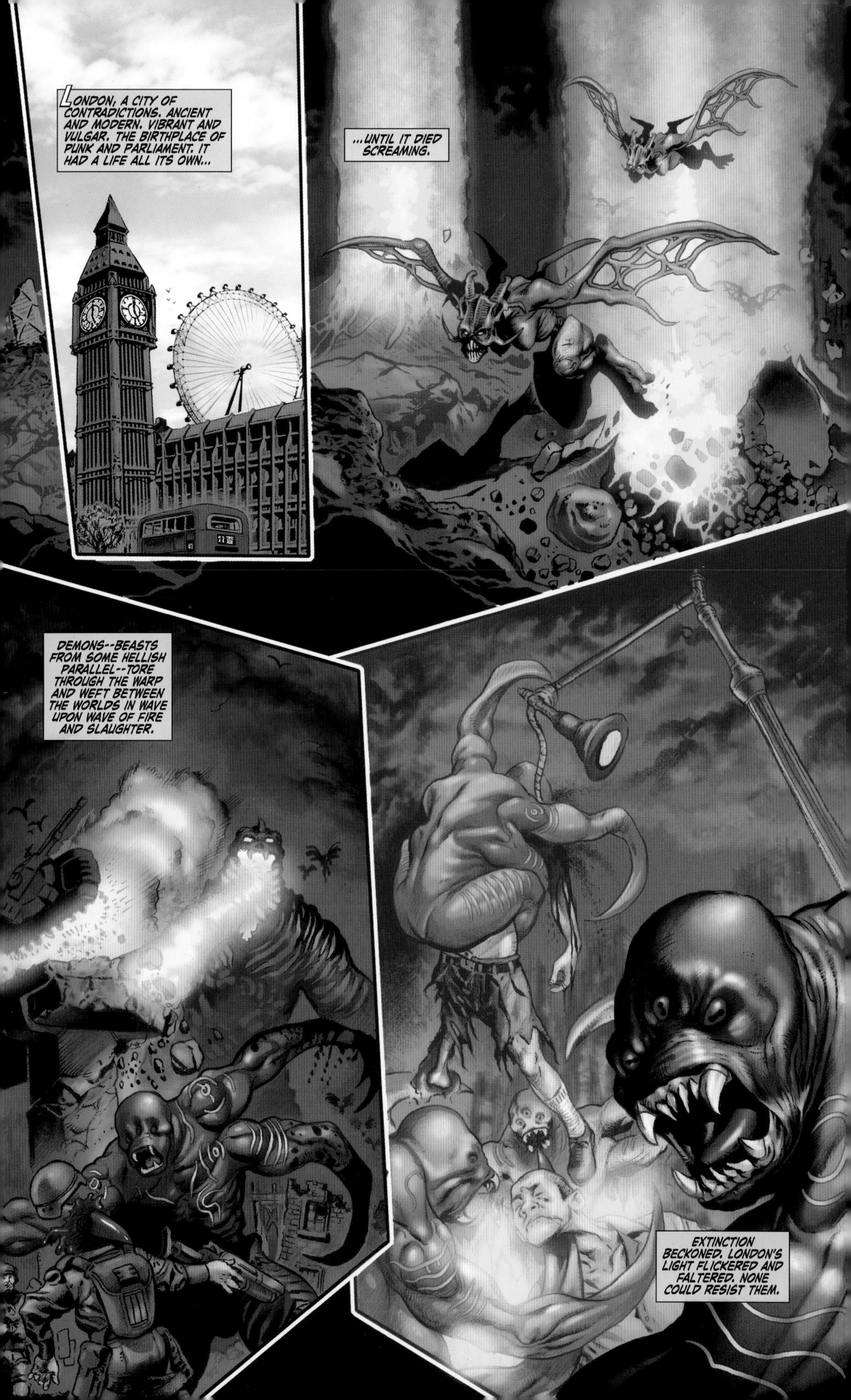
LONDON, A CITY OF CONTRADICTIONS. ANCIENT AND MODERN. VIBRANT AND VULGAR. THE BIRTHPLACE OF PUNK AND PARLIAMENT. IT HAD A LIFE ALL ITS OWN...
...UNTIL IT DIED SCREAMING.
DEMONS--BEASTS FROM SOME HELLISH PARALLEL--TORE THROUGH THE WARP AND WEFT BETWEEN THE WORLDS IN WAVE UPON WAVE OF FIRE AND SLAUGHTER.
EXTINCTION BECKONED. LONDON'S LIGHT FLICKERED AND FALTERED. NONE COULD RESIST THEM.

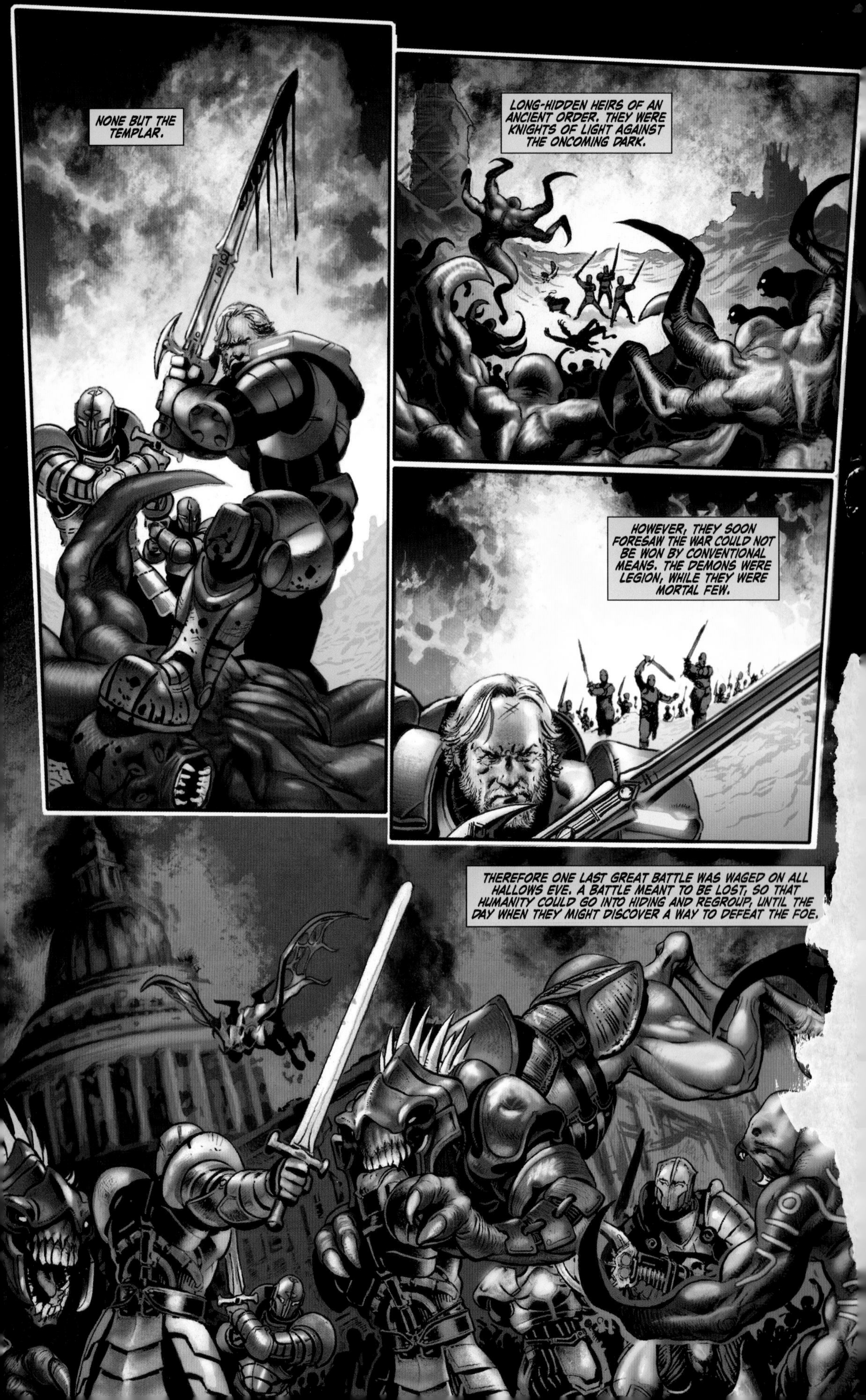
NONE BUT THE TEMPLAR.
LONG-HIDDEN HEIRS OF AN ANCIENT ORDER. THEY WERE KNIGHTS OF LIGHT AGAINST THE ONCOMING DARK.
HOWEVER, THEY SOON FORESAW THE WAR COULD NOT BE WON BY CONVENTIONAL MEANS. THE DEMONS WERE LEGION, WHILE THEY WERE MORTAL FEW.
THEREFORE ONE LAST GREAT BATTLE WAS WAGED ON ALL HALLOWS EVE. A BATTLE MEANT TO BE LOST, SO THAT HUMANITY COULD GO INTO HIDING AND REGROUP, UNTIL THE DAY WHEN THEY MIGHT DISCOVER A WAY TO DEFEAT THE FOE.

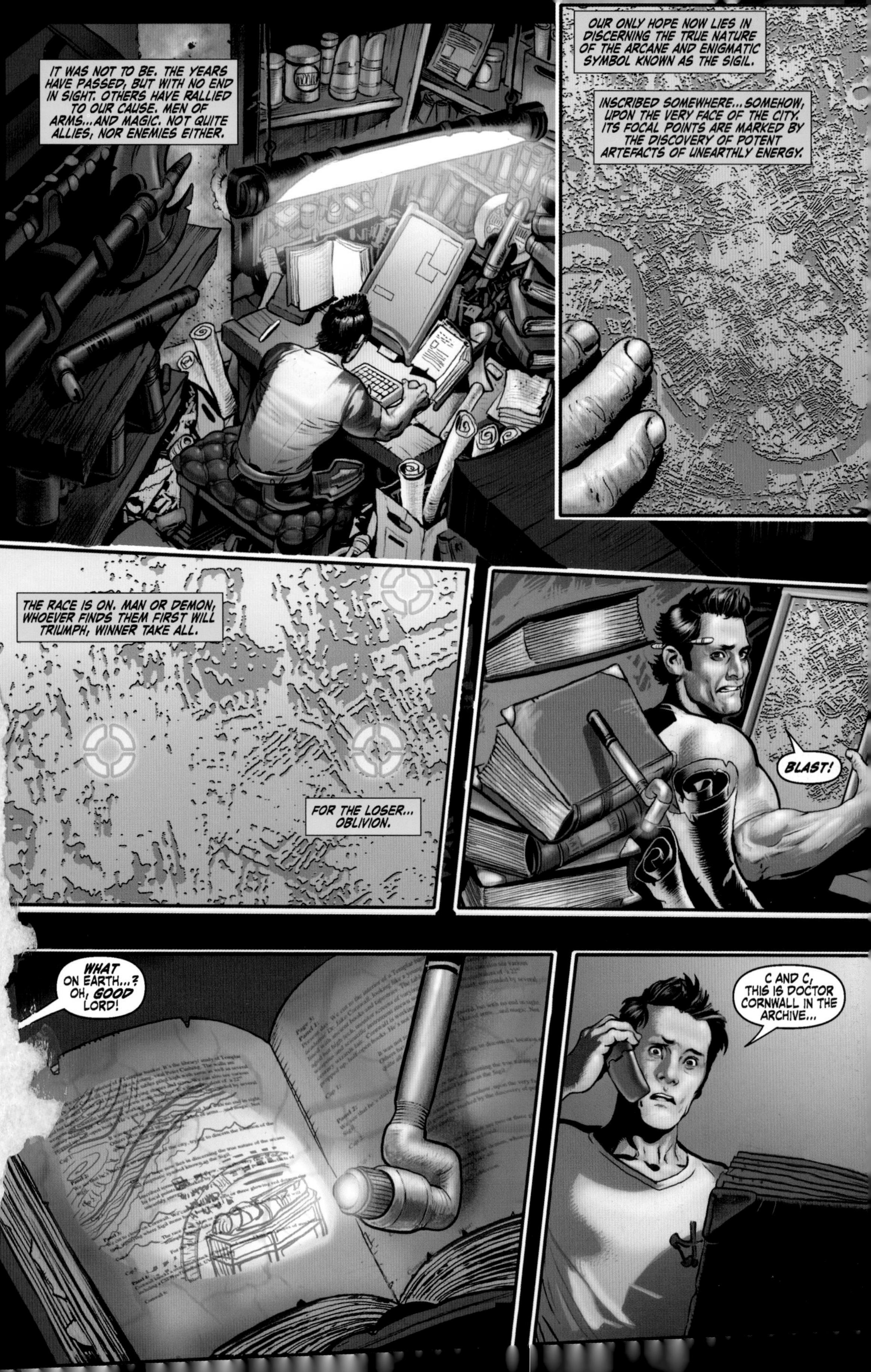
IT WAS NOT TO BE. THE YEARS HAVE PASSED, BUT WITH NO END IN SIGHT. OTHERS HAVE RALLIED TO OUR CAUSE. MEN OF ARMS...AND MAGIC. NOT QUITE ALLIES, NOR ENEMIES EITHER.
OUR ONLY HOPE NOW LIES IN DISCERNING THE TRUE NATURE OF THE ARCANE AND ENIGMATIC SYMBOL KNOWN AS THE SIGIL.
INSCRIBED SOMEWHERE...SOMEHOW, UPON THE VERY FACE OF THE CITY. ITS FOCAL POINTS ARE MARKED BY THE DISCOVERY OF POTENT ARTEFACTS OF UNEARTHLY ENERGY.
THE RACE IS ON. MAN OR DEMON, WHOEVER FINDS THEM FIRST WILL TRIUMPH, WINNER TAKE ALL.
FOR THE LOSER... OBLIVION.
BLAST!
WHAT ON EARTH...? OH, GOOD LORD!
C AND C, THIS IS DOCTOR CORNWALL IN THE ARCHIVE...

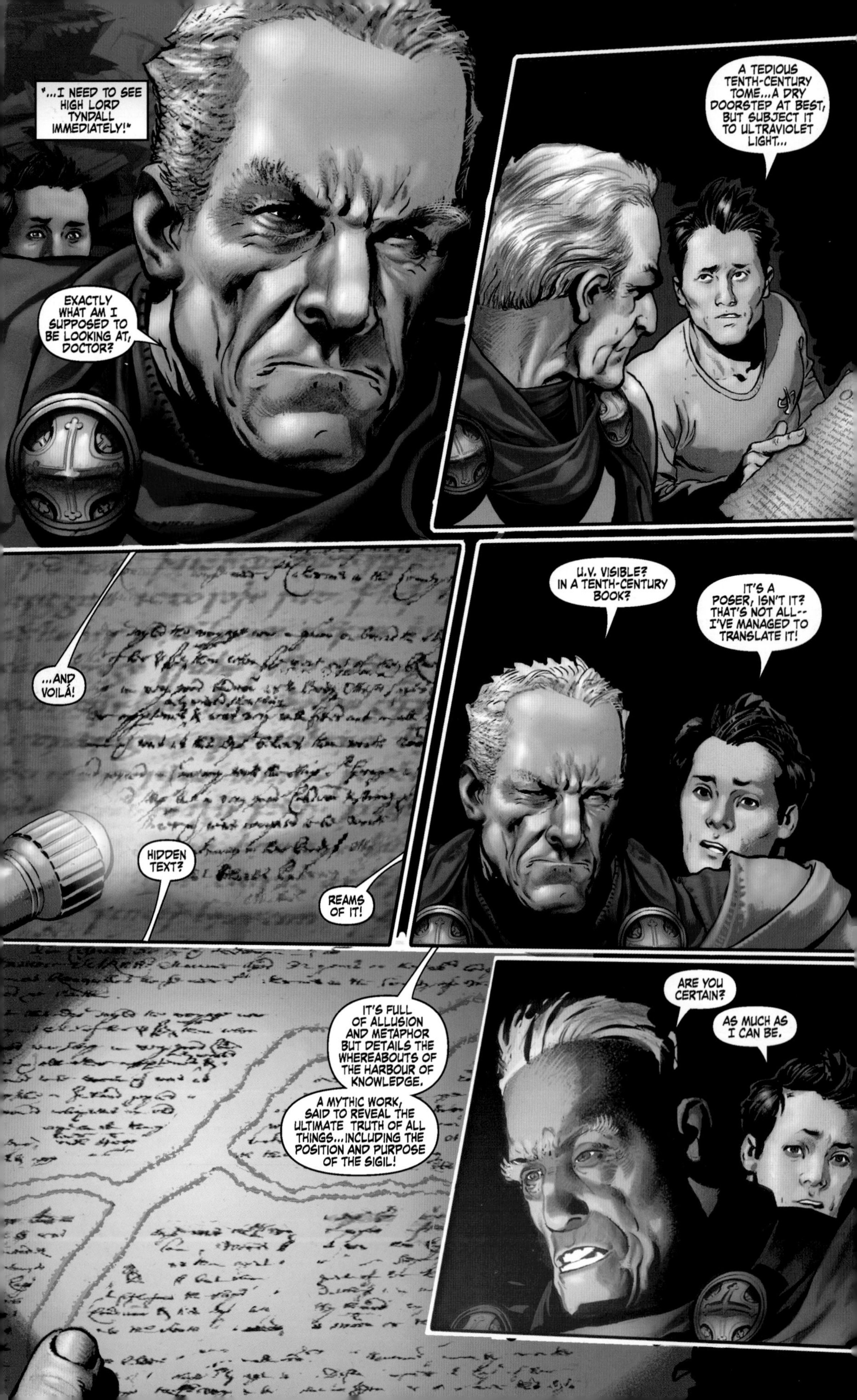
"...I NEED TO SEE HIGH LORD TYNDALL IMMEDIATELY!"
EXACTLY WHAT AM I SUPPOSED TO BE LOOKING AT, DOCTOR?
A TEDIOUS TENTH-CENTURY TOME...A DRY DOORSTEP AT BEST, BUT SUBJECT IT TO ULTRAVIOLET LIGHT...
...AND VOILÁ!
HIDDEN TEXT?
REAMS OF IT!
U.V. VISIBLE? IN A TENTH-CENTURY BOOK?
IT'S A POSER, ISN'T IT? THAT'S NOT ALL-- I'VE MANAGED TO TRANSLATE IT!
IT'S FULL OF ALLUSION AND METAPHOR BUT DETAILS THE WHEREABOUTS OF THE HARBOUR OF KNOWLEDGE.
A MYTHIC WORK, SAID TO REVEAL THE ULTIMATE TRUTH OF ALL THINGS...INCLUDING THE POSITION AND PURPOSE OF THE SIGIL!
ARE YOU CERTAIN?
AS MUCH AS I CAN BE.

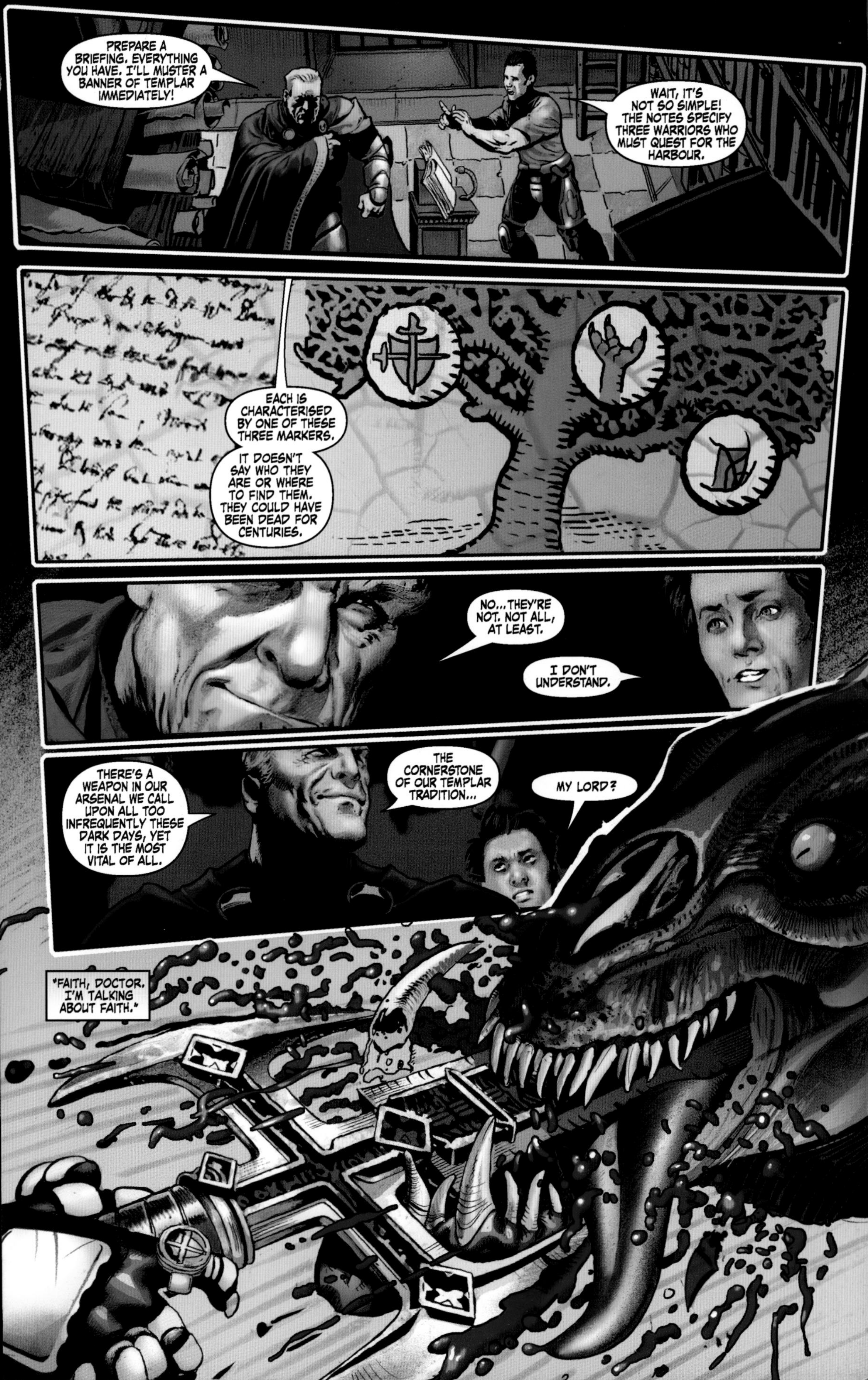
PREPARE A BRIEFING. EVERYTHING YOU HAVE. I'LL MUSTER A BANNER OF TEMPLAR IMMEDIATELY!
WAIT, IT'S NOT SO SIMPLE! THE NOTES SPECIFY THREE WARRIORS WHO MUST QUEST FOR THE HARBOUR.
EACH IS CHARACTERISED BY ONE OF THESE THREE MARKERS.
IT DOESN'T SAY WHO THEY ARE OR WHERE TO FIND THEM. THEY COULD HAVE BEEN DEAD FOR CENTURIES.
NO... THEY'RE NOT. NOT ALL, AT LEAST.
I DON'T UNDERSTAND.
THERE'S A WEAPON IN OUR ARSENAL WE CALL UPON ALL TOO INFREQUENTLY THESE DARK DAYS, YET IT IS THE MOST VITAL OF ALL.
THE CORNERSTONE OF OUR TEMPLAR TRADITION...
MY LORD?
"FAITH, DOCTOR. I'M TALKING ABOUT FAITH."

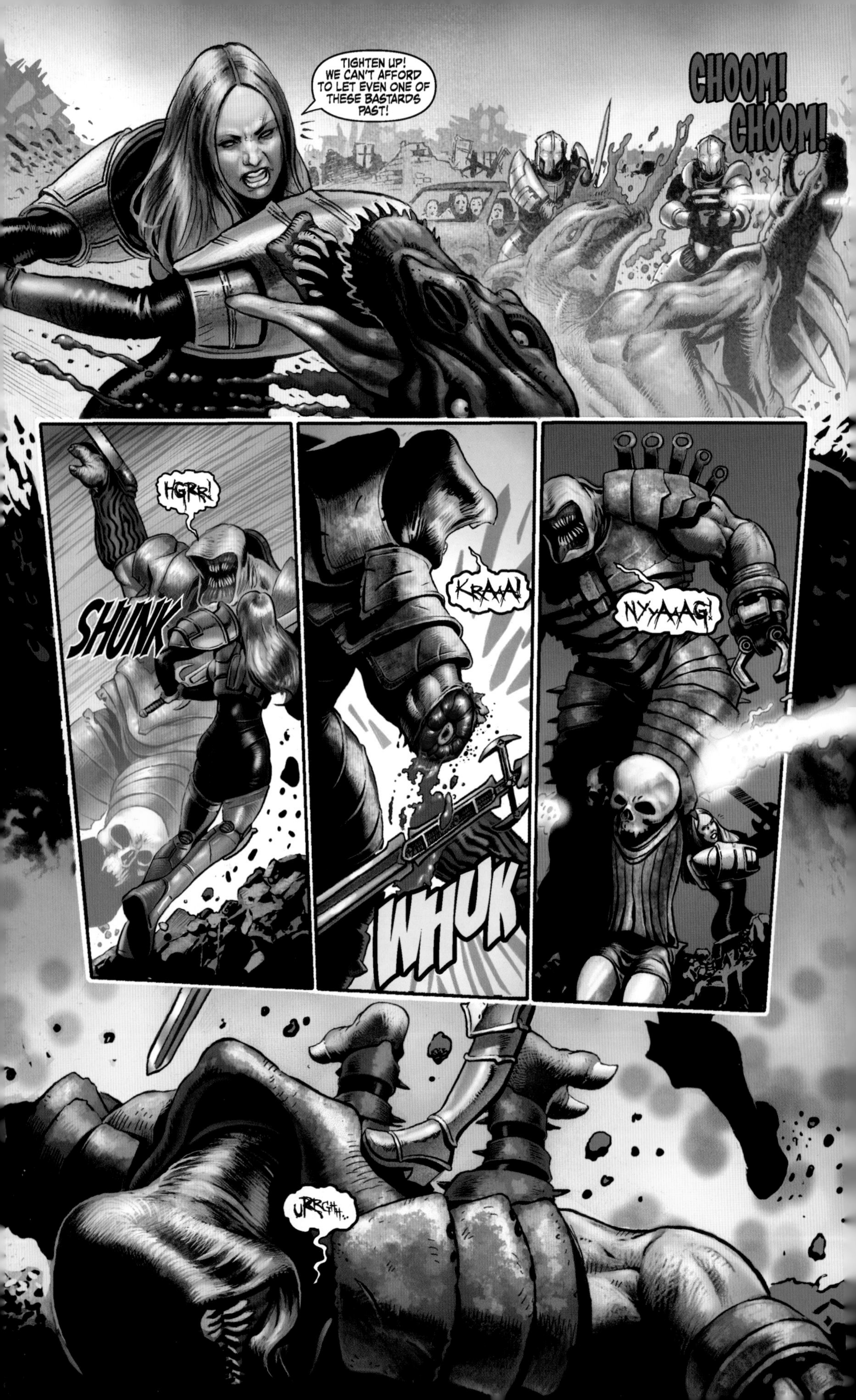
TIGHTEN UP! WE CAN'T AFFORD TO LET EVEN ONE OF THESE BASTARDS PAST!
CHOOM! CHOOM!
HGRR!
SHUNK
KRAAA!
WHUK
NYAAAG!
URRGHH..

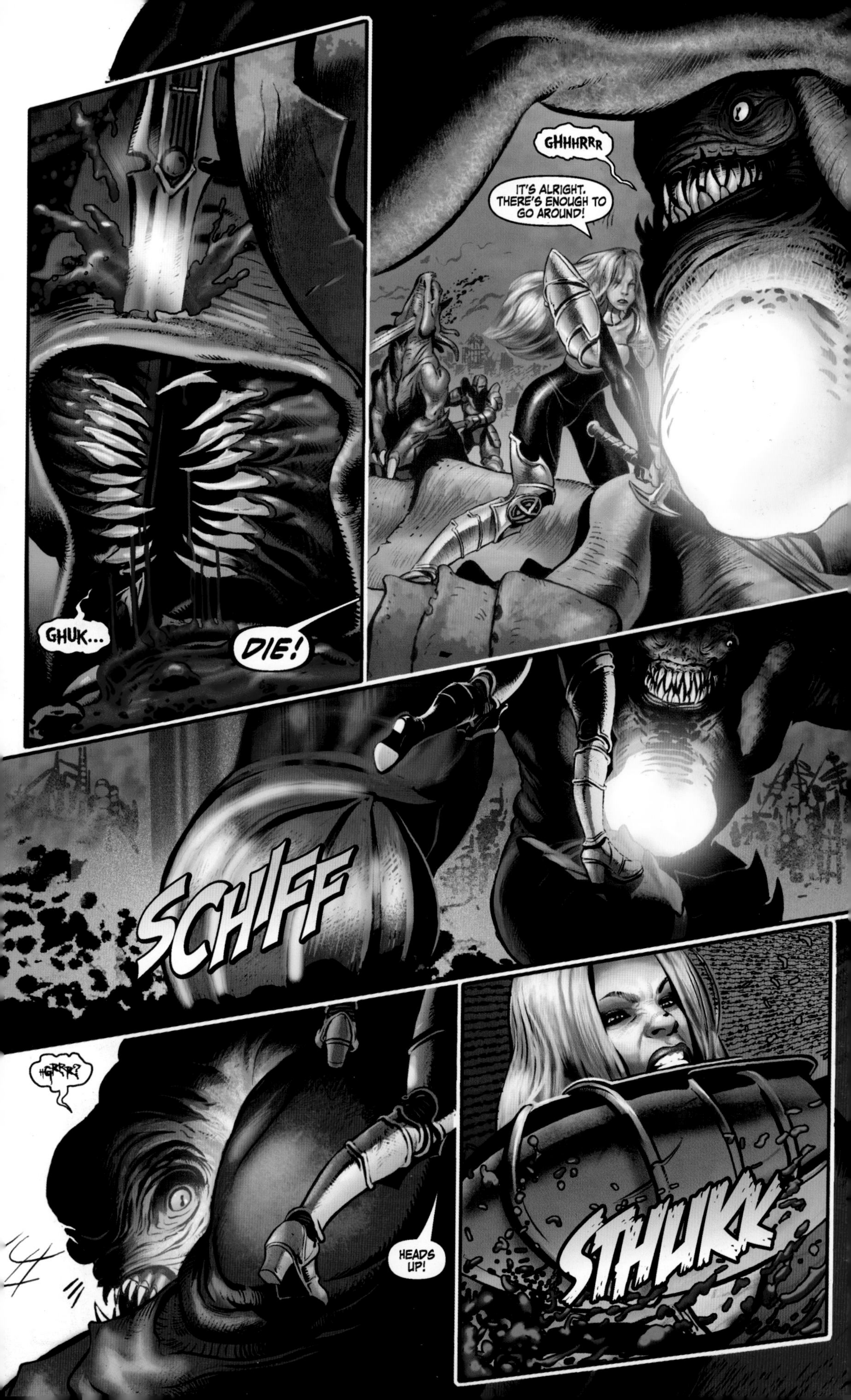
GHUK...
DIE!
GHHHRRR
IT'S ALRIGHT. THERE'S ENOUGH TO GO AROUND!
SCHIFF
HGRRR?
HEADS UP!
SHUKK

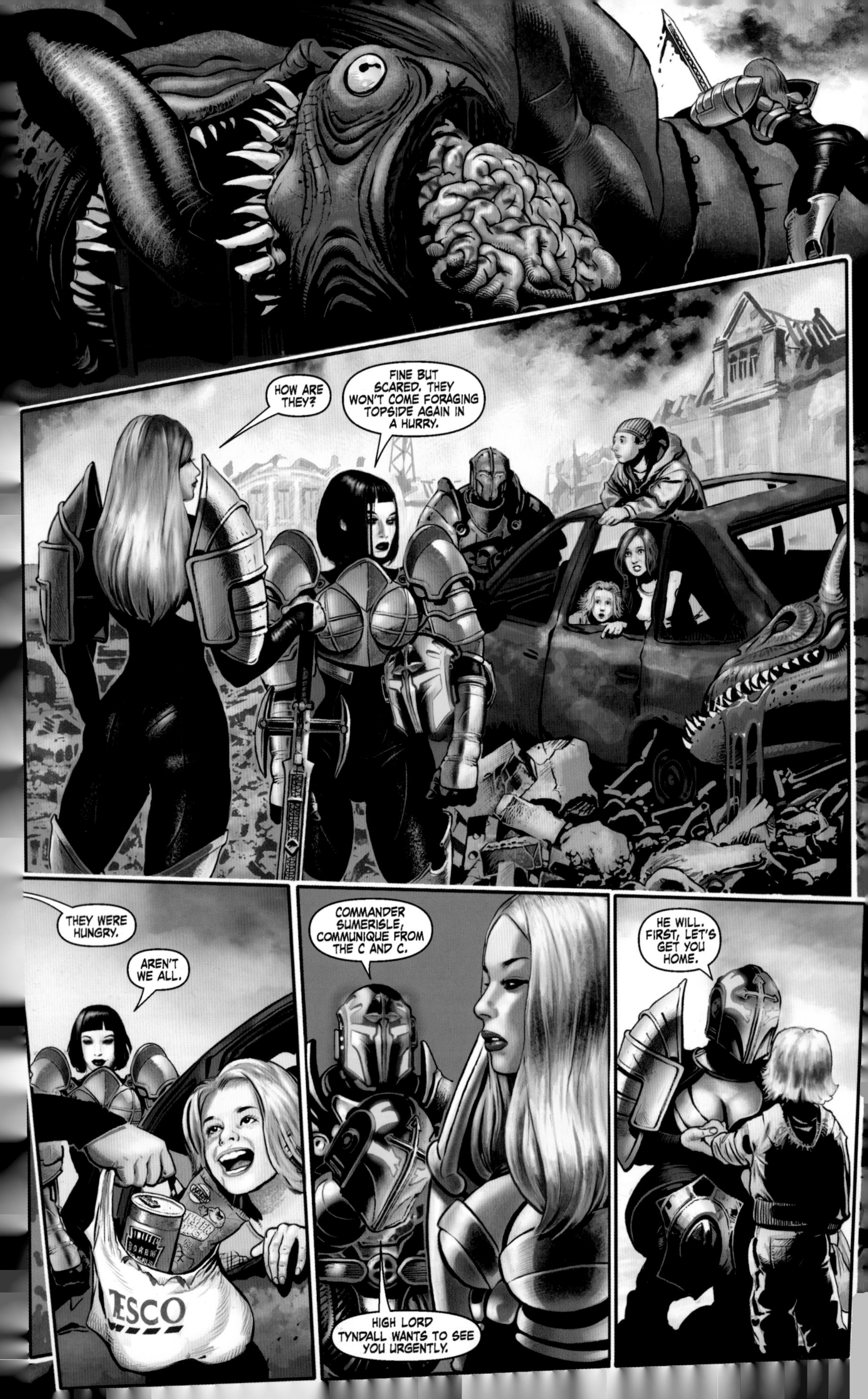
HOW ARE THEY?
FINE BUT SCARED. THEY WON'T COME FORAGING TOPSIDE AGAIN IN A HURRY.
THEY WERE HUNGRY.
AREN'T WE ALL.
TESCO
COMMANDER SUMERISLE, COMMUNIQUE FROM THE C AND C.
HIGH LORD TYNDALL WANTS TO SEE YOU URGENTLY.
HE WILL. FIRST, LET'S GET YOU HOME.

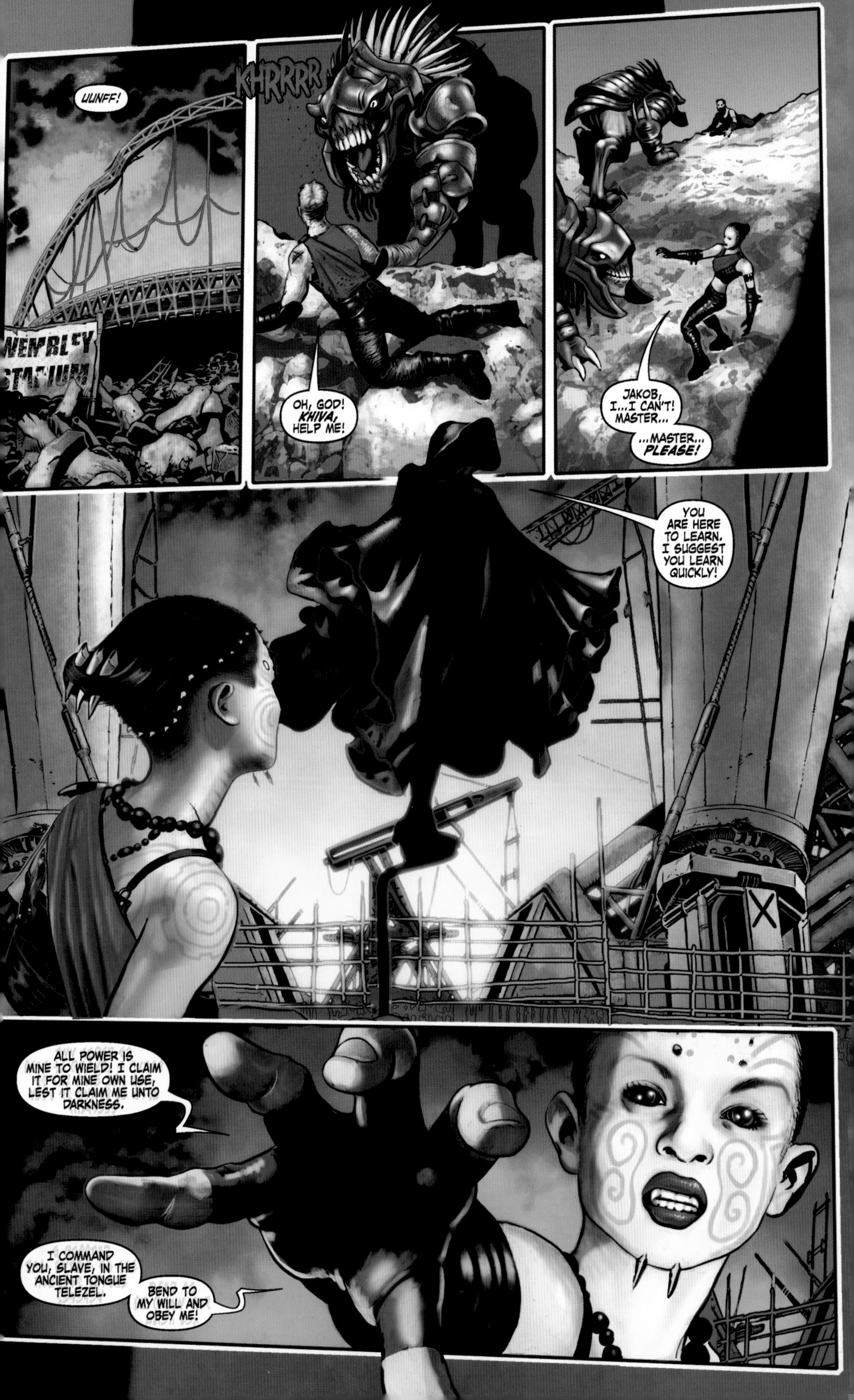
UUNFF!
WEMBLEY STADIUM
KHRRRR
OH, GOD! KHIVA, HELP ME!
JAKOB, I...I CAN'T! MASTER...
...MASTER... PLEASE!
YOU ARE HERE TO LEARN. I SUGGEST YOU LEARN QUICKLY!
ALL POWER IS MINE TO WIELD! I CLAIM IT FOR MINE OWN USE, LEST IT CLAIM ME UNTO DARKNESS.
I COMMAND YOU, SLAVE, IN THE ANCIENT TONGUE TELEZEL.
BEND TO MY WILL AND OBEY ME!

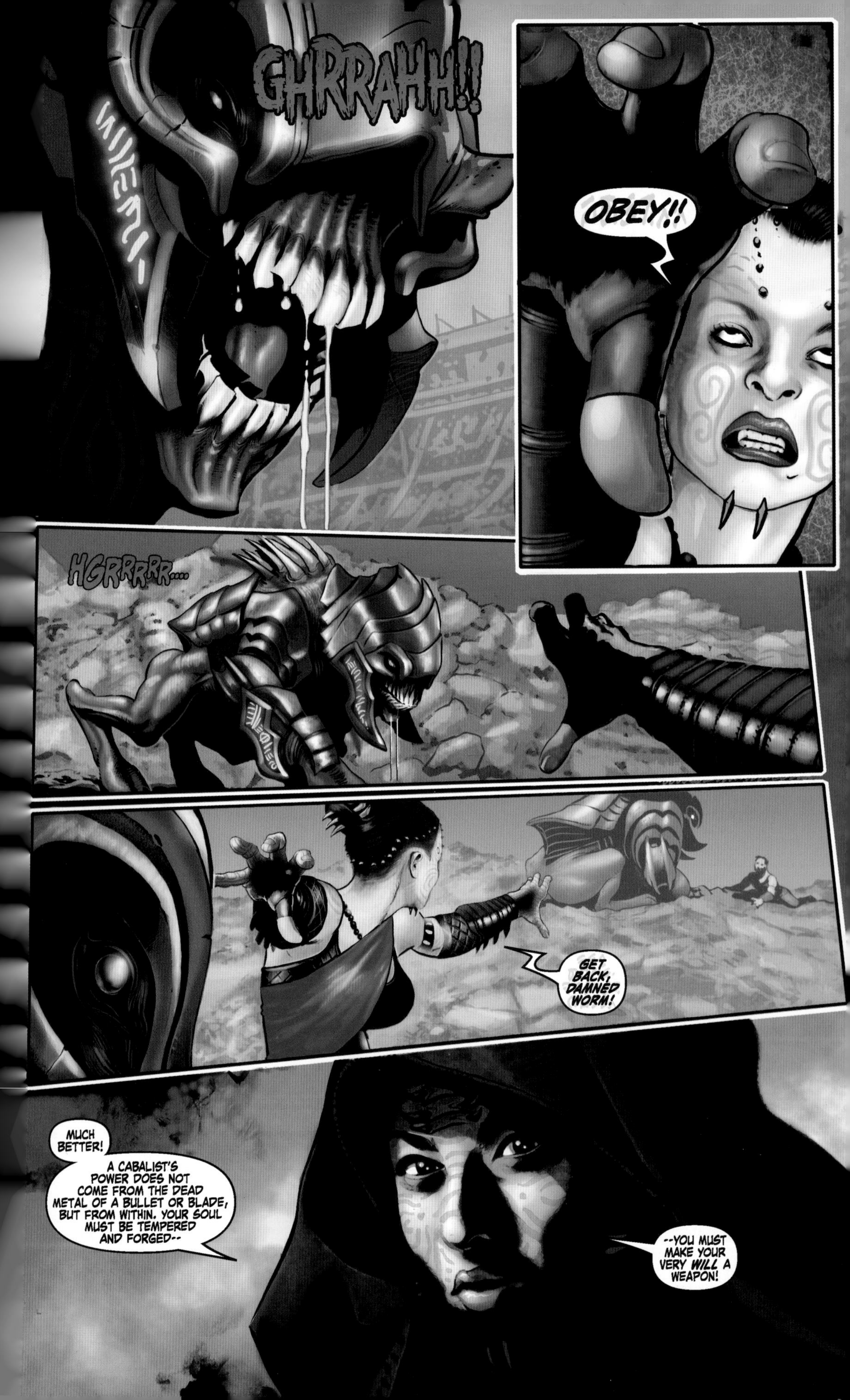

GHRRAHH!!
OBEY!!
HGRRRRR....
GET BACK, DAMNED WORM!
MUCH BETTER!
A CABALIST'S POWER DOES NOT COME FROM THE DEAD METAL OF A BULLET OR BLADE, BUT FROM WITHIN. YOUR SOUL MUST BE TEMPERED AND FORGED--
--YOU MUST MAKE YOUR VERY WILL A WEAPON!

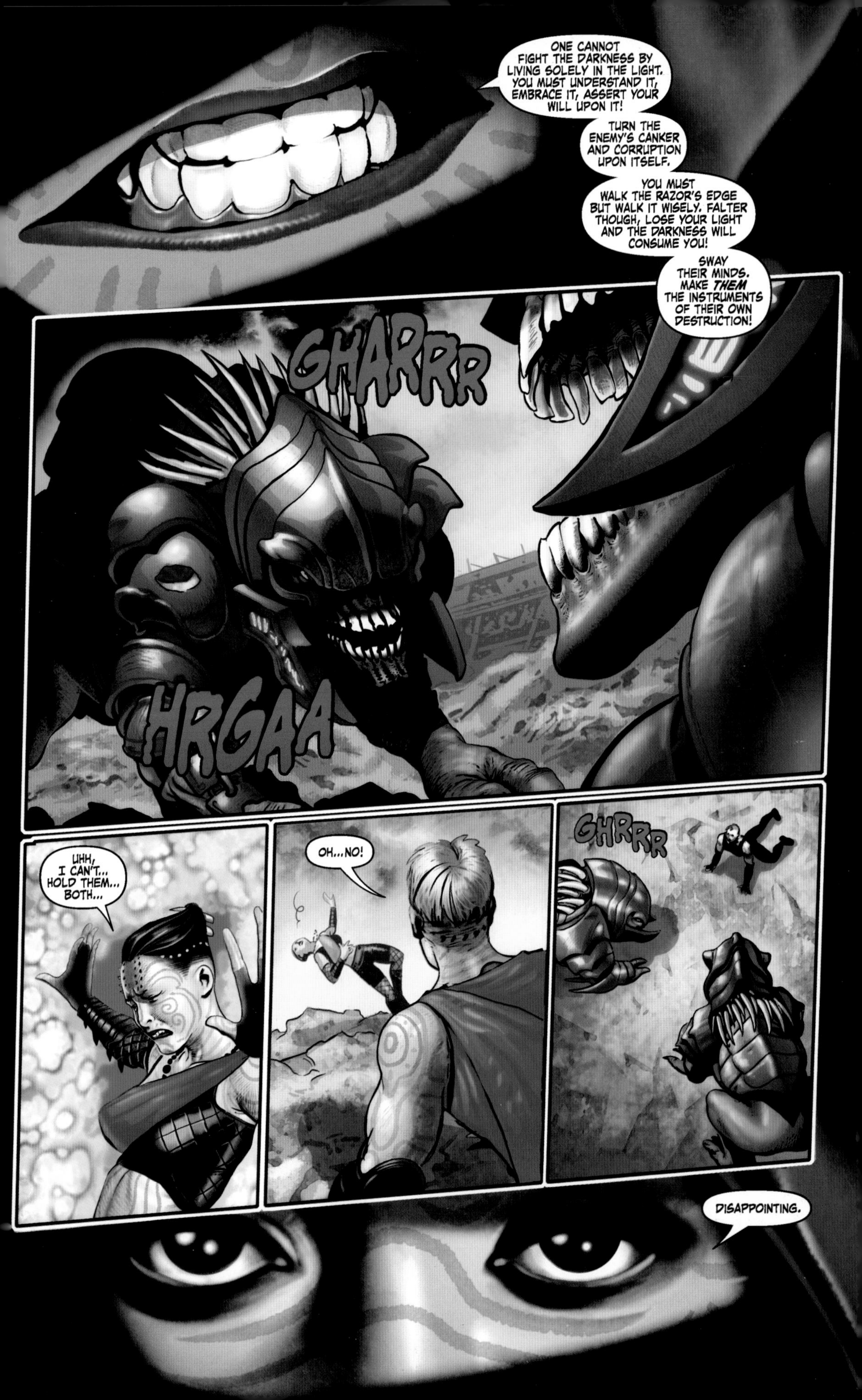
ONE CANNOT FIGHT THE DARKNESS BY LIVING SOLELY IN THE LIGHT. YOU MUST UNDERSTAND IT, EMBRACE IT, ASSERT YOUR WILL UPON IT!
TURN THE ENEMY'S CANKER AND CORRUPTION UPON ITSELF.
YOU MUST WALK THE RAZOR'S EDGE BUT WALK IT WISELY. FALTER THOUGH, LOSE YOUR LIGHT AND THE DARKNESS WILL CONSUME YOU!
SWAY THEIR MINDS. MAKE *THEM* THE INSTRUMENTS OF THEIR OWN DESTRUCTION!
GHARRR
HRGAA
UHH, I CAN'T... HOLD THEM... BOTH...
OH...NO!
GHRRR
DISAPPOINTING.

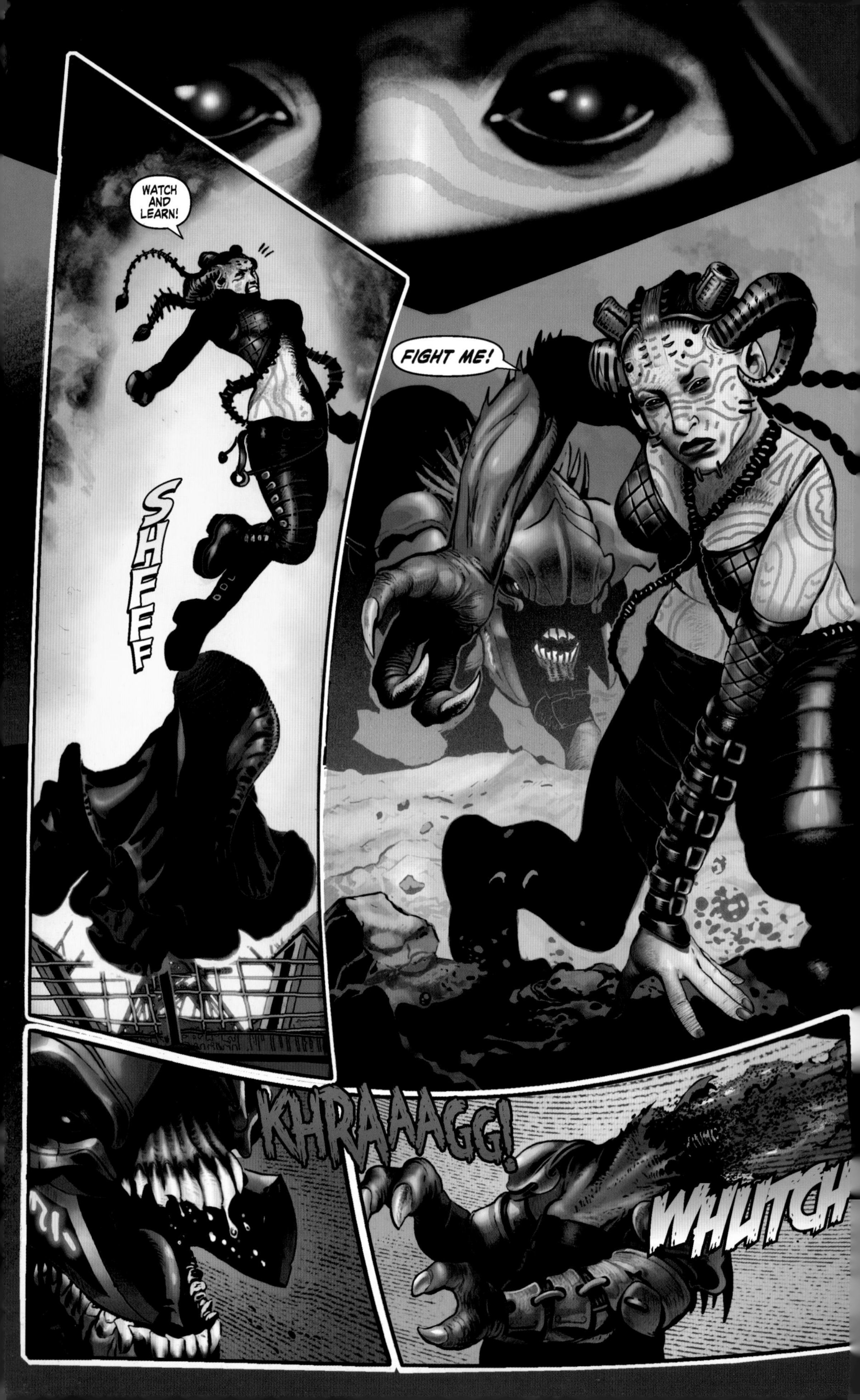
WATCH AND LEARN!
SHFFF
FIGHT ME!
KHRAAAGG!
WHUTCH

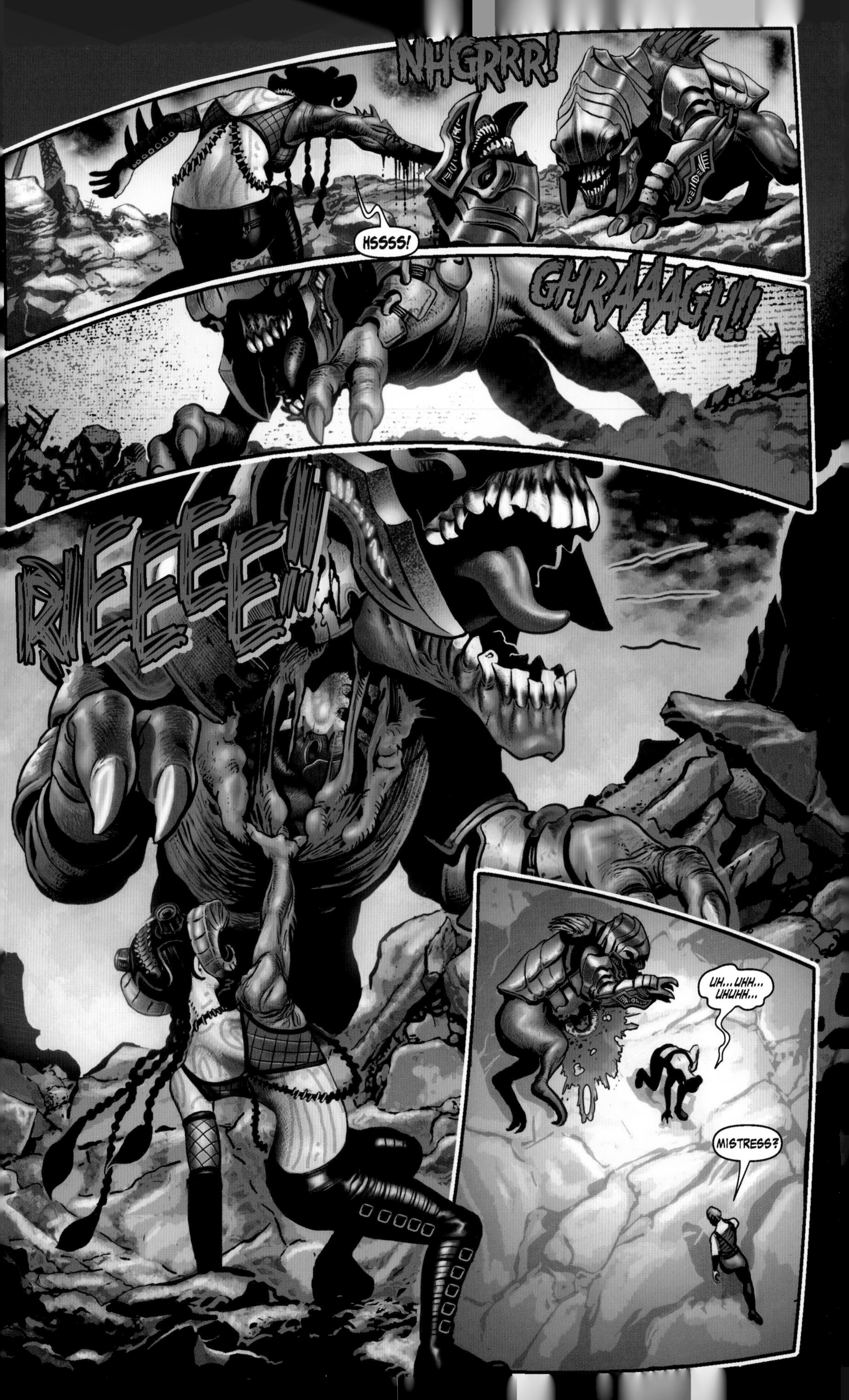
NHGRRR!
HSSSS!
GHRAAAGH!!
RIEEEE!!
UH...UHH...
UHUHH...
MISTRESS?

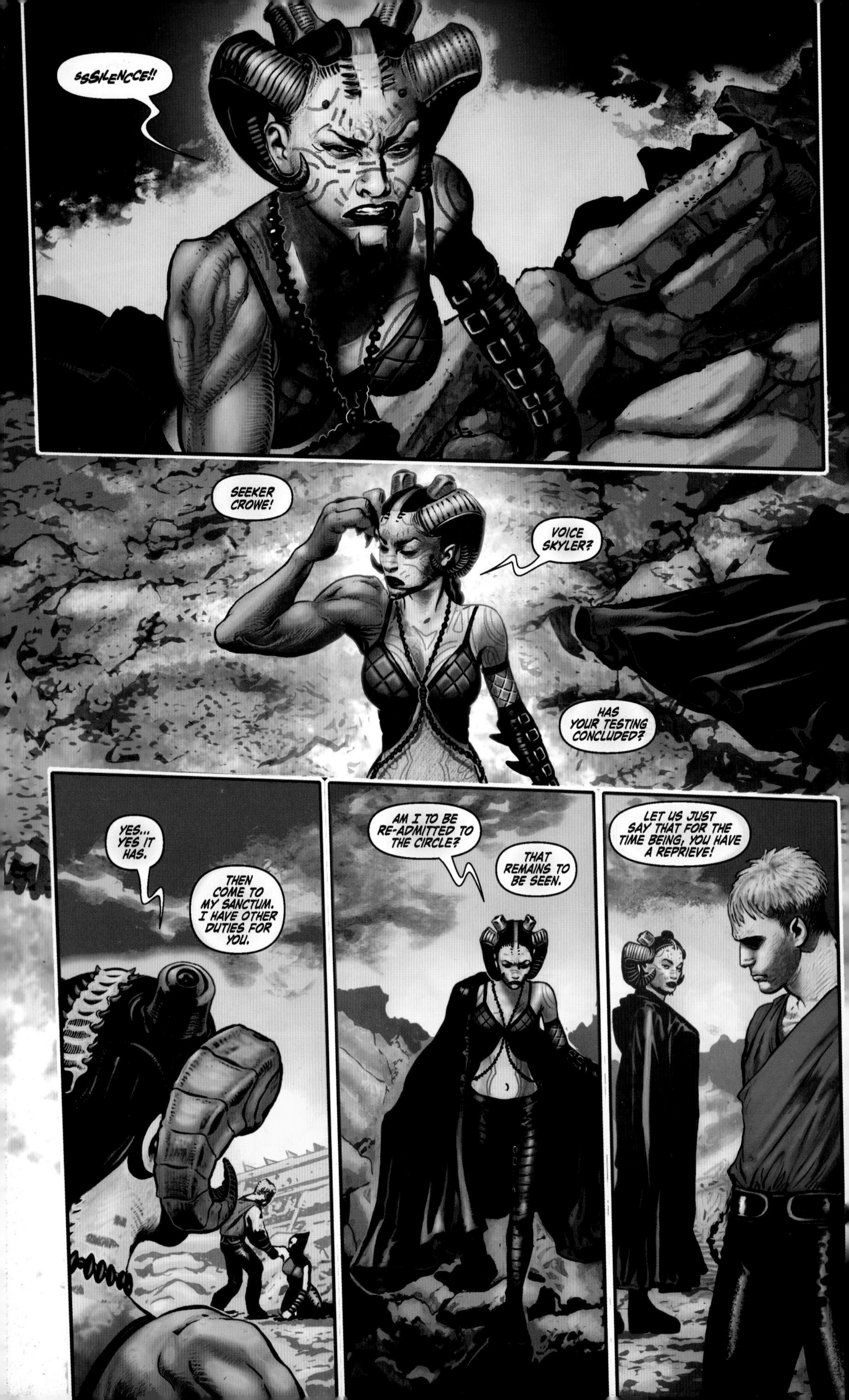
SSSILENCCE!!
SEEKER CROWE!
VOICE SKYLER?
HAS YOUR TESTING CONCLUDED?
YES... YES IT HAS.
THEN COME TO MY SANCTUM. I HAVE OTHER DUTIES FOR YOU.
AM I TO BE RE-ADMITTED TO THE CIRCLE?
THAT REMAINS TO BE SEEN.
LET US JUST SAY THAT FOR THE TIME BEING, YOU HAVE A REPRIEVE!

TWO WEEKS LATER...

FHSSSSS --ETTING THIS? IT'S INCREDIBLE! THE MONSTROUS CREATURES, WHO'D ALL BUT DEFEATED THE COMBINED MIGHT OF THE BRITISH ARMED FORCES, ARE INEXPLICABLY RETREATING?

MY GOD! BOB, GET A SHOT OF THIS, QUICK!

ZOOM IN! THEY'RE BUTCHERING EACH OTHER...SACRIFICING THEMSELVES TO THE RIFT THEY CAME FROM!

LOOK AT ALL THE BODIES! WHY ARE THEY DOING THIS?

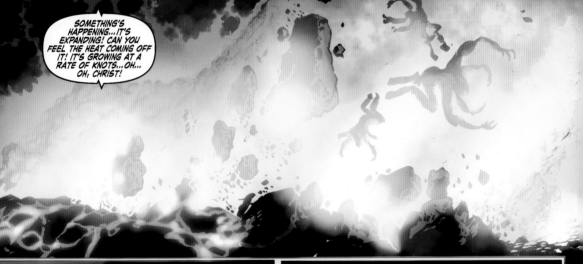

SOMETHING'S HAPPENING...IT'S EXPANDING! CAN YOU FEEL THE HEAT COMING OFF IT! IT'S GROWING AT A RATE OF KNOTS...OH... OH, CHRIST!

RUN! BLOODY MOVE!

RU-- FHHSSSSS

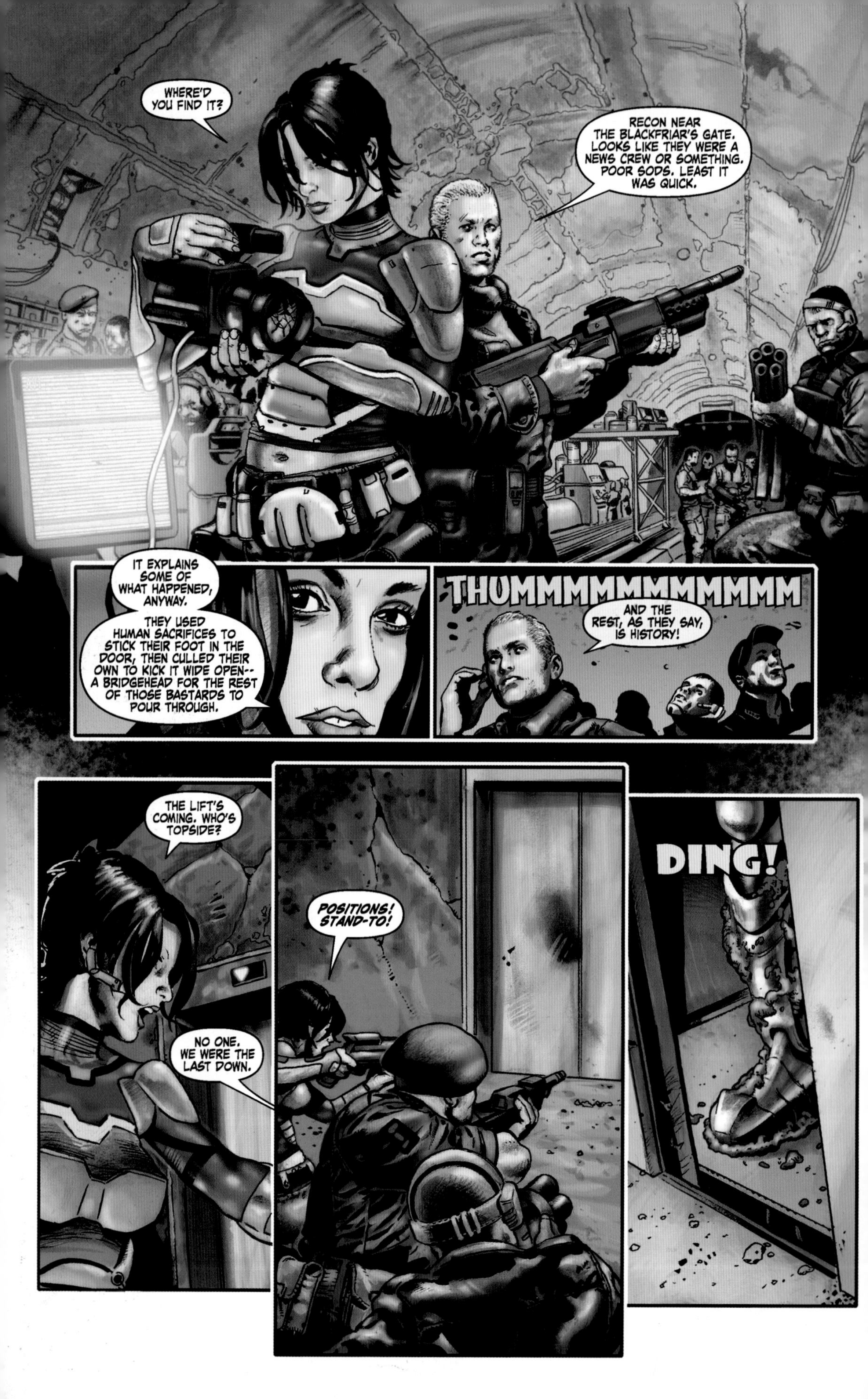

WHERE'D YOU FIND IT?
RECON NEAR THE BLACKFRIAR'S GATE. LOOKS LIKE THEY WERE A NEWS CREW OR SOMETHING. POOR SODS. LEAST IT WAS QUICK.
IT EXPLAINS SOME OF WHAT HAPPENED, ANYWAY.
THEY USED HUMAN SACRIFICES TO STICK THEIR FOOT IN THE DOOR, THEN CULLED THEIR OWN TO KICK IT WIDE OPEN--A BRIDGEHEAD FOR THE REST OF THOSE BASTARDS TO POUR THROUGH.
THOMMMMMMMMMMM
AND THE REST, AS THEY SAY, IS HISTORY!
THE LIFT'S COMING. WHO'S TOPSIDE?
NO ONE. WE WERE THE LAST DOWN.
POSITIONS! STAND-TO!
DING!

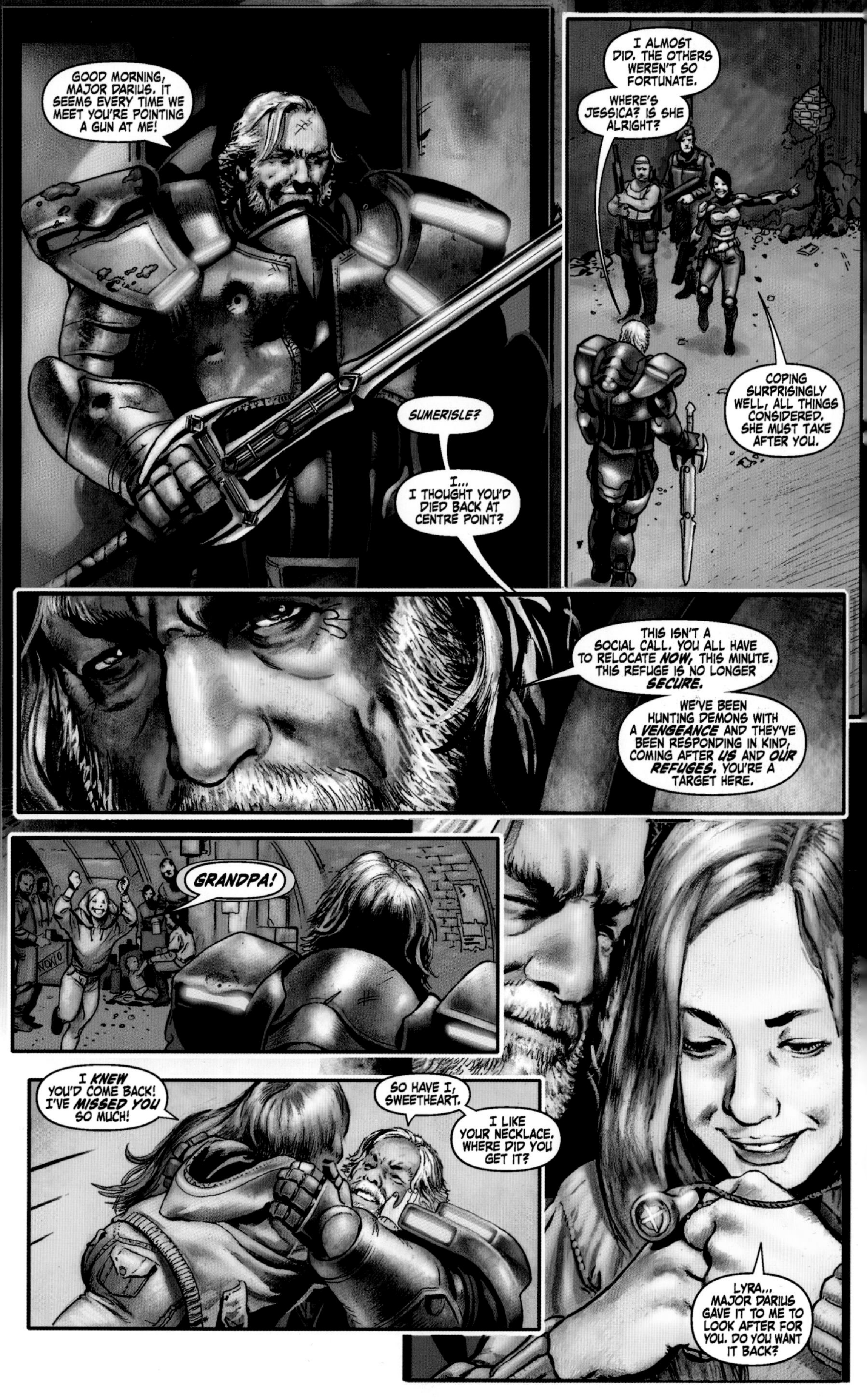
GOOD MORNING, MAJOR DARIUS. IT SEEMS EVERY TIME WE MEET YOU'RE POINTING A GUN AT ME!
SUMERISLE?
I... I THOUGHT YOU'D DIED BACK AT CENTRE POINT?
I ALMOST DID. THE OTHERS WEREN'T SO FORTUNATE.
WHERE'S JESSICA? IS SHE ALRIGHT?
COPING SURPRISINGLY WELL, ALL THINGS CONSIDERED. SHE MUST TAKE AFTER YOU.
THIS ISN'T A SOCIAL CALL. YOU ALL HAVE TO RELOCATE NOW, THIS MINUTE. THIS REFUGE IS NO LONGER SECURE.
WE'VE BEEN HUNTING DEMONS WITH A VENGEANCE AND THEY'VE BEEN RESPONDING IN KIND, COMING AFTER US AND OUR REFUGES. YOU'RE A TARGET HERE.
GRANDPA!
I KNEW YOU'D COME BACK! I'VE MISSED YOU SO MUCH!
SO HAVE I, SWEETHEART.
I LIKE YOUR NECKLACE. WHERE DID YOU GET IT?
LYRA... MAJOR DARIUS GAVE IT TO ME TO LOOK AFTER FOR YOU. DO YOU WANT IT BACK?

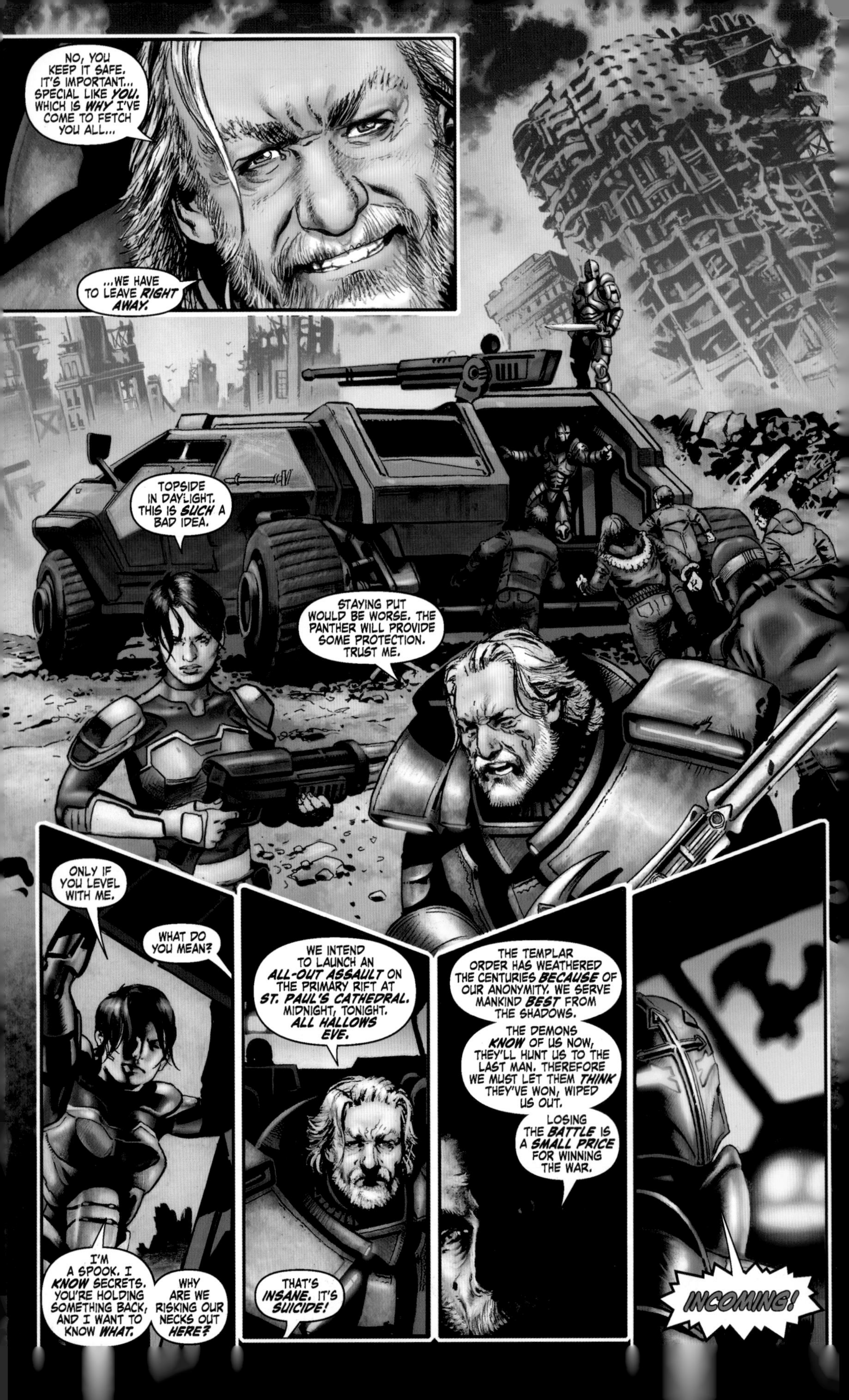
NO, YOU KEEP IT SAFE. IT'S IMPORTANT... SPECIAL LIKE *YOU.* WHICH IS *WHY* I'VE COME TO FETCH YOU ALL...
...WE HAVE TO LEAVE *RIGHT AWAY.*
TOPSIDE IN DAYLIGHT. THIS IS *SUCH* A BAD IDEA.
STAYING PUT WOULD BE WORSE. THE PANTHER WILL PROVIDE SOME PROTECTION. TRUST ME.
ONLY IF YOU LEVEL WITH ME.
WHAT DO YOU MEAN?
I'M A SPOOK. I *KNOW* SECRETS. YOU'RE HOLDING SOMETHING BACK, AND I WANT TO KNOW *WHAT.*
WHY ARE WE RISKING OUR NECKS OUT *HERE?*
WE INTEND TO LAUNCH AN *ALL-OUT ASSAULT* ON THE PRIMARY RIFT AT *ST. PAUL'S CATHEDRAL.* MIDNIGHT, TONIGHT. *ALL HALLOWS EVE.*
THAT'S *INSANE.* IT'S *SUICIDE!*
THE TEMPLAR ORDER HAS WEATHERED THE CENTURIES *BECAUSE* OF OUR ANONYMITY. WE SERVE MANKIND *BEST* FROM THE SHADOWS.
THE DEMONS *KNOW* OF US NOW, THEY'LL HUNT US TO THE LAST MAN. THEREFORE WE MUST LET THEM *THINK* THEY'VE WON, WIPED US OUT.
LOSING THE *BATTLE* IS A *SMALL PRICE* FOR WINNING THE WAR.
INCOMING!

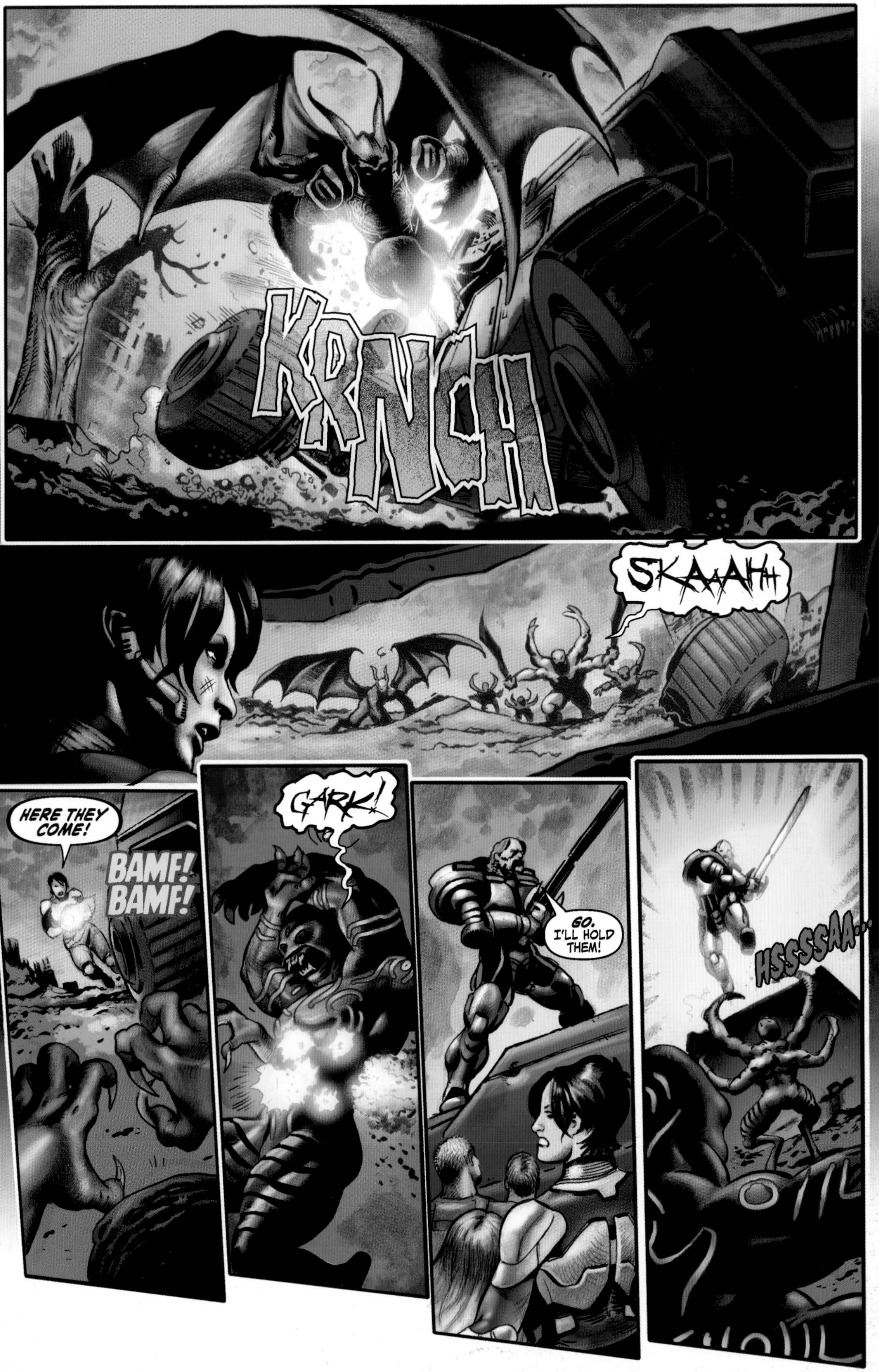
KRNCH
SKAAAHH
HERE THEY COME!
BAMF! BAMF!
GARK!
GO. I'LL HOLD THEM!
HSSSSAA...

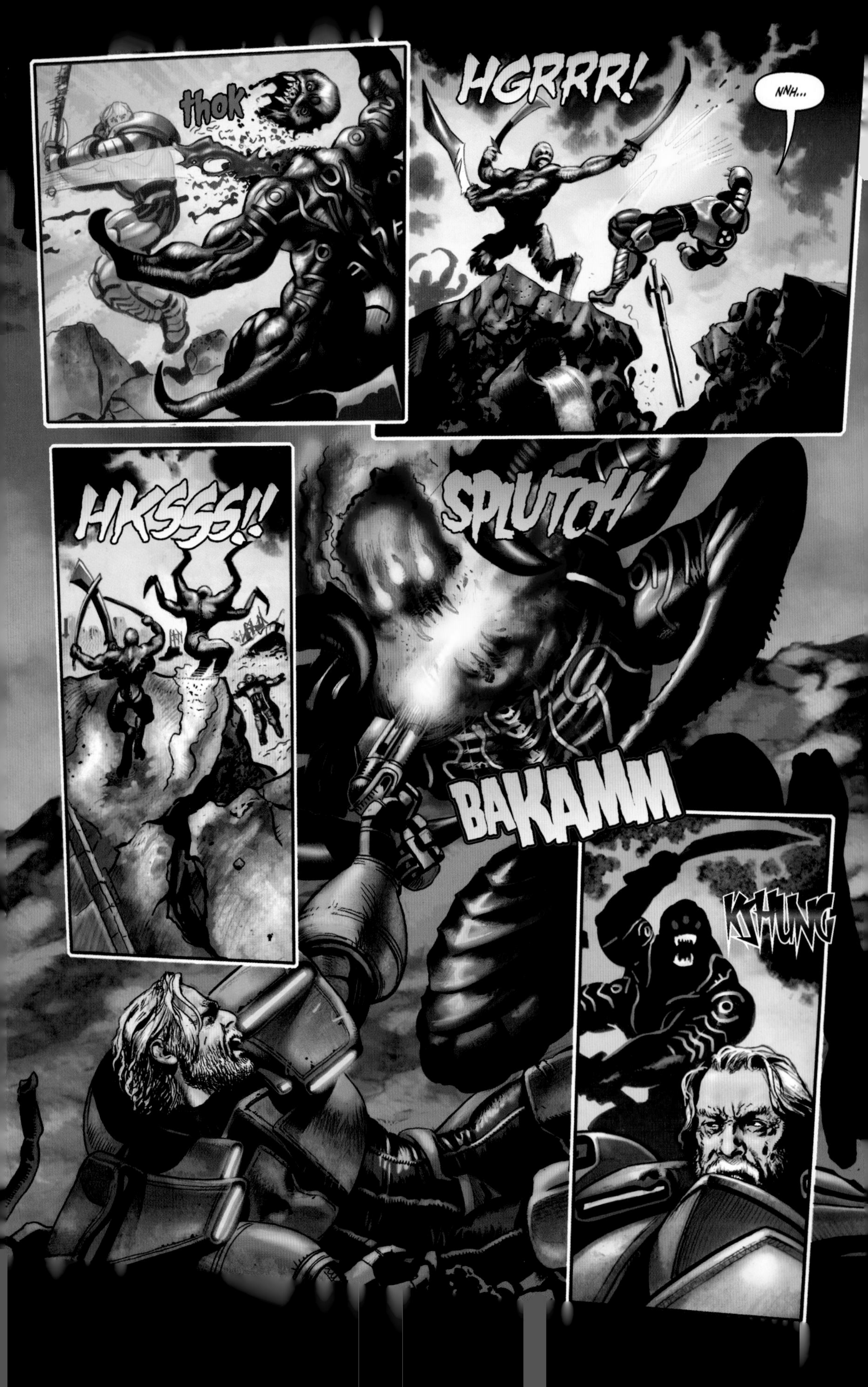
thok
HGRRR!
NNH...
HKSSS!!
SPLUTCH
BAKAMM
KSHUNG

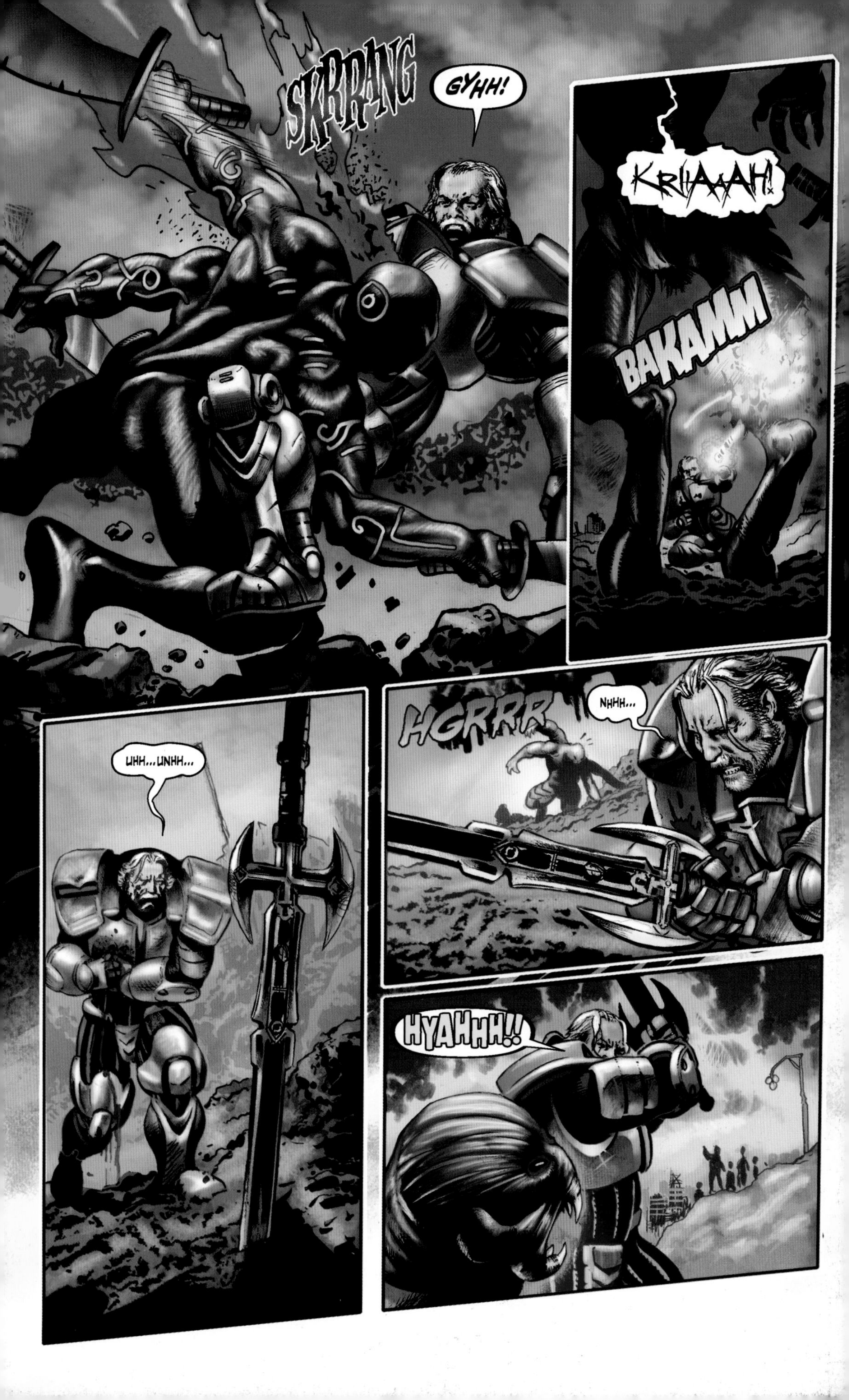
SKRRANG
GYHH!
KRIIAAAH!
BAKAMM
UHH...UNHH...
HGRRR
NHHH...
HYAHHH!!

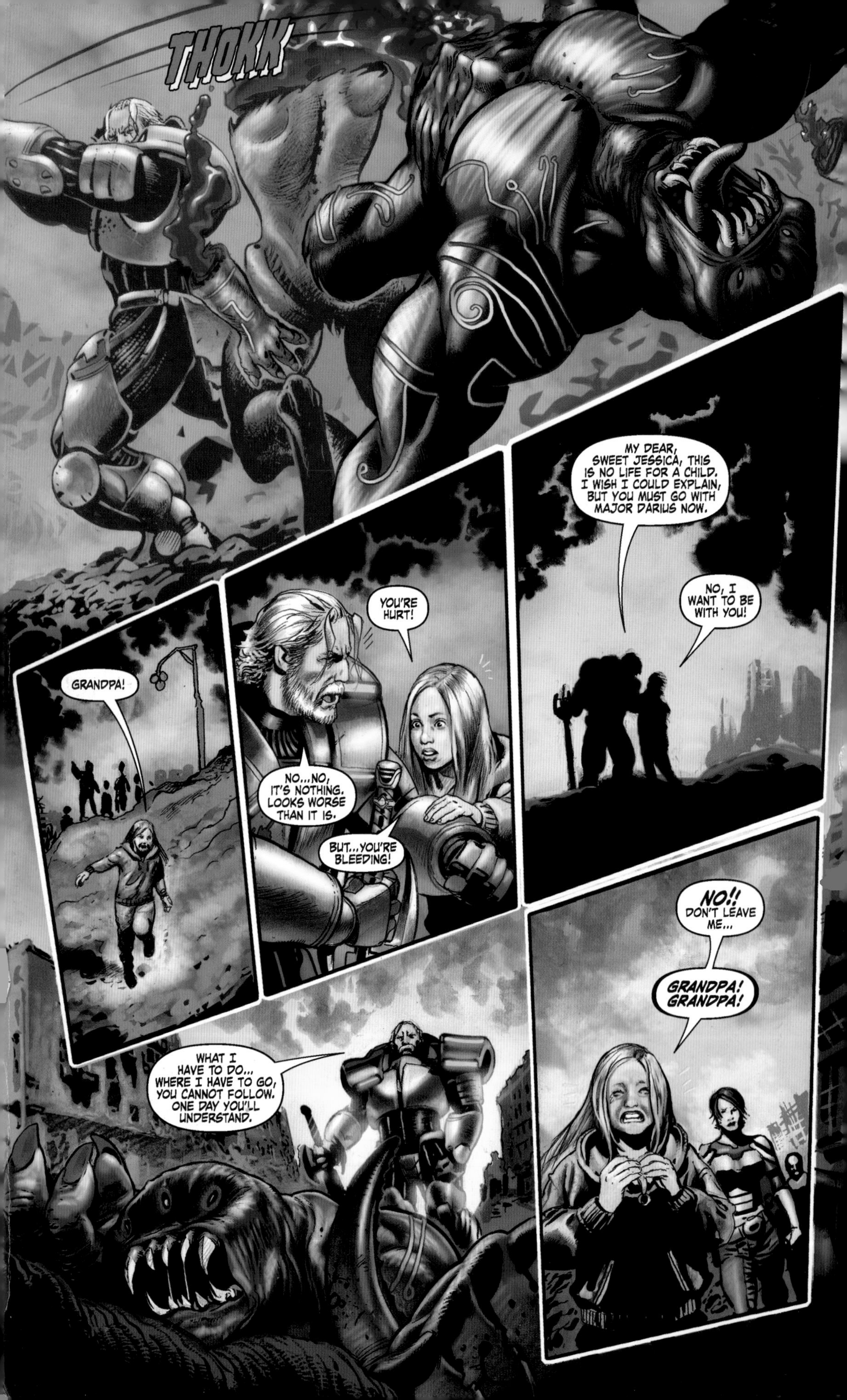
THOKK
GRANDPA!
YOU'RE HURT!
NO...NO, IT'S NOTHING. LOOKS WORSE THAN IT IS.
BUT...YOU'RE BLEEDING!
MY DEAR, SWEET JESSICA, THIS IS NO LIFE FOR A CHILD. I WISH I COULD EXPLAIN, BUT YOU MUST GO WITH MAJOR DARIUS NOW.
NO, I WANT TO BE WITH YOU!
WHAT I HAVE TO DO... WHERE I HAVE TO GO, YOU CANNOT FOLLOW. ONE DAY YOU'LL UNDERSTAND.
NO!! DON'T LEAVE ME...
GRANDPA! GRANDPA!

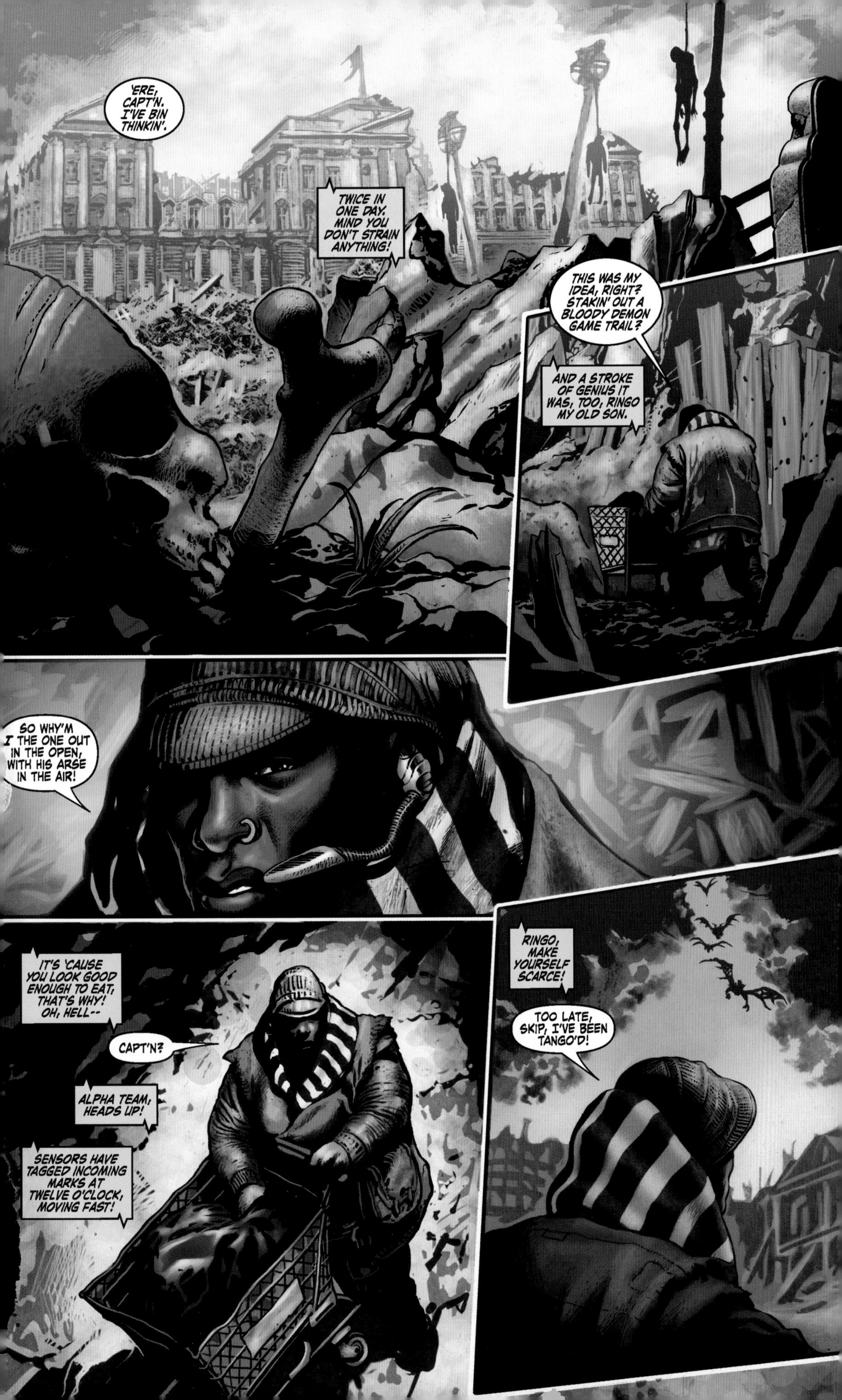
'ERE, CAPT'N. I'VE BIN THINKIN'.
TWICE IN ONE DAY. MIND YOU DON'T STRAIN ANYTHING!
THIS WAS MY IDEA, RIGHT? STAKIN' OUT A BLOODY DEMON GAME TRAIL?
AND A STROKE OF GENIUS IT WAS, TOO, RINGO MY OLD SON.
SO WHY'M I THE ONE OUT IN THE OPEN, WITH HIS ARSE IN THE AIR!
IT'S 'CAUSE YOU LOOK GOOD ENOUGH TO EAT, THAT'S WHY! OH, HELL--
CAPT'N?
ALPHA TEAM, HEADS UP!
SENSORS HAVE TAGGED INCOMING MARKS AT TWELVE O'CLOCK, MOVING FAST!
RINGO, MAKE YOURSELF SCARCE!
TOO LATE, SKIP, I'VE BEEN TANGO'D!

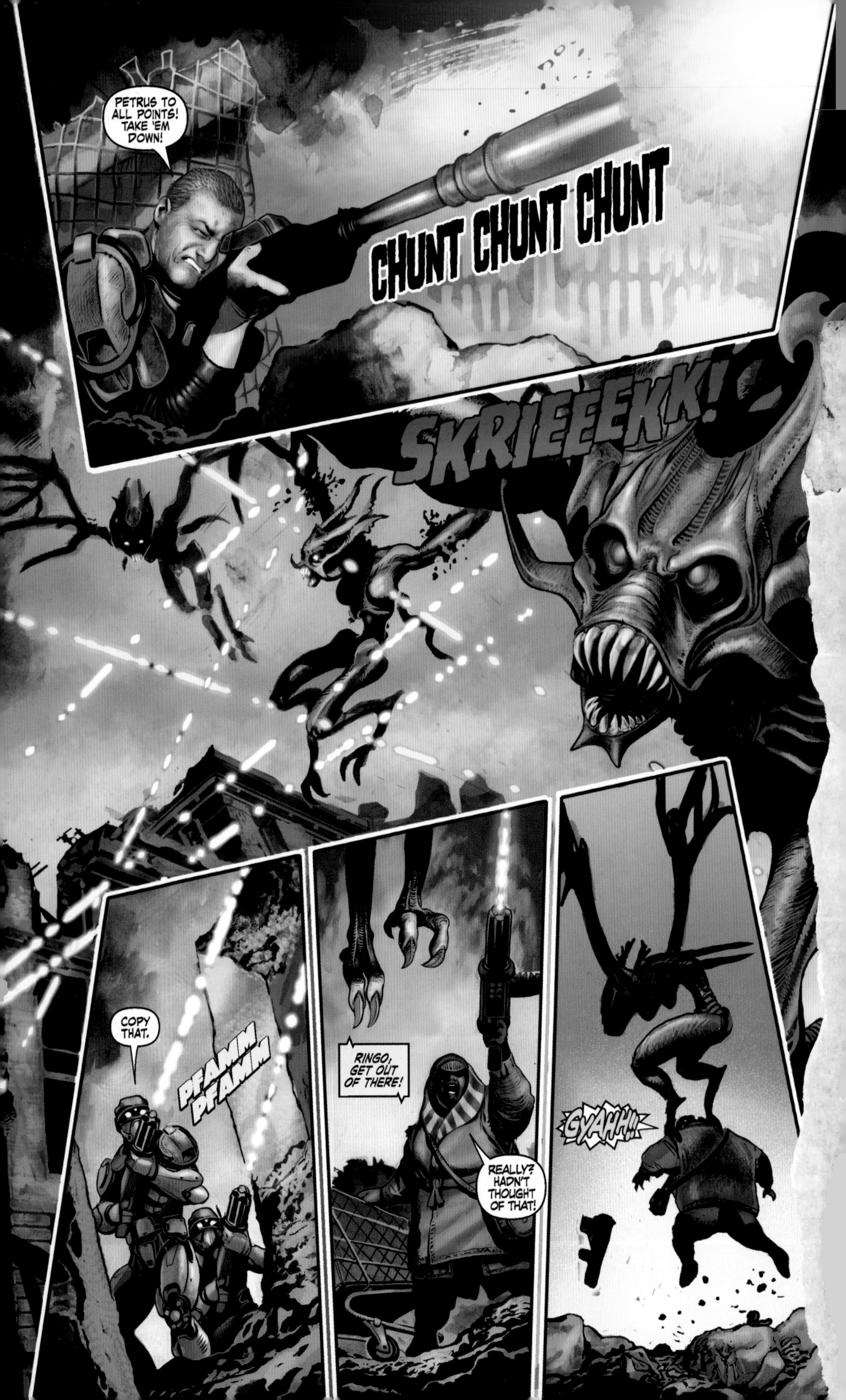
PETRUS TO ALL POINTS! TAKE 'EM DOWN!
CHUNT CHUNT CHUNT
SKRIEEEEKK!
COPY THAT.
PFAMM PFAMM
RINGO, GET OUT OF THERE!
REALLY? HADN'T THOUGHT OF THAT!
GYAHH!!

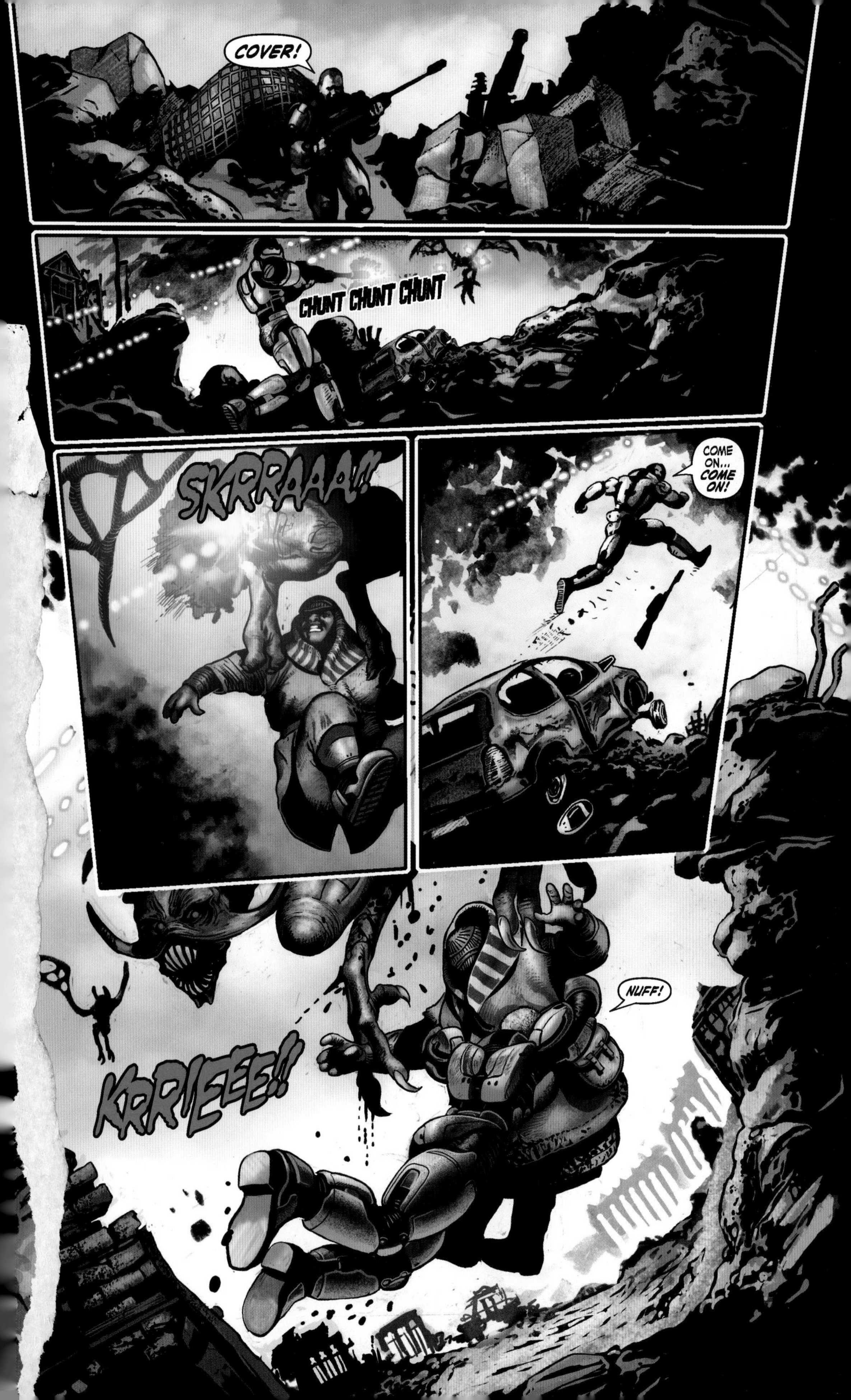
COVER!
CHUNT CHUNT CHUNT
SKRRAAA!!
COME ON... COME ON!
NUFF!
KRRIEEE!!

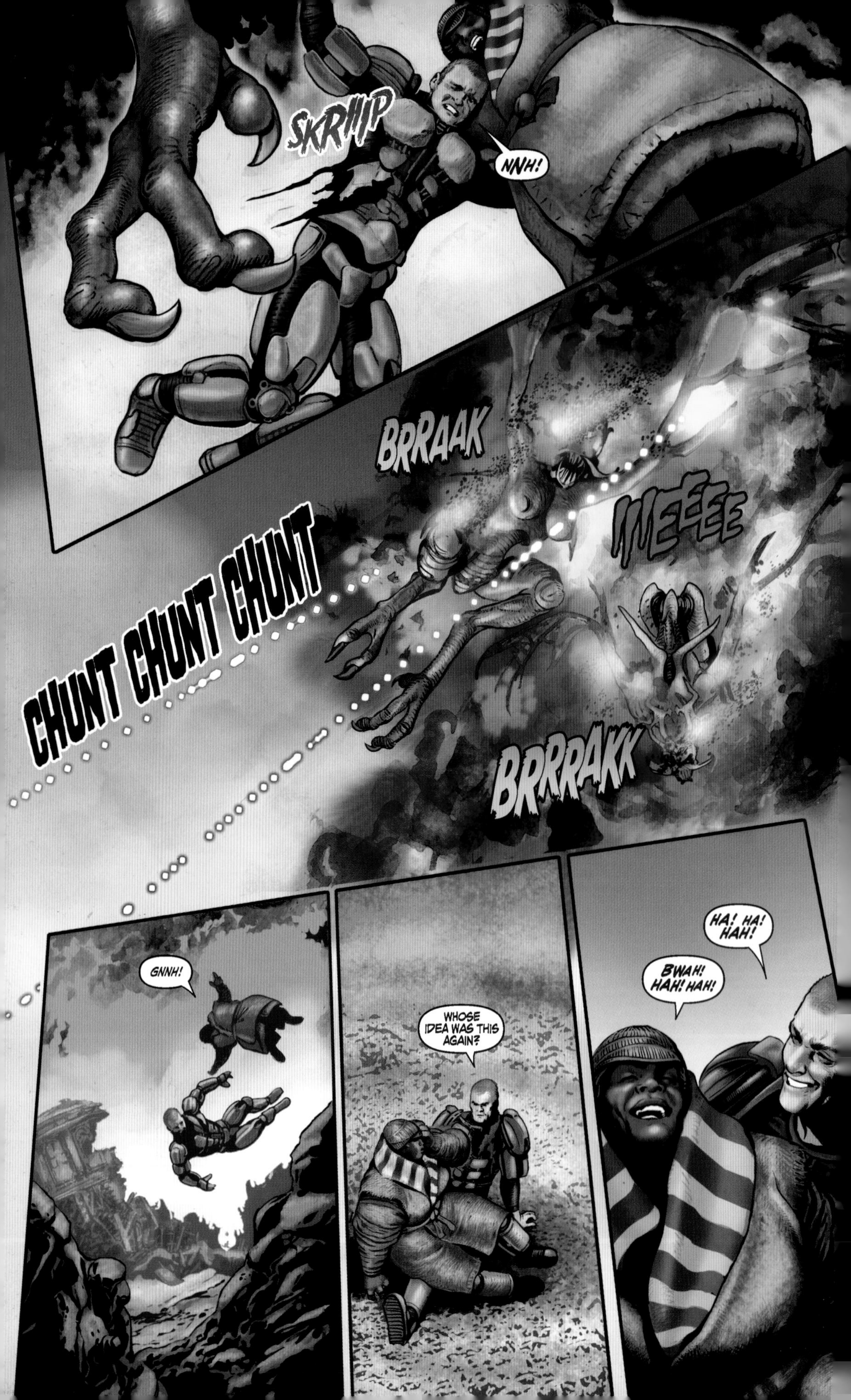
SKRIIIP
NNH!
BRRAAK
CHUNT CHUNT CHUNT
IIIEEEEE
BRRRAKK
GNNH!
WHOSE IDEA WAS THIS AGAIN?
HA! HA! HAH!
BWAH! HAH! HAH!

CAPTAIN PETRUS!

YES, SIR! COMMANDER WYVERN!

STAND DOWN YOUR TEAM AND RETURN TO THE COMMAND BUNKER. YOU'RE BEING REASSIGNED.

BUT, SIR...

THAT'S AN ORDER, CAPTAIN! I'LL EXPECT YOU WITHIN THE HOUR. WYVERN OUT!

UNDERSTOOD.

CAPT'N, YOUR ARMOUR. THE FREAK SLICED RIGHT THROUGH...YOU'RE WOUNDED?

IT'S OKAY. DON'T SWEAT IT. IT'S A BURN... CHILDHOOD ACCIDENT FROM A LIFETIME AGO.

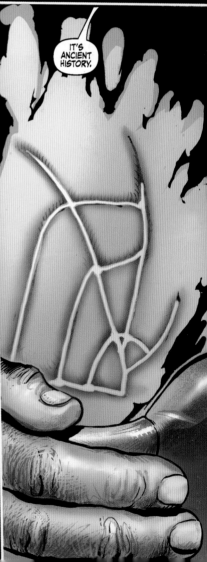

IT'S ANCIENT HISTORY.

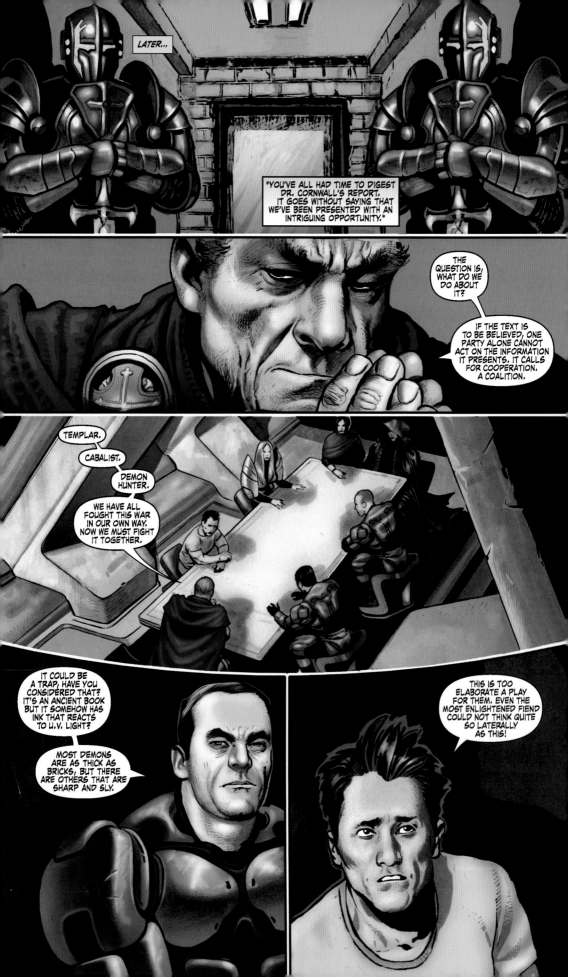

LATER...

"YOU'VE ALL HAD TIME TO DIGEST DR. CORNWALL'S REPORT. IT GOES WITHOUT SAYING THAT WE'VE BEEN PRESENTED WITH AN INTRIGUING OPPORTUNITY."

THE QUESTION IS, WHAT DO WE DO ABOUT IT?

IF THE TEXT IS TO BE BELIEVED, ONE PARTY ALONE CANNOT ACT ON THE INFORMATION IT PRESENTS. IT CALLS FOR COOPERATION. A COALITION.

TEMPLAR.

CABALIST.

DEMON HUNTER.

WE HAVE ALL FOUGHT THIS WAR IN OUR OWN WAY. NOW WE MUST FIGHT IT TOGETHER.

IT COULD BE A TRAP, HAVE YOU CONSIDERED THAT? IT'S AN ANCIENT BOOK BUT IT SOMEHOW HAS INK THAT REACTS TO U.V. LIGHT?

MOST DEMONS ARE AS THICK AS BRICKS, BUT THERE ARE OTHERS THAT ARE SHARP AND SLY.

THIS IS TOO ELABORATE A PLAY FOR THEM. EVEN THE MOST ENLIGHTENED FIEND COULD NOT THINK QUITE SO LATERALLY AS THIS!

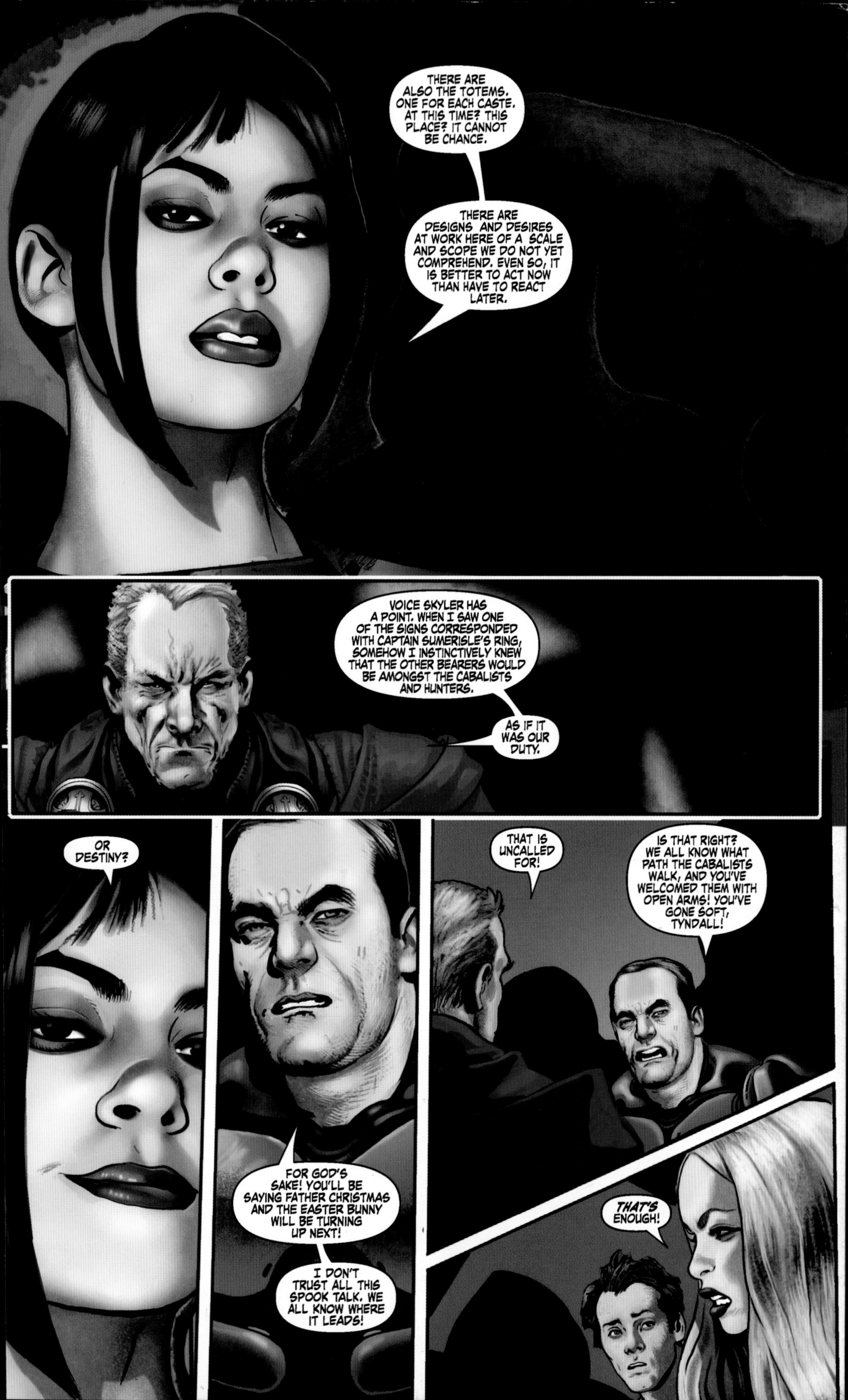

THERE ARE ALSO THE TOTEMS. ONE FOR EACH CASTE. AT THIS TIME? THIS PLACE? IT CANNOT BE CHANCE.
THERE ARE DESIGNS AND DESIRES AT WORK HERE OF A SCALE AND SCOPE WE DO NOT YET COMPREHEND. EVEN SO, IT IS BETTER TO ACT NOW THAN HAVE TO REACT LATER.
VOICE SKYLER HAS A POINT. WHEN I SAW ONE OF THE SIGNS CORRESPONDED WITH CAPTAIN SUMERISLE'S RING, SOMEHOW I INSTINCTIVELY KNEW THAT THE OTHER BEARERS WOULD BE AMONGST THE CABALISTS AND HUNTERS.
AS IF IT WAS OUR DUTY.
OR DESTINY?
FOR GOD'S SAKE! YOU'LL BE SAYING FATHER CHRISTMAS AND THE EASTER BUNNY WILL BE TURNING UP NEXT!
I DON'T TRUST ALL THIS SPOOK TALK. WE ALL KNOW WHERE IT LEADS!
THAT IS UNCALLED FOR!
IS THAT RIGHT? WE ALL KNOW WHAT PATH THE CABALISTS WALK, AND YOU'VE WELCOMED THEM WITH OPEN ARMS! YOU'VE GONE SOFT, TYNDALL!
THAT'S ENOUGH!

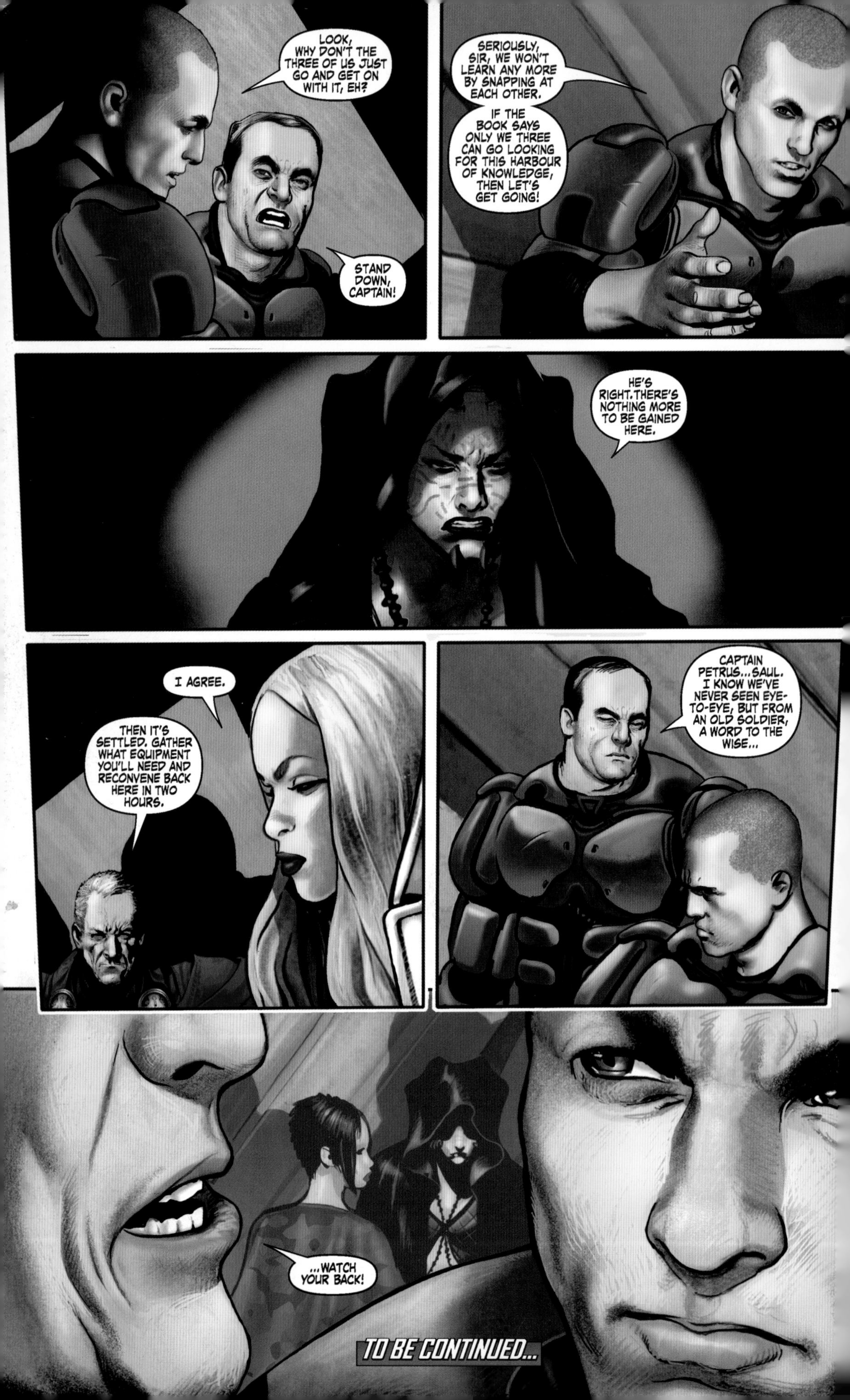
LOOK, WHY DON'T THE THREE OF US JUST GO AND GET ON WITH IT, EH?
STAND DOWN, CAPTAIN!
SERIOUSLY, SIR, WE WON'T LEARN ANY MORE BY SNAPPING AT EACH OTHER.
IF THE BOOK SAYS ONLY WE THREE CAN GO LOOKING FOR THIS HARBOUR OF KNOWLEDGE, THEN LET'S GET GOING!
HE'S RIGHT. THERE'S NOTHING MORE TO BE GAINED HERE.
I AGREE.
THEN IT'S SETTLED. GATHER WHAT EQUIPMENT YOU'LL NEED AND RECONVENE BACK HERE IN TWO HOURS.
CAPTAIN PETRUS... SAUL. I KNOW WE'VE NEVER SEEN EYE-TO-EYE, BUT FROM AN OLD SOLDIER, A WORD TO THE WISE...
...WATCH YOUR BACK!
TO BE CONTINUED...

CHAPTER
Three

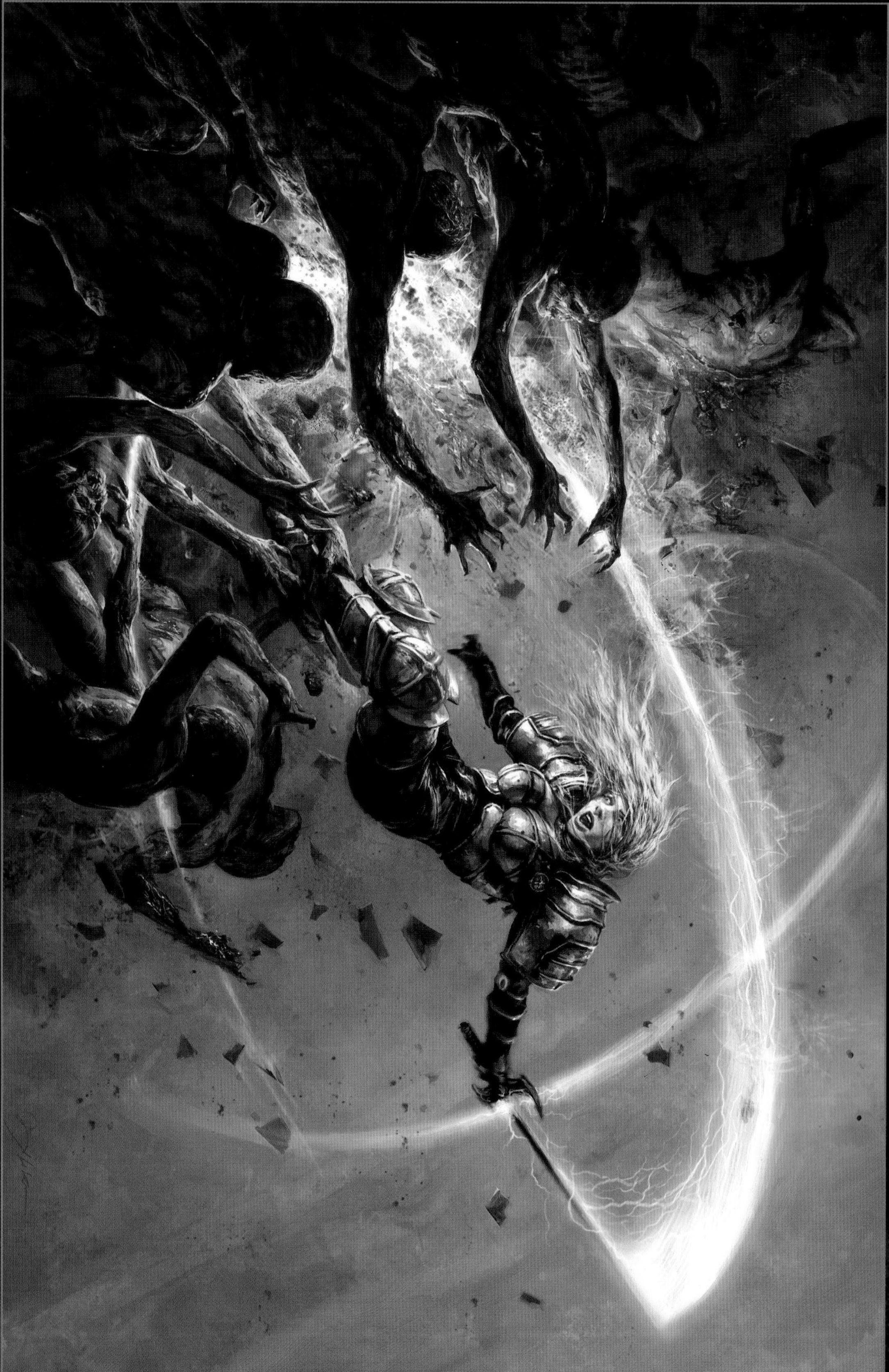

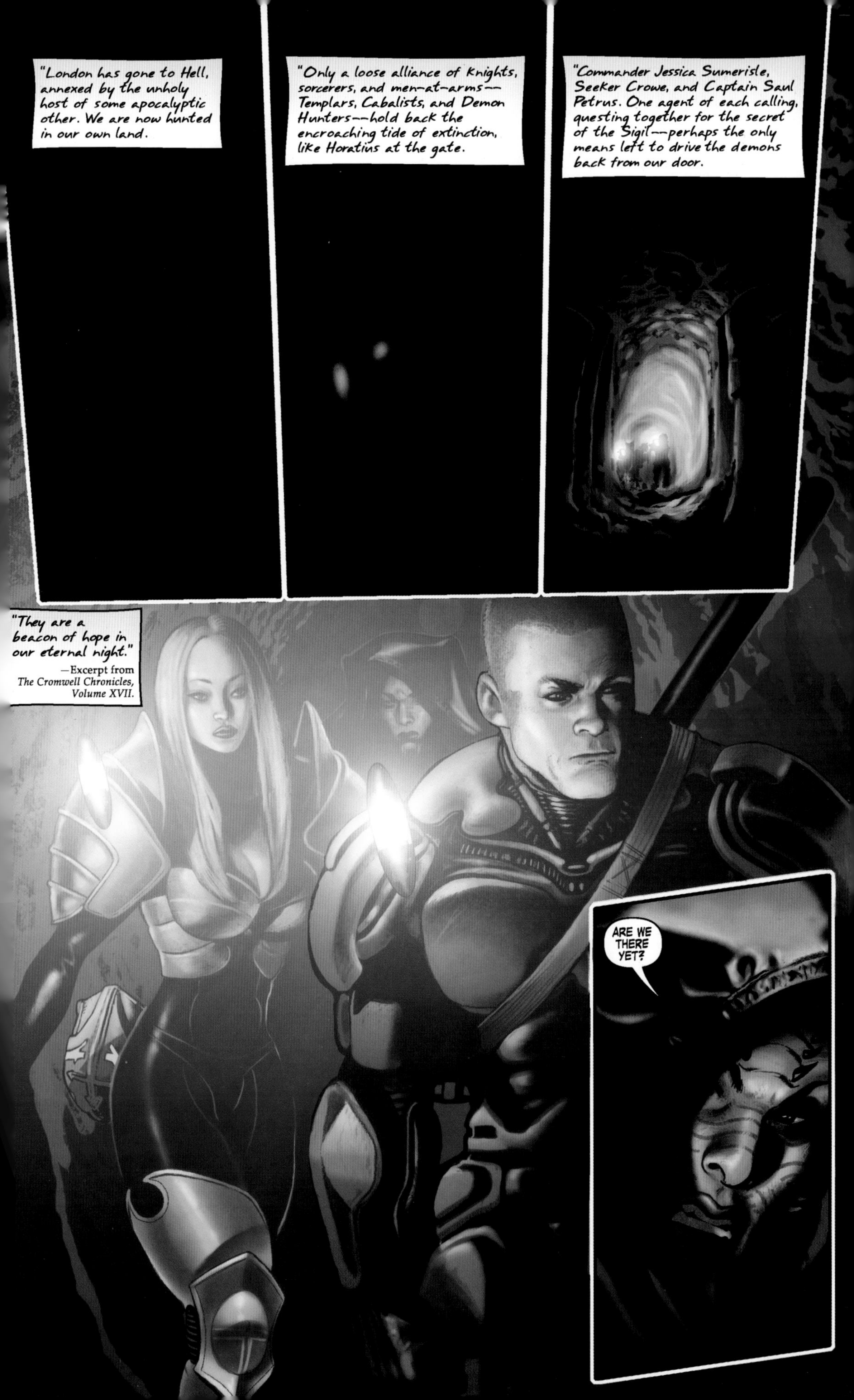
"London has gone to Hell, annexed by the unholy host of some apocalyptic other. We are now hunted in our own land.
"Only a loose alliance of knights, sorcerers, and men-at-arms-- Templars, Cabalists, and Demon Hunters--hold back the encroaching tide of extinction, like Horatius at the gate.
"Commander Jessica Sumerisle, Seeker Crowe, and Captain Saul Petrus. One agent of each calling, questing together for the secret of the Sigil--perhaps the only means left to drive the demons back from our door.
"They are a beacon of hope in our eternal night."
—Excerpt from The Cromwell Chronicles, Volume XVII.
ARE WE THERE YET?

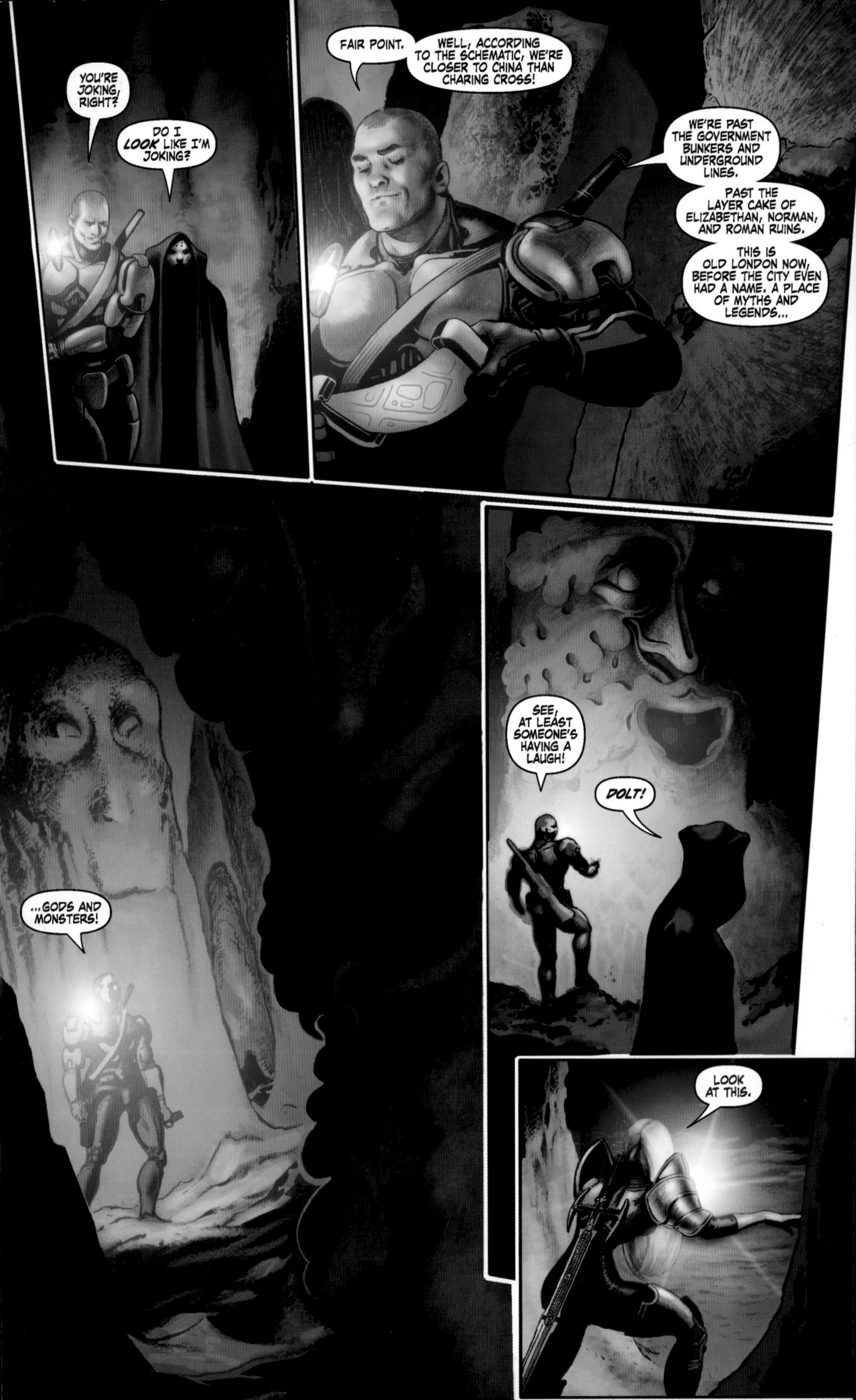
YOU'RE JOKING, RIGHT?
DO I LOOK LIKE I'M JOKING?
FAIR POINT.
WELL, ACCORDING TO THE SCHEMATIC, WE'RE CLOSER TO CHINA THAN CHARING CROSS!
WE'RE PAST THE GOVERNMENT BUNKERS AND UNDERGROUND LINES.
PAST THE LAYER CAKE OF ELIZABETHAN, NORMAN, AND ROMAN RUINS.
THIS IS OLD LONDON NOW, BEFORE THE CITY EVEN HAD A NAME. A PLACE OF MYTHS AND LEGENDS...
...GODS AND MONSTERS!
SEE, AT LEAST SOMEONE'S HAVING A LAUGH!
DOLT!
LOOK AT THIS.

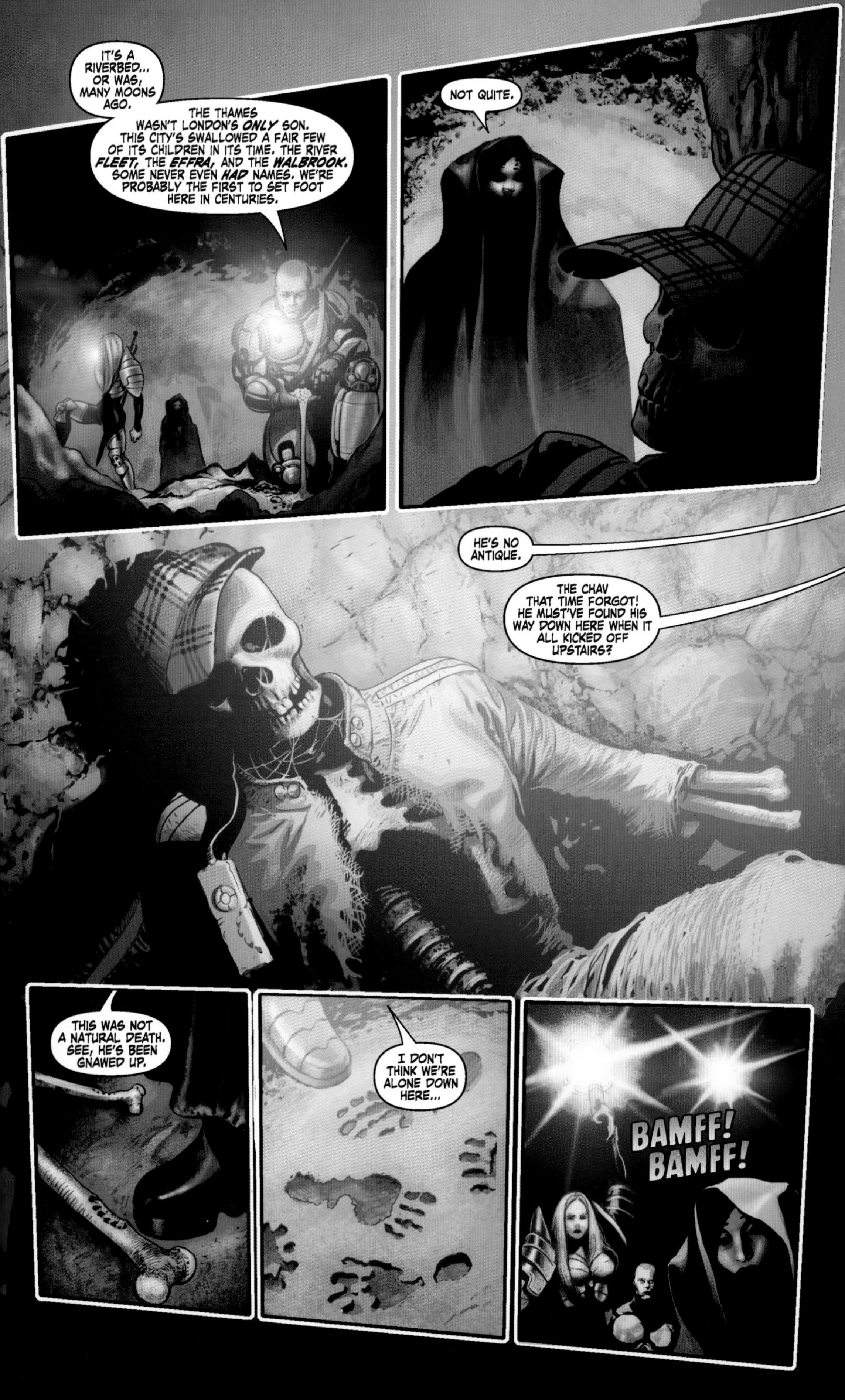
IT'S A RIVERBED... OR WAS, MANY MOONS AGO.
THE THAMES WASN'T LONDON'S ONLY SON. THIS CITY'S SWALLOWED A FAIR FEW OF ITS CHILDREN IN ITS TIME. THE RIVER FLEET, THE EFFRA, AND THE WALBROOK. SOME NEVER EVEN HAD NAMES. WE'RE PROBABLY THE FIRST TO SET FOOT HERE IN CENTURIES.
NOT QUITE.
HE'S NO ANTIQUE.
THE CHAV THAT TIME FORGOT! HE MUST'VE FOUND HIS WAY DOWN HERE WHEN IT ALL KICKED OFF UPSTAIRS?
THIS WAS NOT A NATURAL DEATH. SEE, HE'S BEEN GNAWED UP.
I DON'T THINK WE'RE ALONE DOWN HERE...
BAMFF! BAMFF!

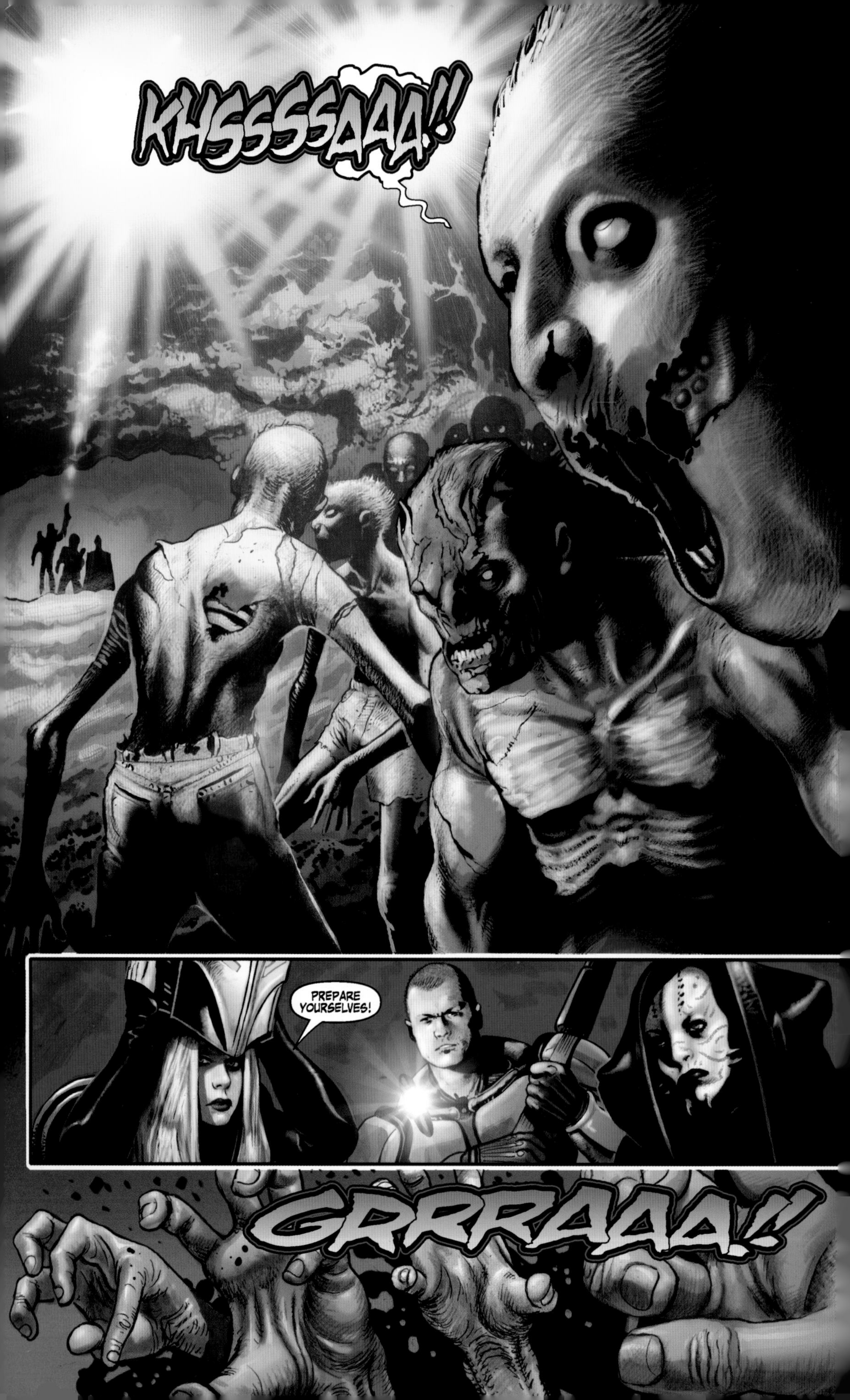
KHSSSSAAA!!
PREPARE YOURSELVES!
GRRRAAA!!

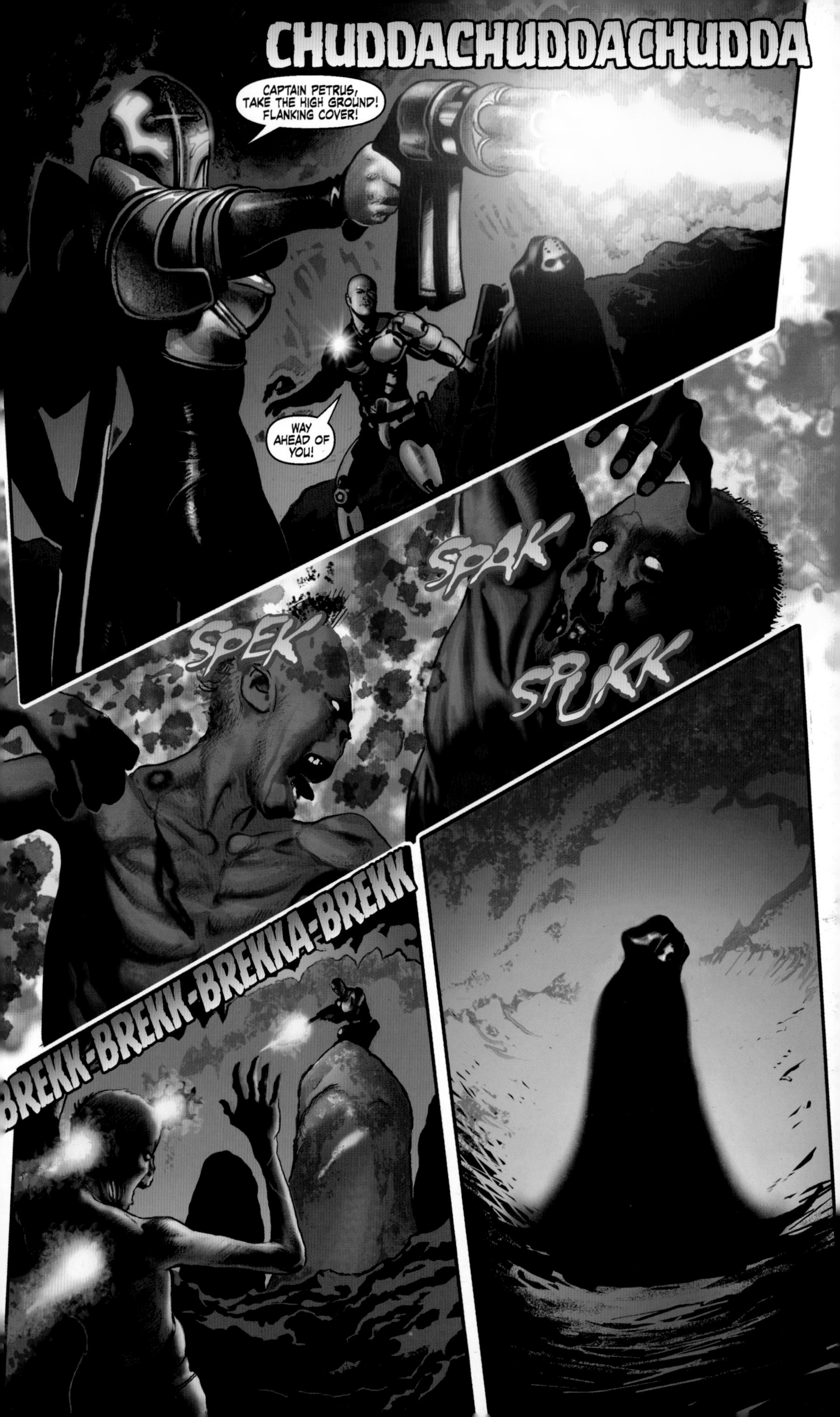
CHUDDACHUDDACHUDDA
CAPTAIN PETRUS, TAKE THE HIGH GROUND! FLANKING COVER!
WAY AHEAD OF YOU!
SPAK
SPEK
SPUKK
BREKK-BREKK-BREKKA-BREKK

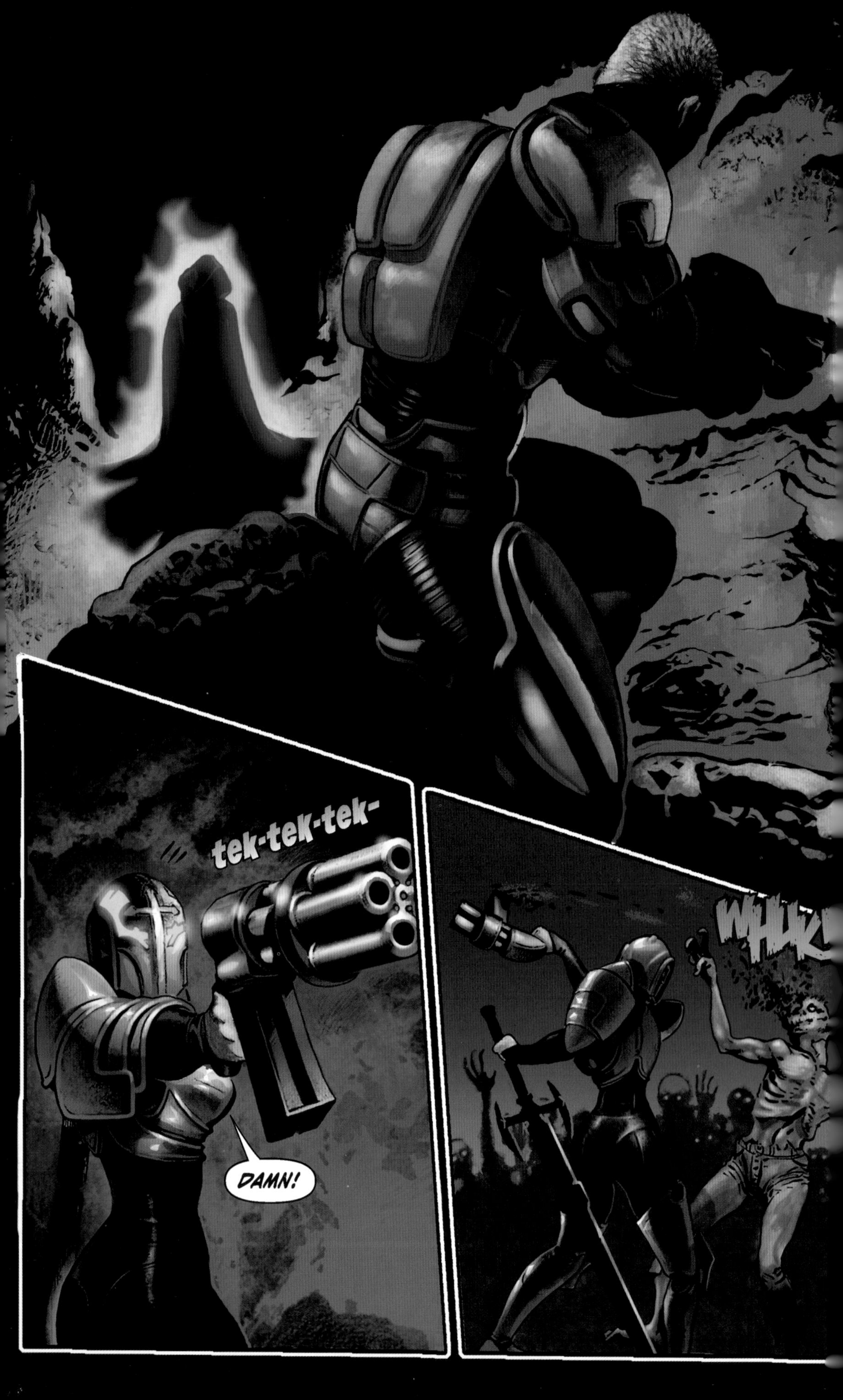
tek-tek-tek-
DAMN!

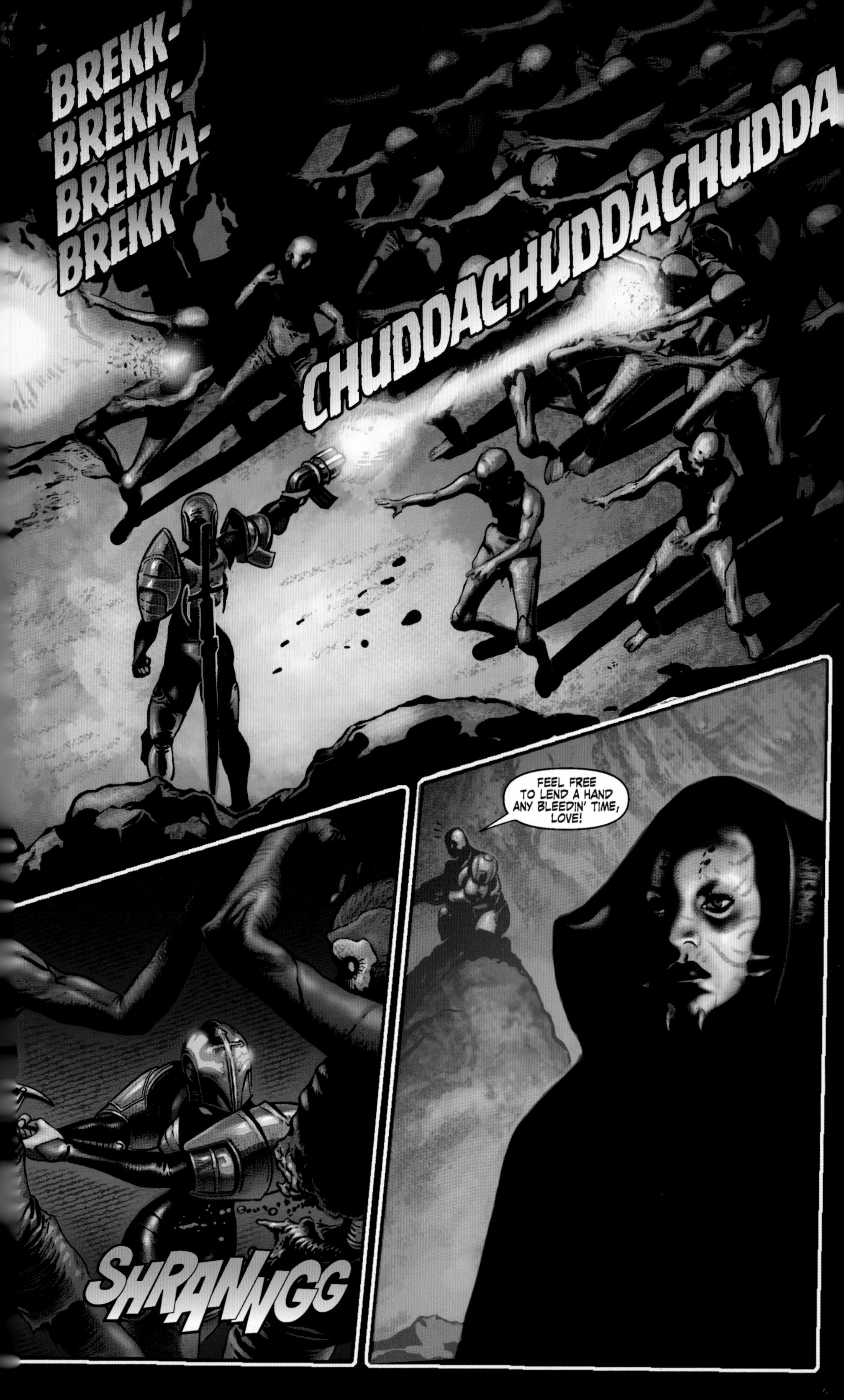
BREKK-
BREKK-
BREKKA-
BREKK
CHUDDACHUDDACHUDDA
FEEL FREE TO LEND A HAND ANY BLEEDIN' TIME, LOVE!
SHRANNGG

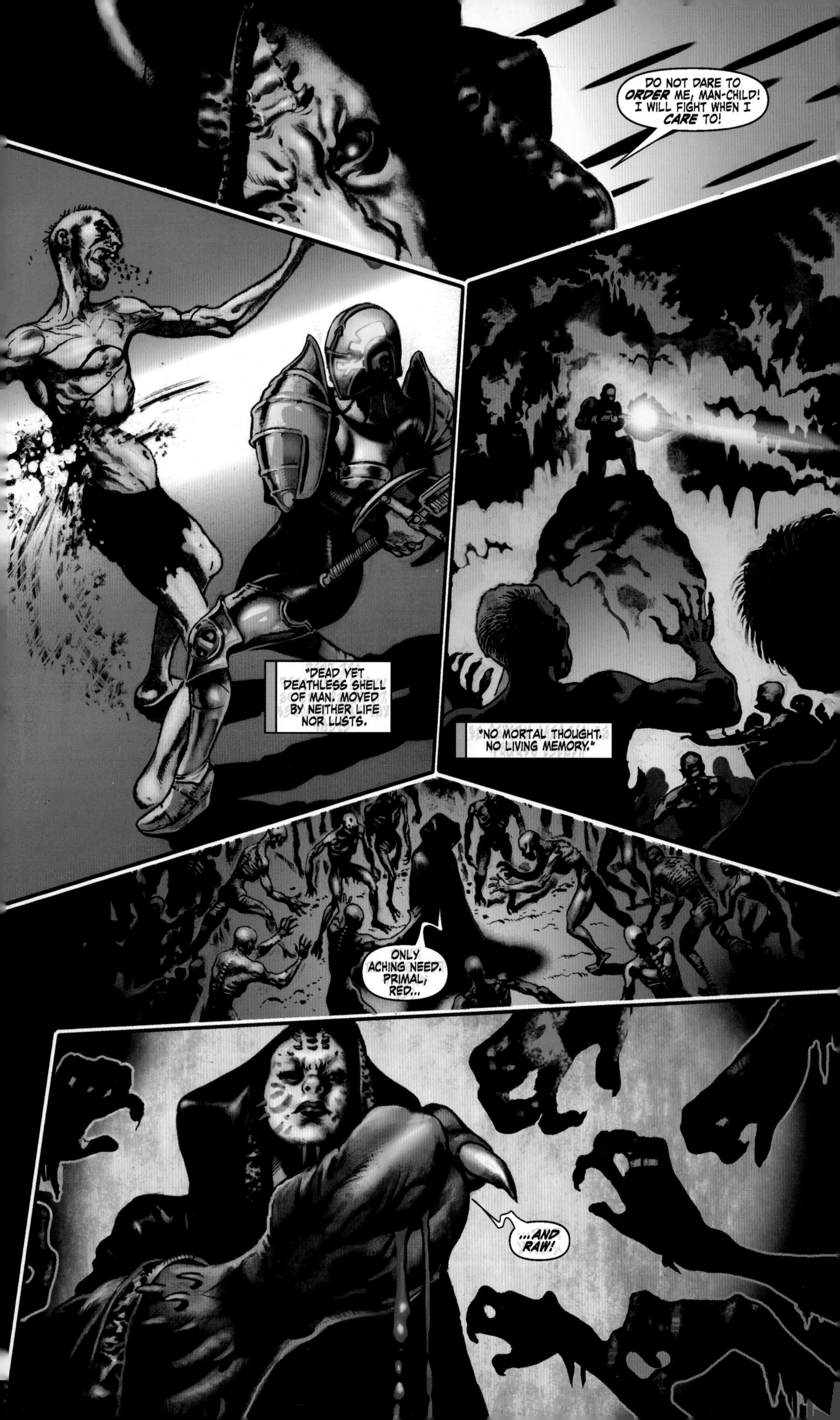
DO NOT DARE TO ORDER ME, MAN-CHILD! I WILL FIGHT WHEN I CARE TO!
"DEAD YET DEATHLESS SHELL OF MAN. MOVED BY NEITHER LIFE NOR LUSTS.
"NO MORTAL THOUGHT. NO LIVING MEMORY."
ONLY ACHING NEED. PRIMAL, RED...
...AND RAW!

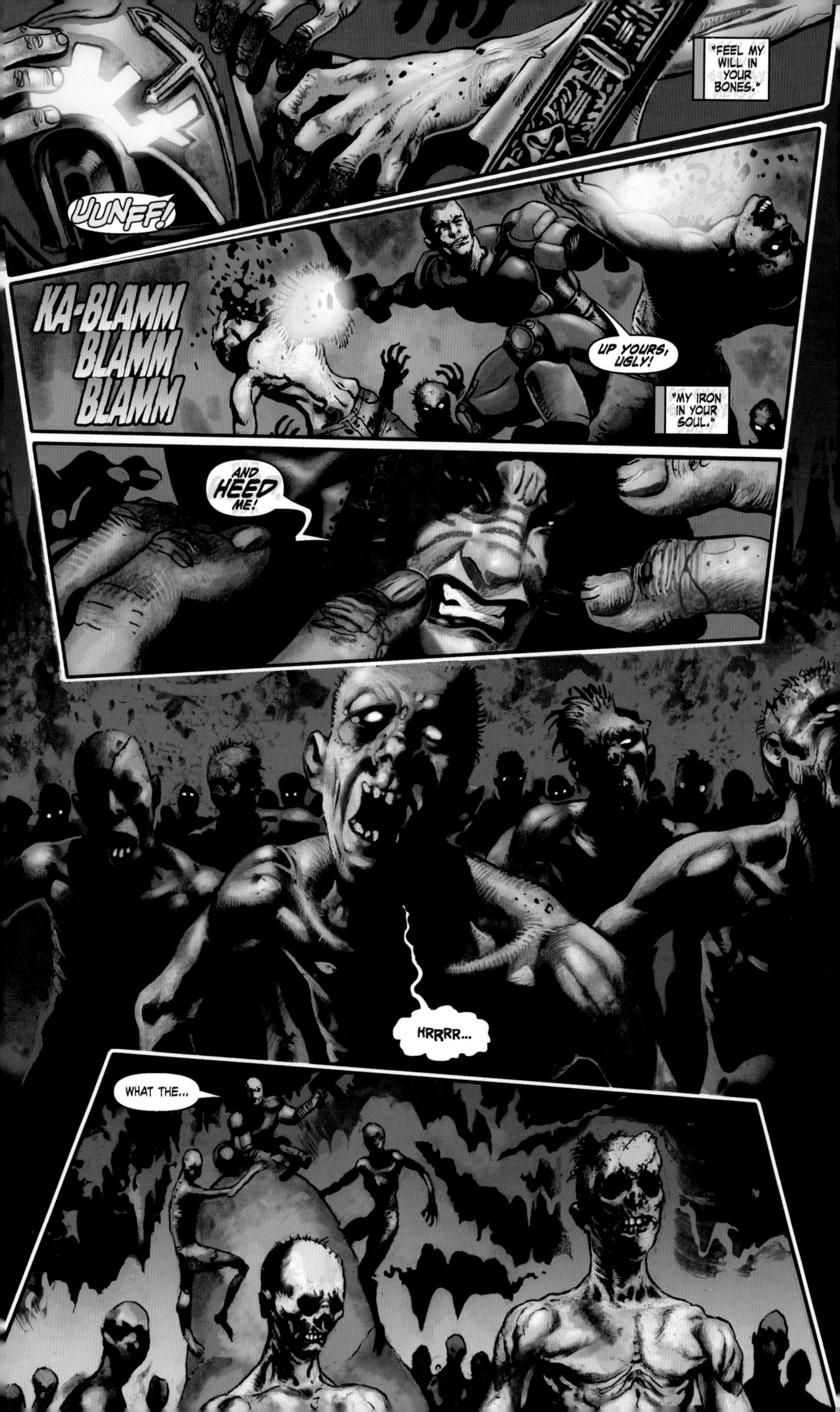
"FEEL MY WILL IN YOUR BONES."
UUNFF!
KA-BLAMM BLAMM BLAMM
UP YOURS, UGLY!
"MY IRON IN YOUR SOUL."
AND HEED ME!
HRRRR...
WHAT THE...

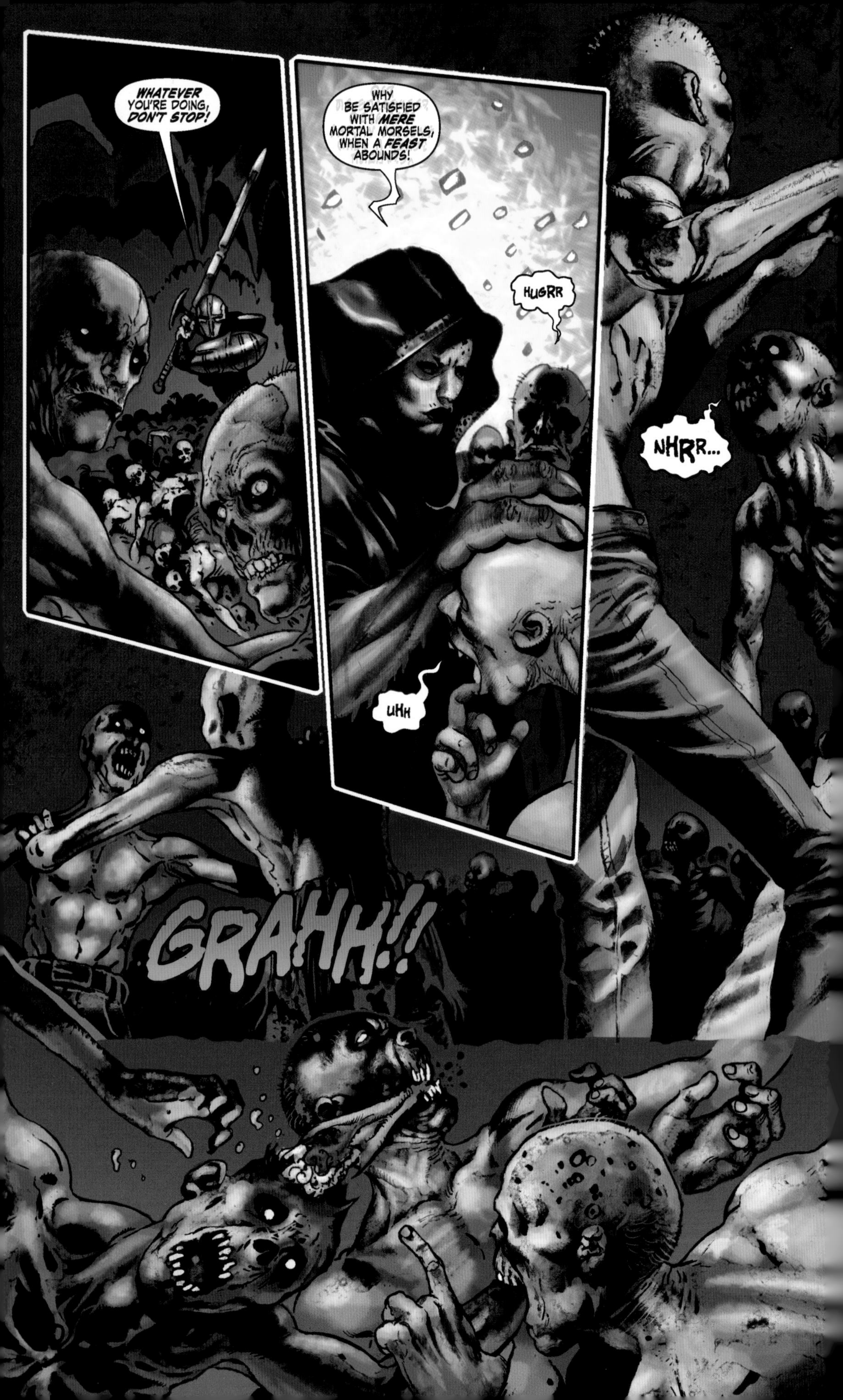
WHATEVER YOU'RE DOING, DON'T STOP!
WHY BE SATISFIED WITH MERE MORTAL MORSELS, WHEN A FEAST ABOUNDS!
HUGRR
NHRR...
UHH
GRAHH!!

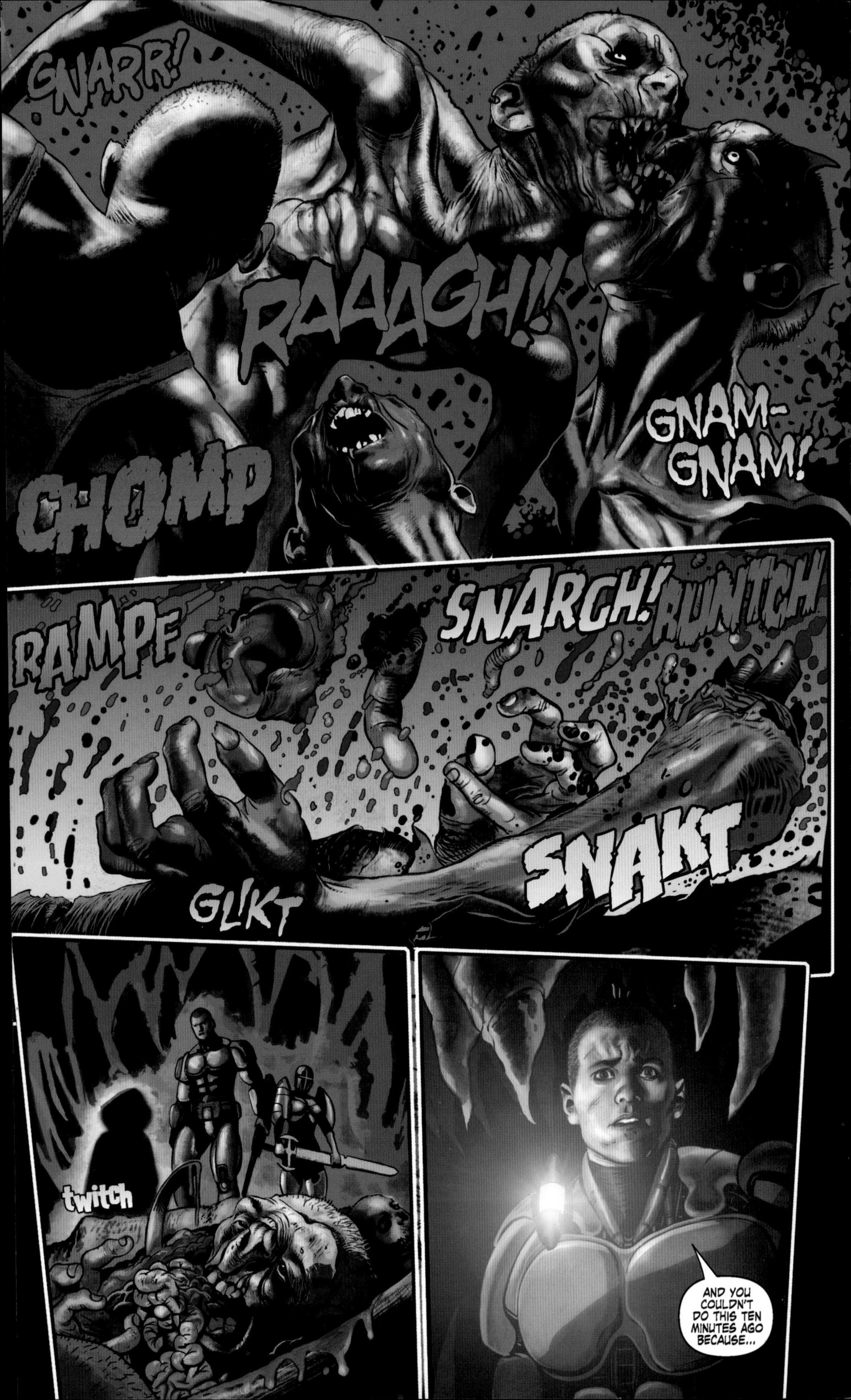
GNARR!
RAAAGH!!
GNAM-GNAM!
CHOMP
RAMPF
SNARCH!
RUNTCH
SNAKT
GLIKT
twitch
AND YOU COULDN'T DO THIS TEN MINUTES AGO BECAUSE...

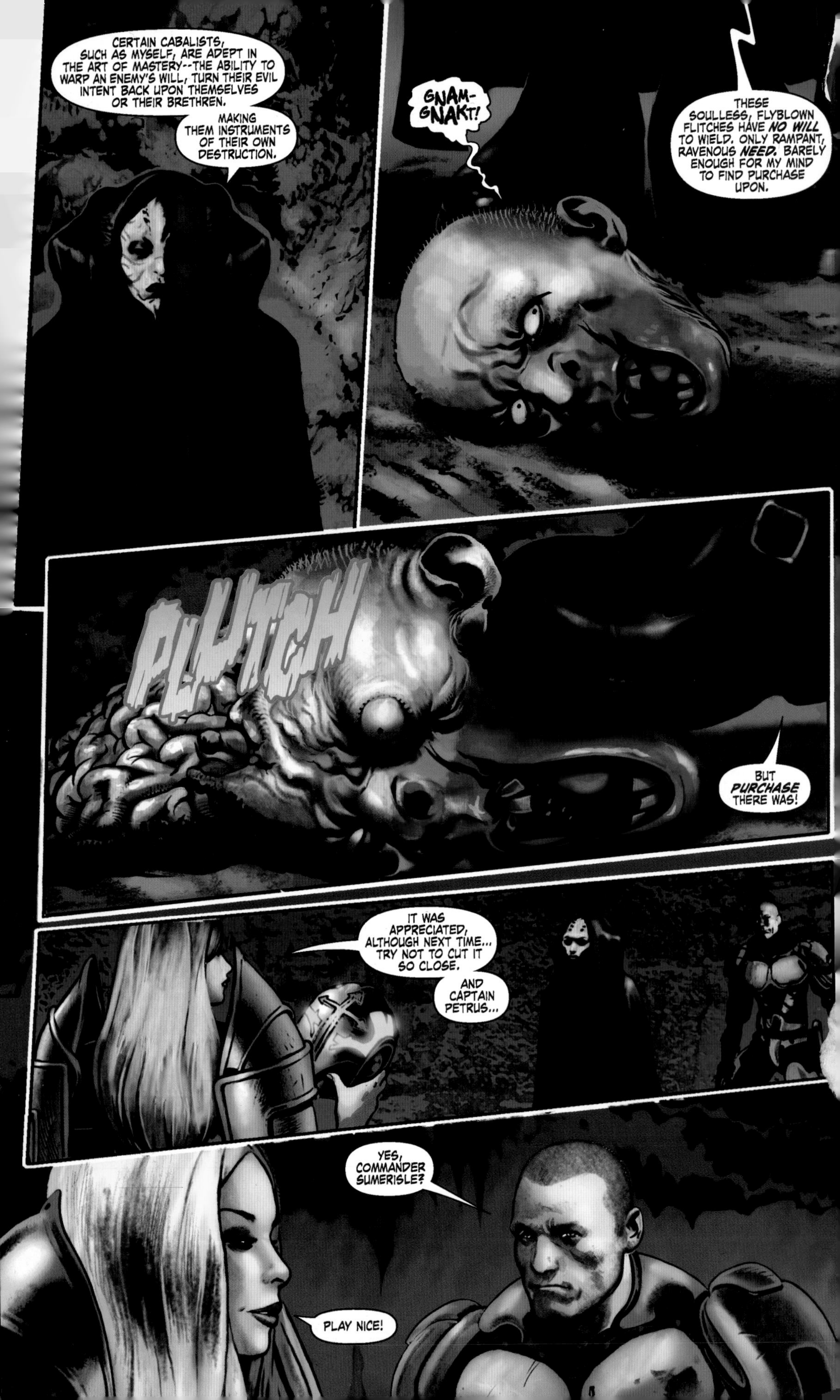
CERTAIN CABALISTS, SUCH AS MYSELF, ARE ADEPT IN THE ART OF MASTERY--THE ABILITY TO WARP AN ENEMY'S WILL, TURN THEIR EVIL INTENT BACK UPON THEMSELVES OR THEIR BRETHREN.
MAKING THEM INSTRUMENTS OF THEIR OWN DESTRUCTION.
GNAM-GNAKT!
THESE SOULLESS, FLYBLOWN FLITCHES HAVE NO WILL TO WIELD. ONLY RAMPANT, RAVENOUS NEED. BARELY ENOUGH FOR MY MIND TO FIND PURCHASE UPON.
PLUTCH
BUT PURCHASE THERE WAS!
IT WAS APPRECIATED, ALTHOUGH NEXT TIME... TRY NOT TO CUT IT SO CLOSE.
AND CAPTAIN PETRUS...
YES, COMMANDER SUMERISLE?
PLAY NICE!

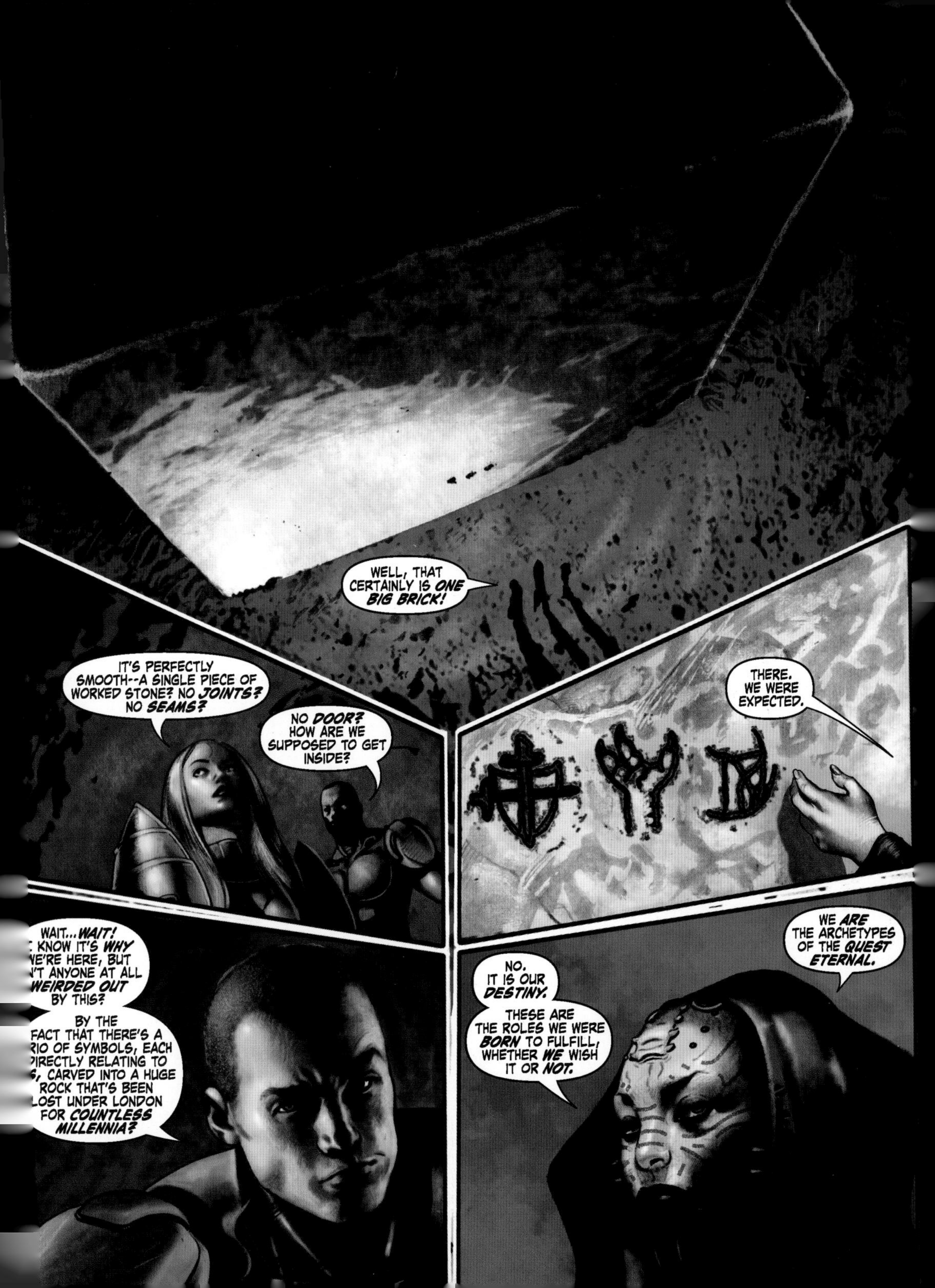
WELL, THAT CERTAINLY IS ONE BIG BRICK!
IT'S PERFECTLY SMOOTH--A SINGLE PIECE OF WORKED STONE? NO JOINTS? NO SEAMS?
NO DOOR? HOW ARE WE SUPPOSED TO GET INSIDE?
THERE. WE WERE EXPECTED.
WAIT...WAIT! KNOW IT'S WHY E'RE HERE, BUT 'T ANYONE AT ALL WEIRDED OUT BY THIS?
BY THE FACT THAT THERE'S A RIO OF SYMBOLS, EACH DIRECTLY RELATING TO , CARVED INTO A HUGE ROCK THAT'S BEEN LOST UNDER LONDON FOR COUNTLESS MILLENNIA?
NO. IT IS OUR DESTINY.
THESE ARE THE ROLES WE WERE BORN TO FULFILL, WHETHER WE WISH IT OR NOT.
WE ARE THE ARCHETYPES OF THE QUEST ETERNAL.

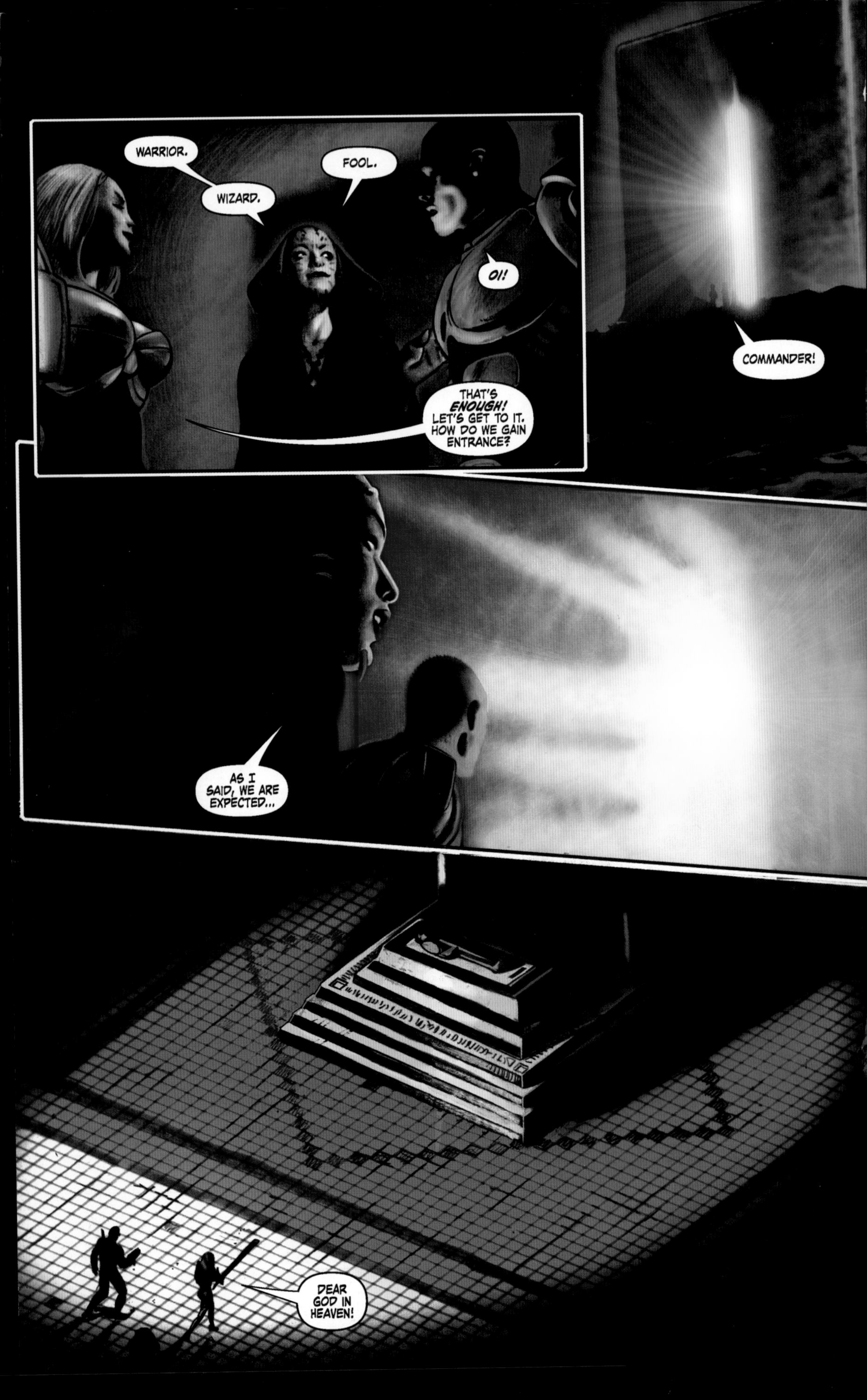
COMMANDER!
WARRIOR.
WIZARD.
FOOL.
OI!
THAT'S ENOUGH! LET'S GET TO IT. HOW DO WE GAIN ENTRANCE?
AS I SAID, WE ARE EXPECTED...
DEAR GOD IN HEAVEN!

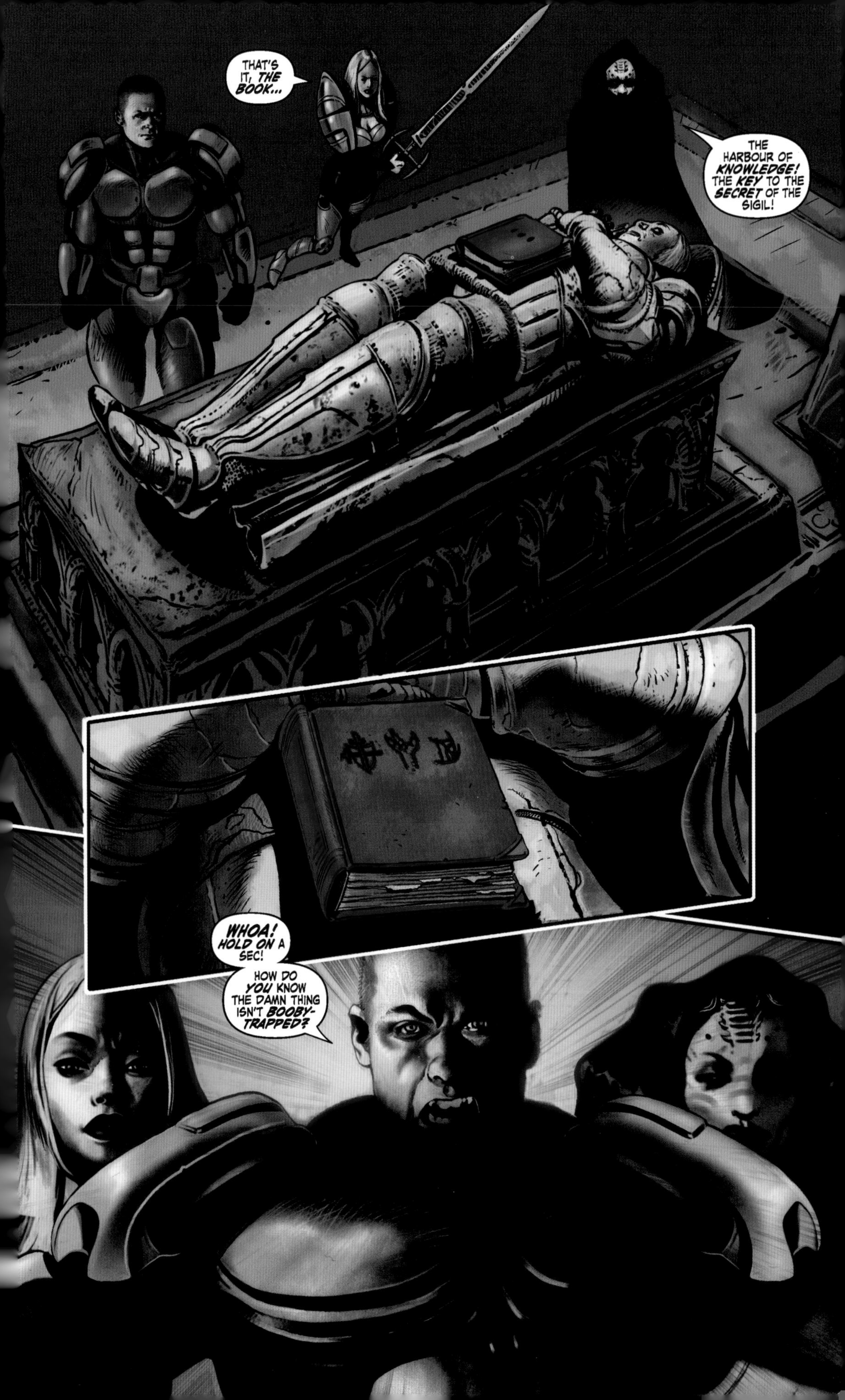
THAT'S IT, *THE BOOK...*
THE HARBOUR OF *KNOWLEDGE!* THE *KEY* TO THE *SECRET* OF THE SIGIL!
WHOA! HOLD ON A SEC!
HOW DO *YOU* KNOW THE DAMN THING ISN'T *BOOBY-TRAPPED?*

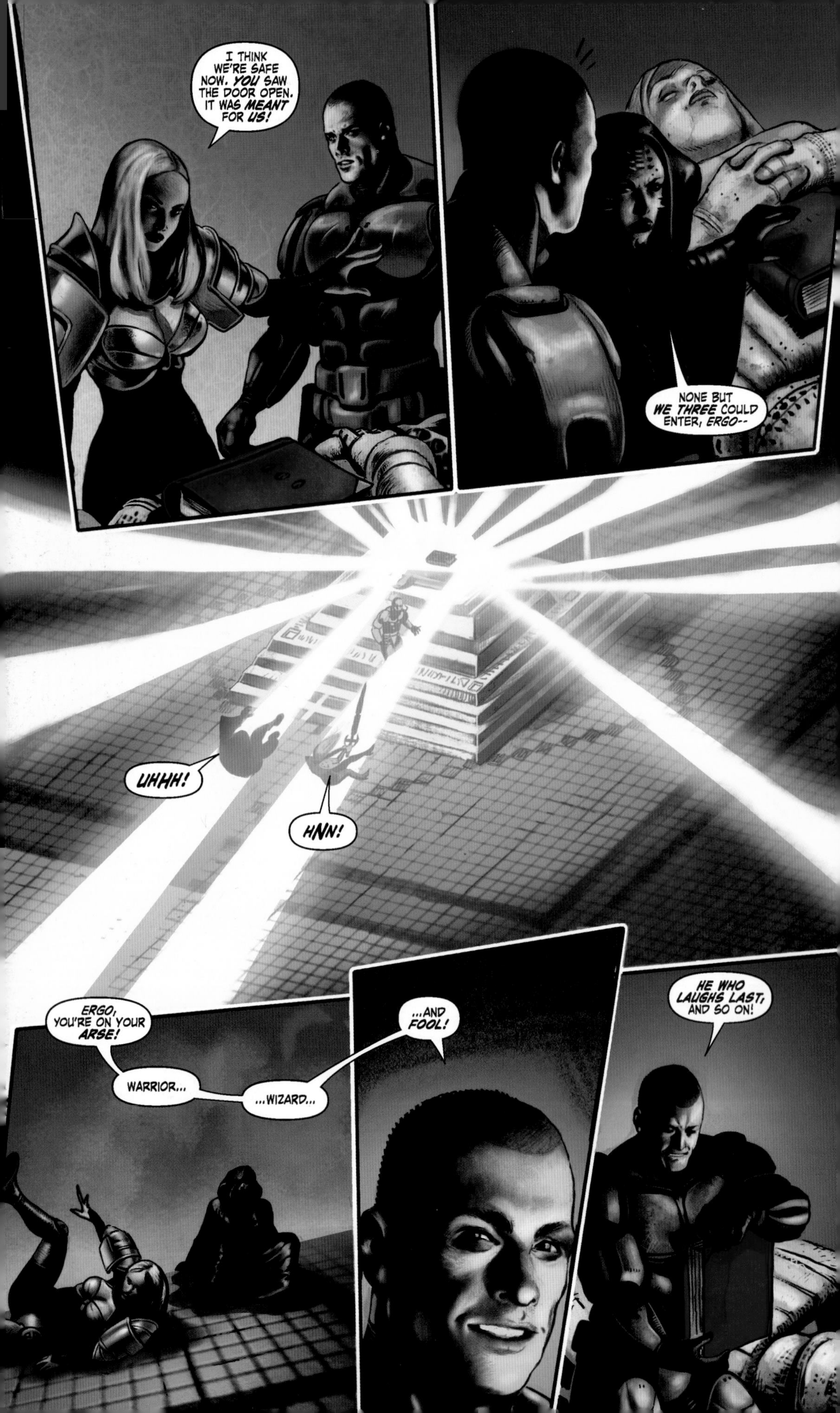
I THINK WE'RE SAFE NOW. *YOU* SAW THE DOOR OPEN. IT WAS *MEANT* FOR *US!*
NONE BUT *WE THREE* COULD ENTER, *ERGO*--
UHHH!
HNN!
ERGO, YOU'RE ON YOUR *ARSE!*
WARRIOR...
...WIZARD...
...AND *FOOL!*
HE WHO LAUGHS LAST, AND SO ON!

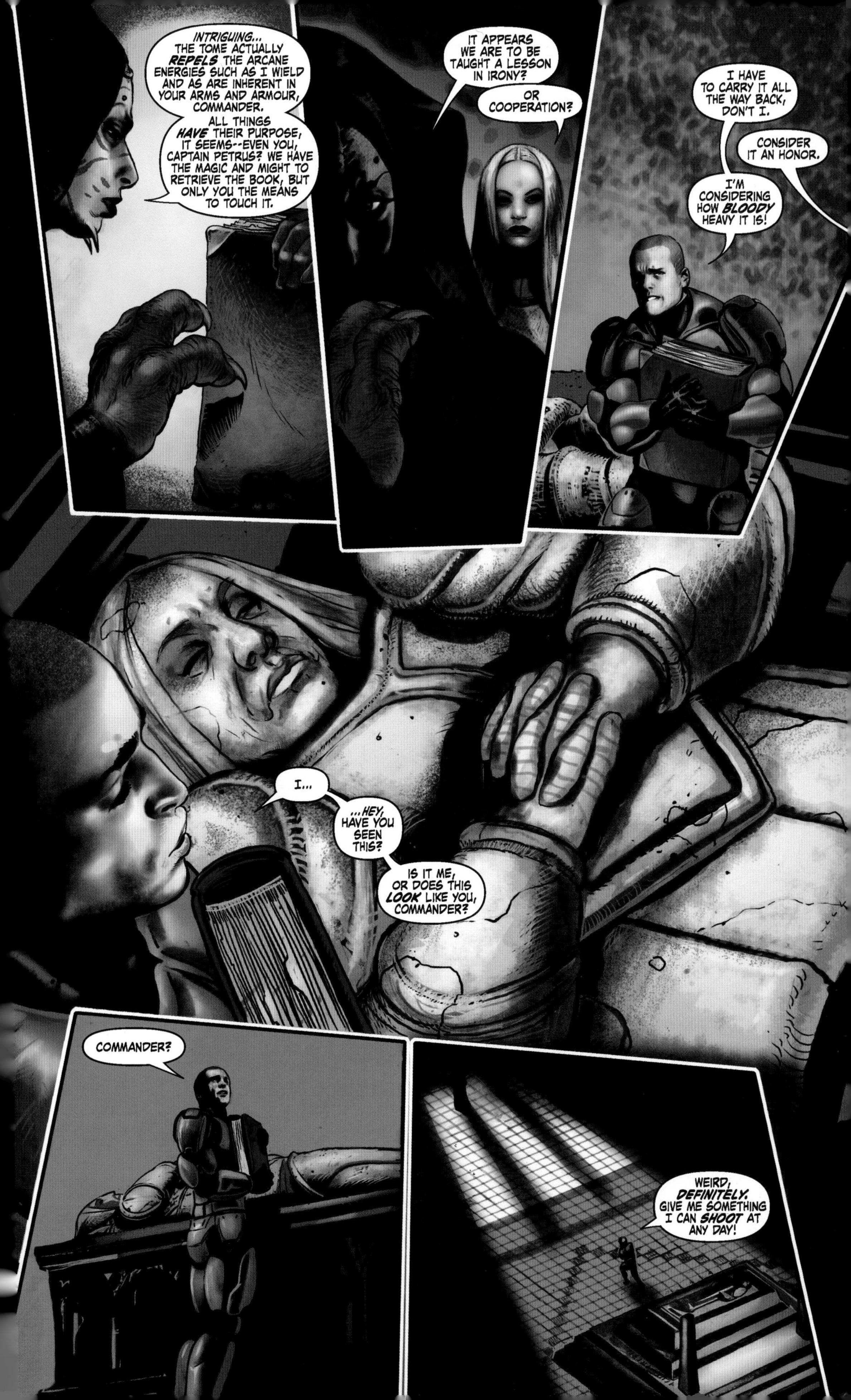
INTRIGUING... THE TOME ACTUALLY REPELS THE ARCANE ENERGIES SUCH AS I WIELD AND AS ARE INHERENT IN YOUR ARMS AND ARMOUR, COMMANDER.
ALL THINGS HAVE THEIR PURPOSE, IT SEEMS--EVEN YOU, CAPTAIN PETRUS? WE HAVE THE MAGIC AND MIGHT TO RETRIEVE THE BOOK, BUT ONLY YOU THE MEANS TO TOUCH IT.
IT APPEARS WE ARE TO BE TAUGHT A LESSON IN IRONY?
OR COOPERATION?
I HAVE TO CARRY IT ALL THE WAY BACK, DON'T I.
CONSIDER IT AN HONOR.
I'M CONSIDERING HOW BLOODY HEAVY IT IS!
I...
...HEY, HAVE YOU SEEN THIS?
IS IT ME, OR DOES THIS LOOK LIKE YOU, COMMANDER?
COMMANDER?
WEIRD, DEFINITELY. GIVE ME SOMETHING I CAN SHOOT AT ANY DAY!

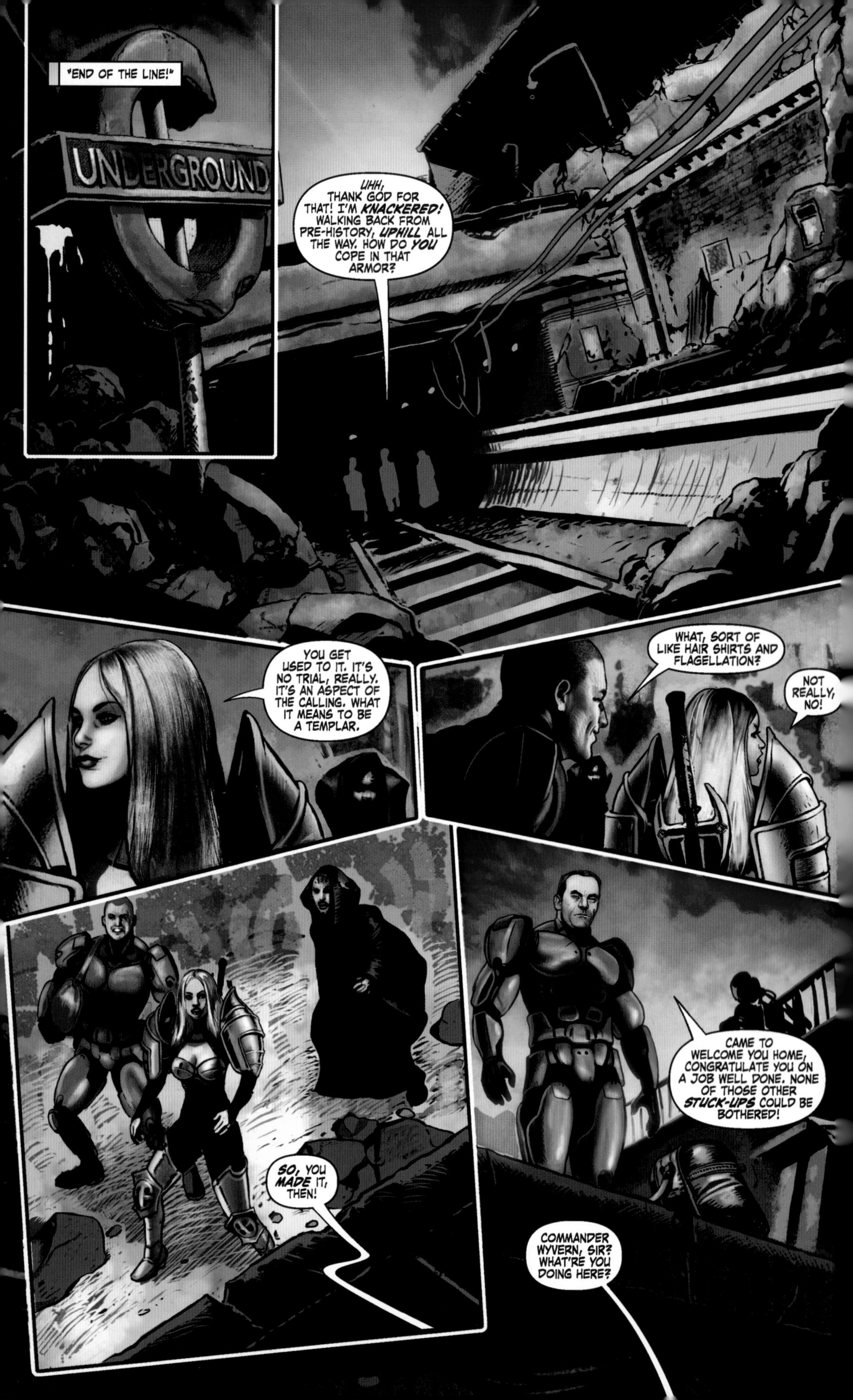
"END OF THE LINE!"
UNDERGROUND
UHH, THANK GOD FOR THAT! I'M KNACKERED! WALKING BACK FROM PRE-HISTORY, UPHILL ALL THE WAY. HOW DO YOU COPE IN THAT ARMOR?
YOU GET USED TO IT. IT'S NO TRIAL, REALLY. IT'S AN ASPECT OF THE CALLING. WHAT IT MEANS TO BE A TEMPLAR.
WHAT, SORT OF LIKE HAIR SHIRTS AND FLAGELLATION?
NOT REALLY, NO!
SO, YOU MADE IT, THEN!
COMMANDER WYVERN, SIR? WHAT'RE YOU DOING HERE?
CAME TO WELCOME YOU HOME, CONGRATULATE YOU ON A JOB WELL DONE. NONE OF THOSE OTHER STUCK-UPS COULD BE BOTHERED!

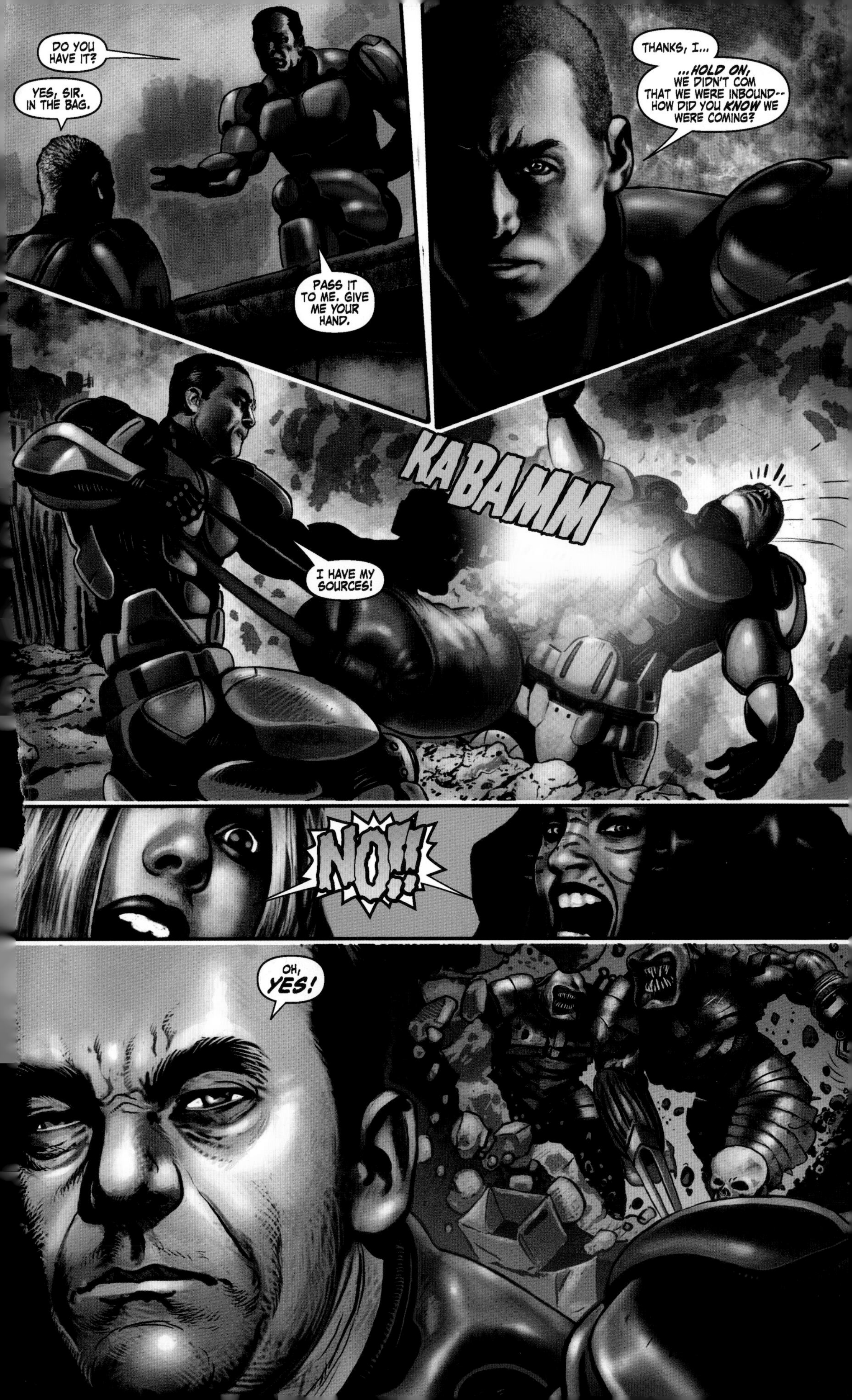
DO YOU HAVE IT?
YES, SIR. IN THE BAG.
PASS IT TO ME. GIVE ME YOUR HAND.
THANKS, I...
...HOLD ON, WE DIDN'T COM THAT WE WERE INBOUND-- HOW DID YOU KNOW WE WERE COMING?
KA BAMM
I HAVE MY SOURCES!
NO!!
OH, YES!

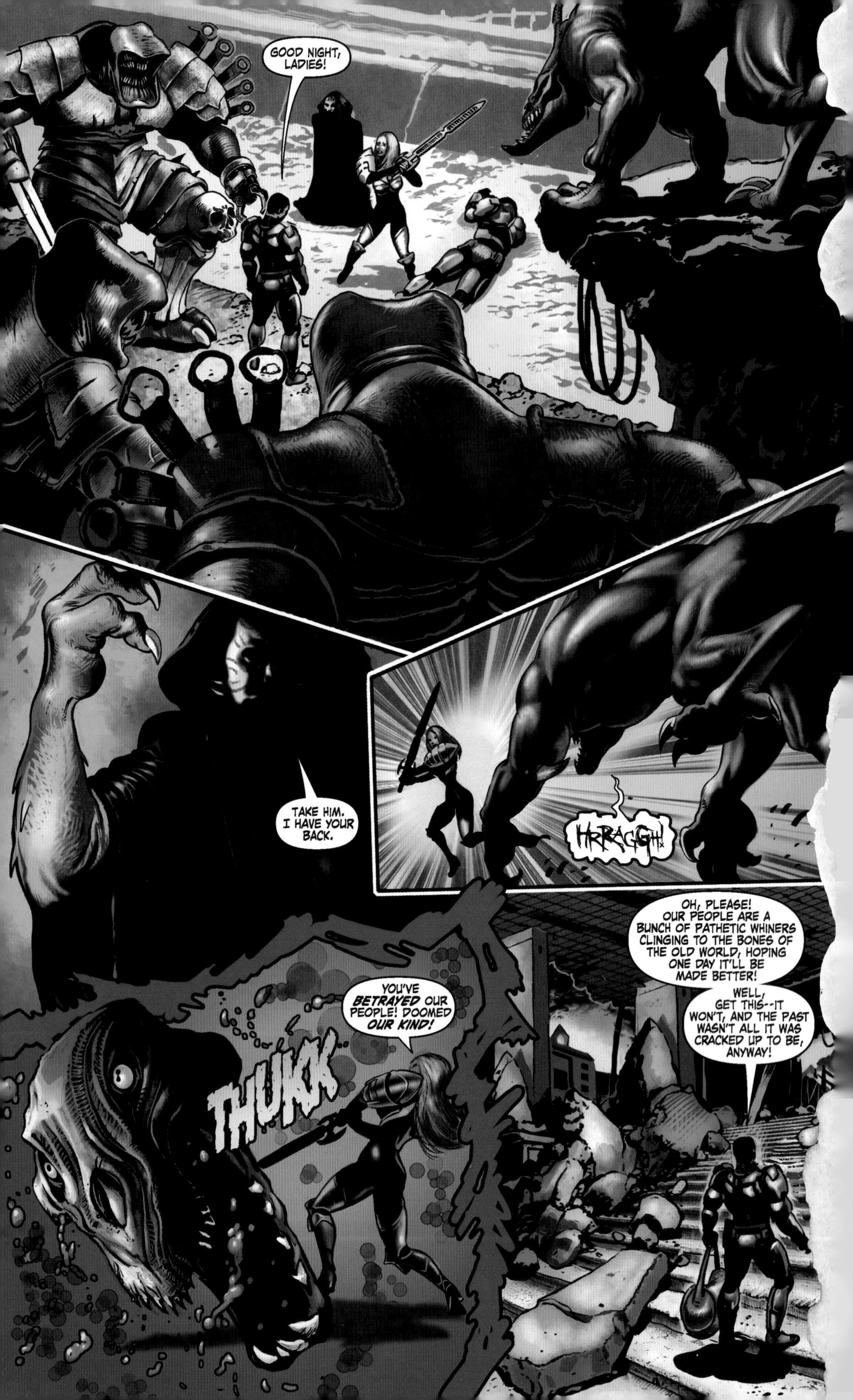
GOOD NIGHT, LADIES!
TAKE HIM. I HAVE YOUR BACK.
HRRAGGH!
YOU'VE BETRAYED OUR PEOPLE! DOOMED OUR KIND!
THUKK
OH, PLEASE! OUR PEOPLE ARE A BUNCH OF PATHETIC WHINERS CLINGING TO THE BONES OF THE OLD WORLD, HOPING ONE DAY IT'LL BE MADE BETTER!
WELL, GET THIS--IT WON'T, AND THE PAST WASN'T ALL IT WAS CRACKED UP TO BE, ANYWAY!

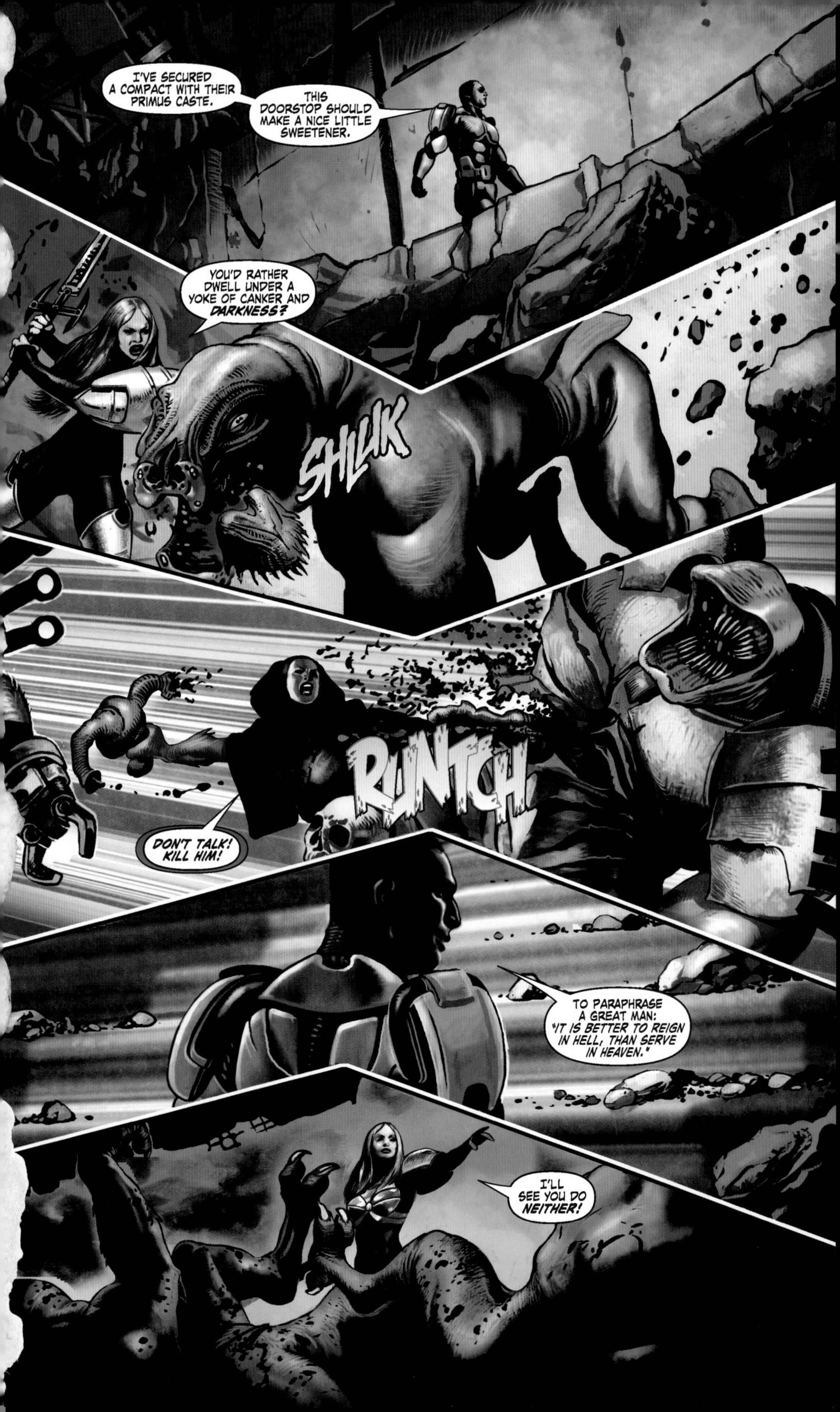
I'VE SECURED A COMPACT WITH THEIR PRIMUS CASTE.
THIS DOORSTOP SHOULD MAKE A NICE LITTLE SWEETENER.
YOU'D RATHER DWELL UNDER A YOKE OF CANKER AND *DARKNESS?*
SHLLIK
RUNTCH
DON'T TALK! KILL HIM!
TO PARAPHRASE A GREAT MAN: *"IT IS BETTER TO REIGN IN HELL, THAN SERVE IN HEAVEN."*
I'LL SEE YOU DO *NEITHER!*

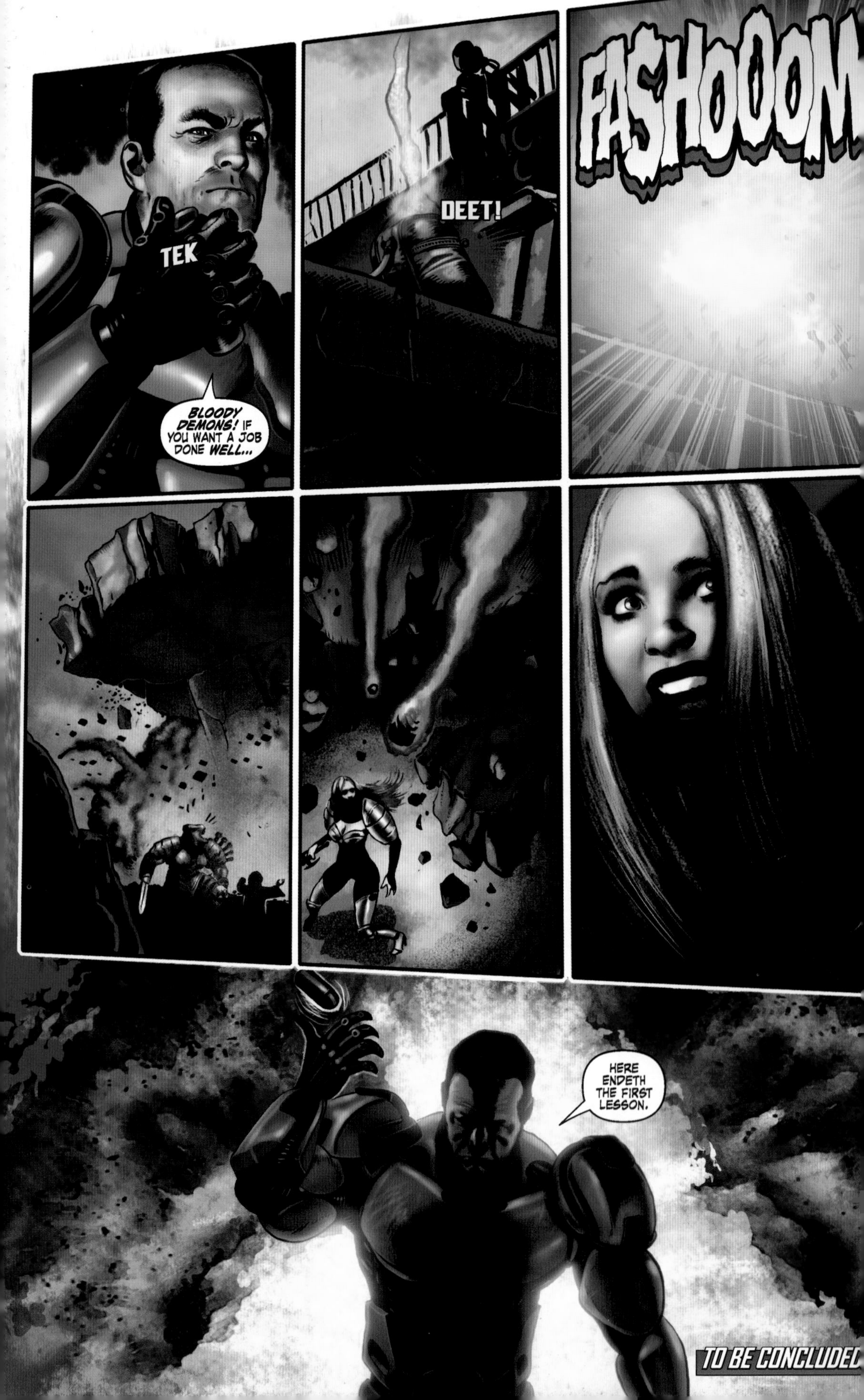
TEK
BLOODY DEMONS! IF YOU WANT A JOB DONE WELL...
DEET!
FASHOOOM
HERE ENDETH THE FIRST LESSON.
TO BE CONCLUDED

Chapter

four

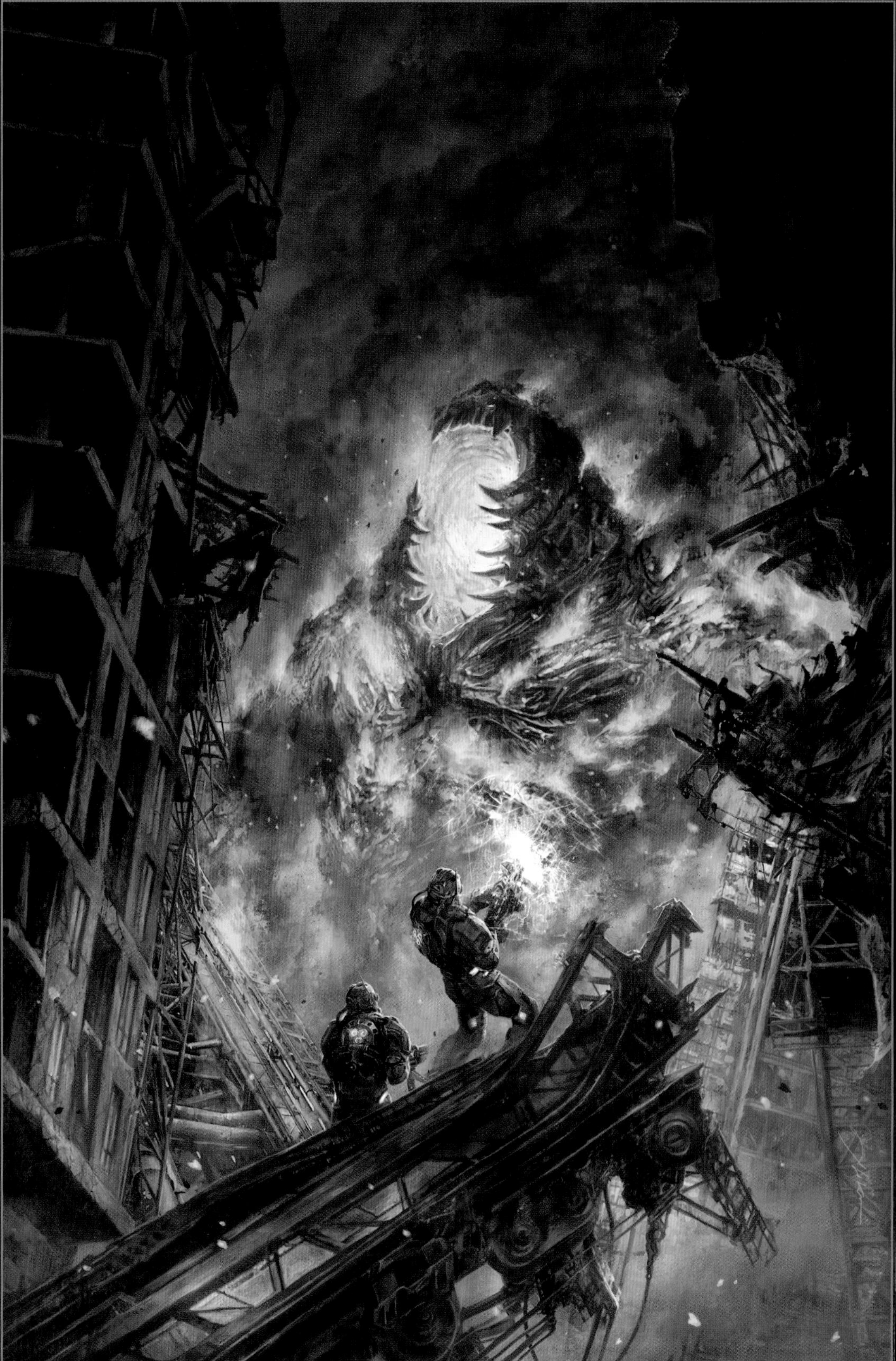

It is always darkest before the dawn, or so it's said. In our demon-haunted world, what illumination here is serves only to highlight the yoke of despair we labour under.

"What scant hope we had lay with Templar Commander Sumerisle, Cabalist Seeker Crowe, and Demon Hunter Captain Petrus. Together they quested for the secret of the Sigil, the mythic means by which the demons may be banished from our world.

"Having retrieved the Harbour of Knowledge, an ancient tome of vital scripture, they were betrayed by the quisling Wyvern, who had bartered his soul and species for an alliance with things unholy.

GROUND

YYYAAHHH!!

However, while his lack of faith in humanity was his weakness, for others it was a source of strength and inspiration."

—Excerpt from *The Cromwell Chronicles,*
Volume XVII.

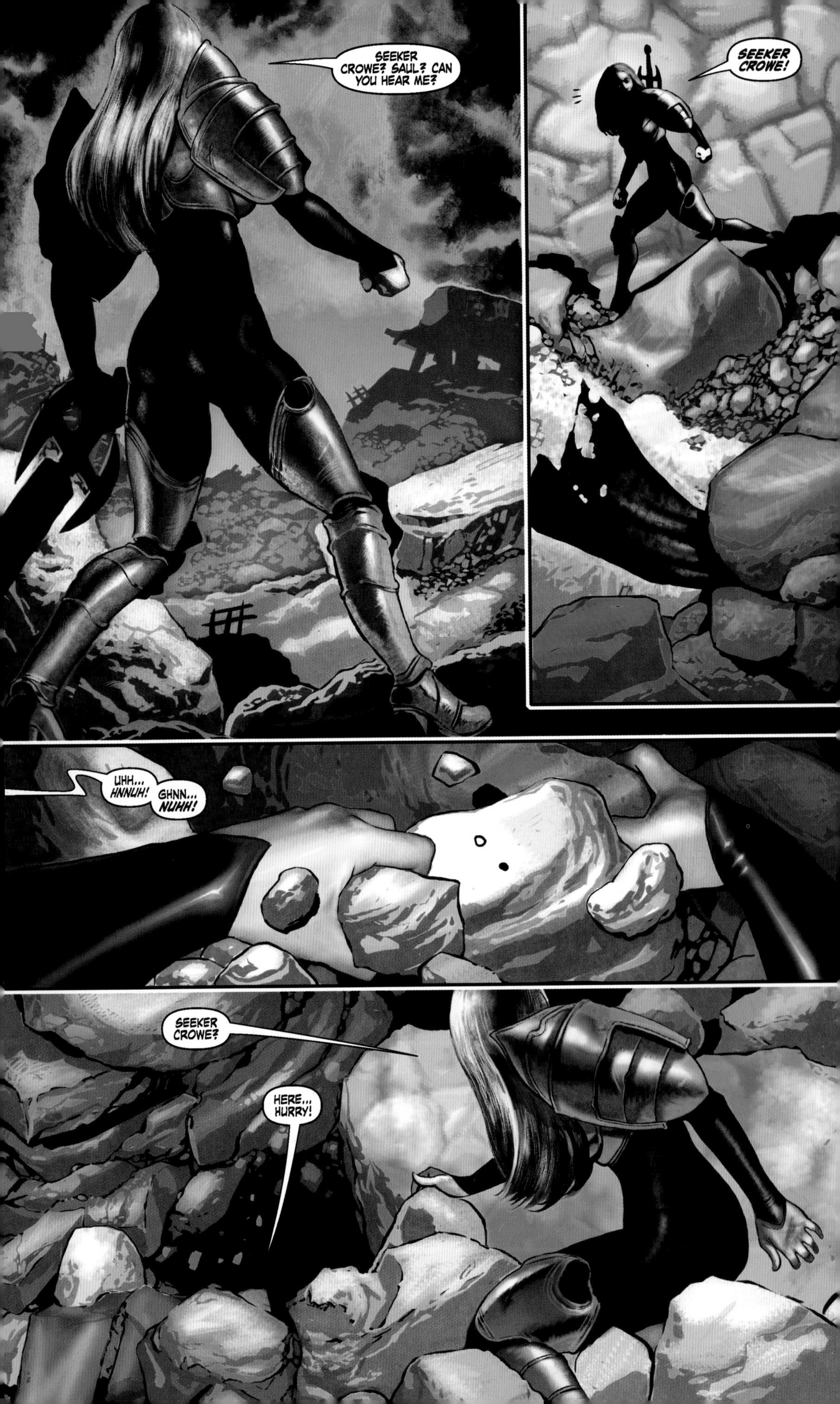
SEEKER CROWE? SAUL? CAN YOU HEAR ME?
SEEKER CROWE!
UHH... HNNUH!
GHNN... NUHH!
SEEKER CROWE?
HERE... HURRY!

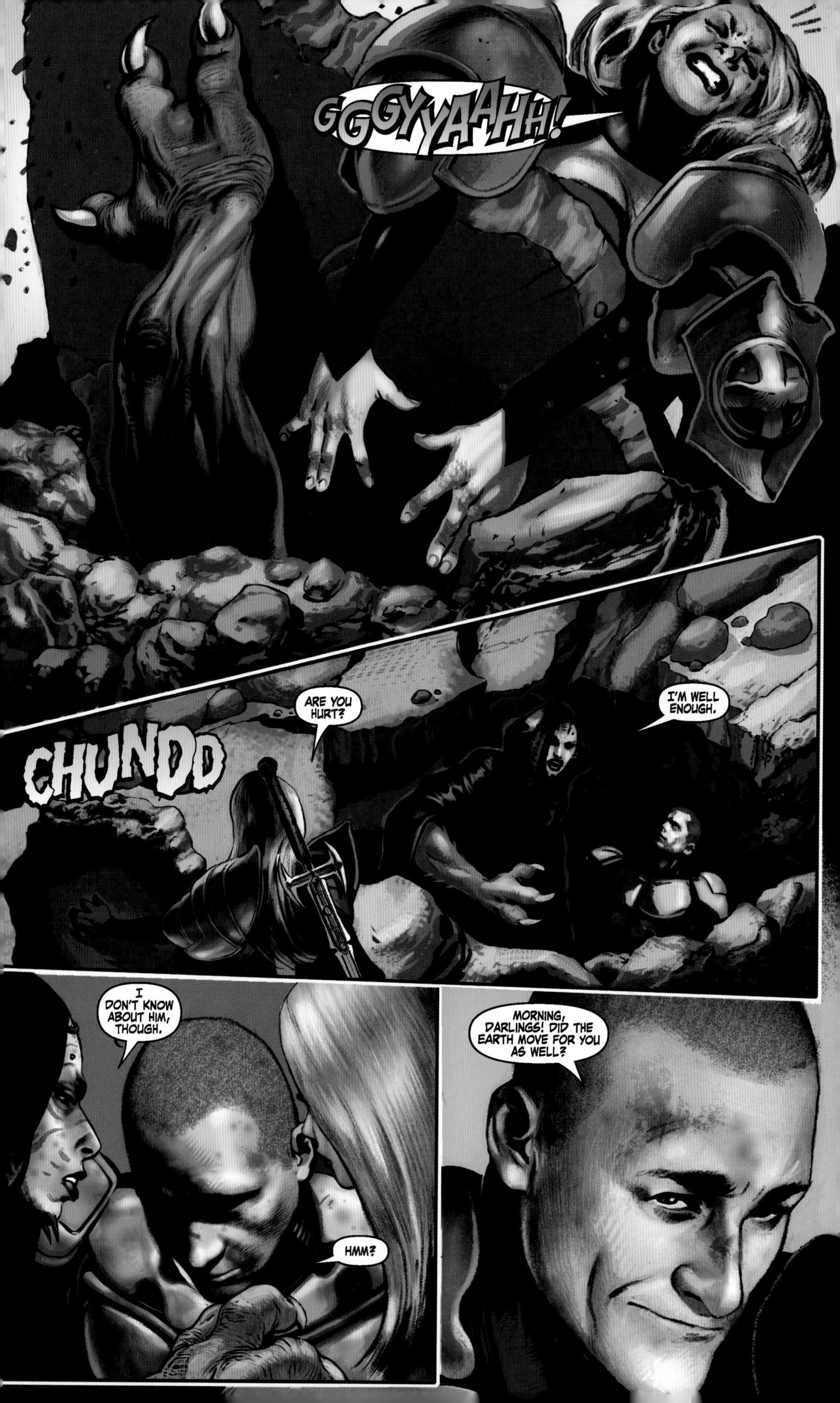
GGGYYAAHH!
CHUNDD
ARE YOU HURT?
I'M WELL ENOUGH.
I DON'T KNOW ABOUT HIM, THOUGH.
HMM?
MORNING, DARLINGS! DID THE EARTH MOVE FOR YOU AS WELL?

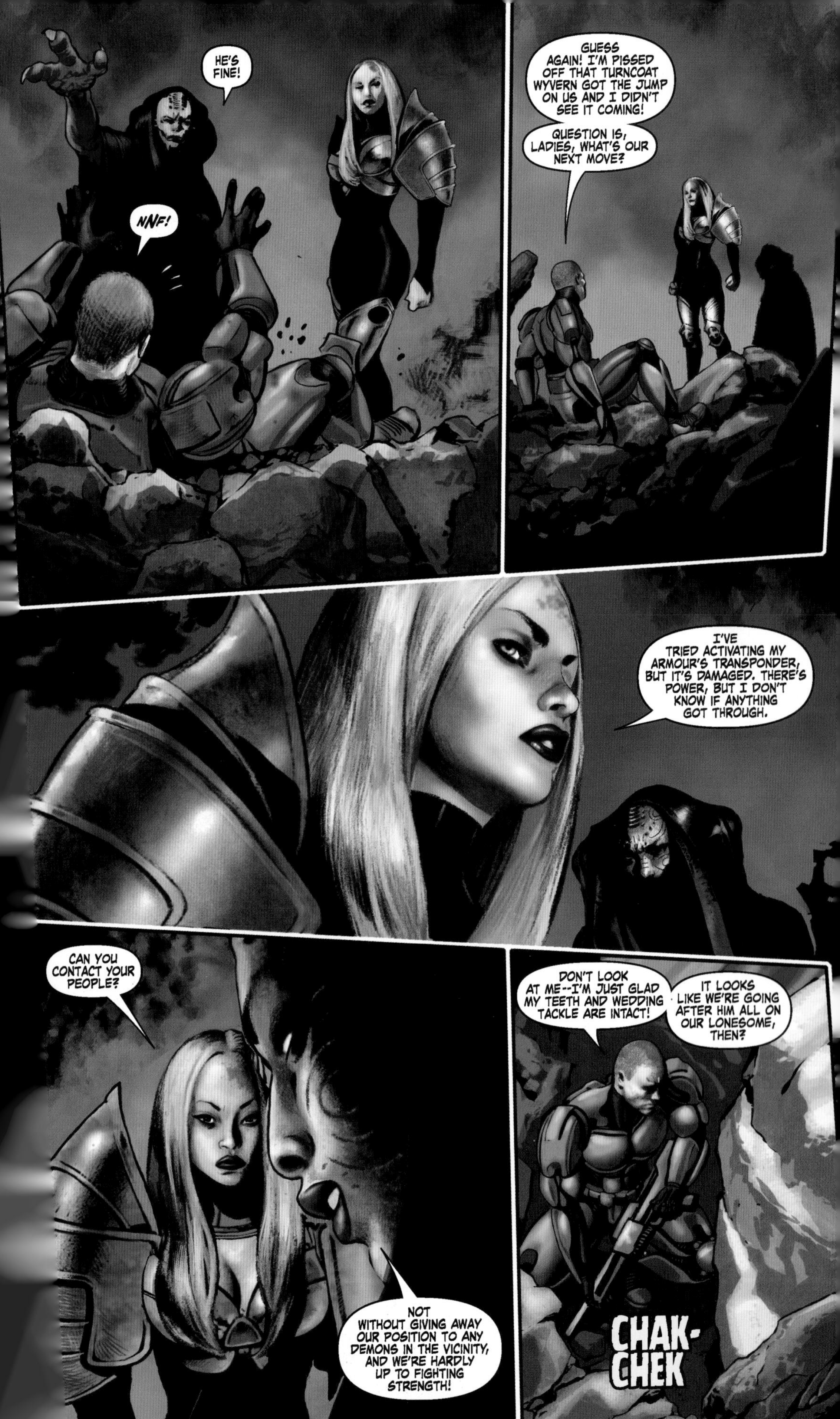
HE'S FINE!
NNF!
GUESS AGAIN! I'M PISSED OFF THAT TURNCOAT WYVERN GOT THE JUMP ON US AND I DIDN'T SEE IT COMING!
QUESTION IS, LADIES, WHAT'S OUR NEXT MOVE?
I'VE TRIED ACTIVATING MY ARMOUR'S TRANSPONDER, BUT IT'S DAMAGED. THERE'S POWER, BUT I DON'T KNOW IF ANYTHING GOT THROUGH.
CAN YOU CONTACT YOUR PEOPLE?
NOT WITHOUT GIVING AWAY OUR POSITION TO ANY DEMONS IN THE VICINITY, AND WE'RE HARDLY UP TO FIGHTING STRENGTH!
DON'T LOOK AT ME--I'M JUST GLAD MY TEETH AND WEDDING TACKLE ARE INTACT!
IT LOOKS LIKE WE'RE GOING AFTER HIM ALL ON OUR LONESOME, THEN?
CHAK-CHEK

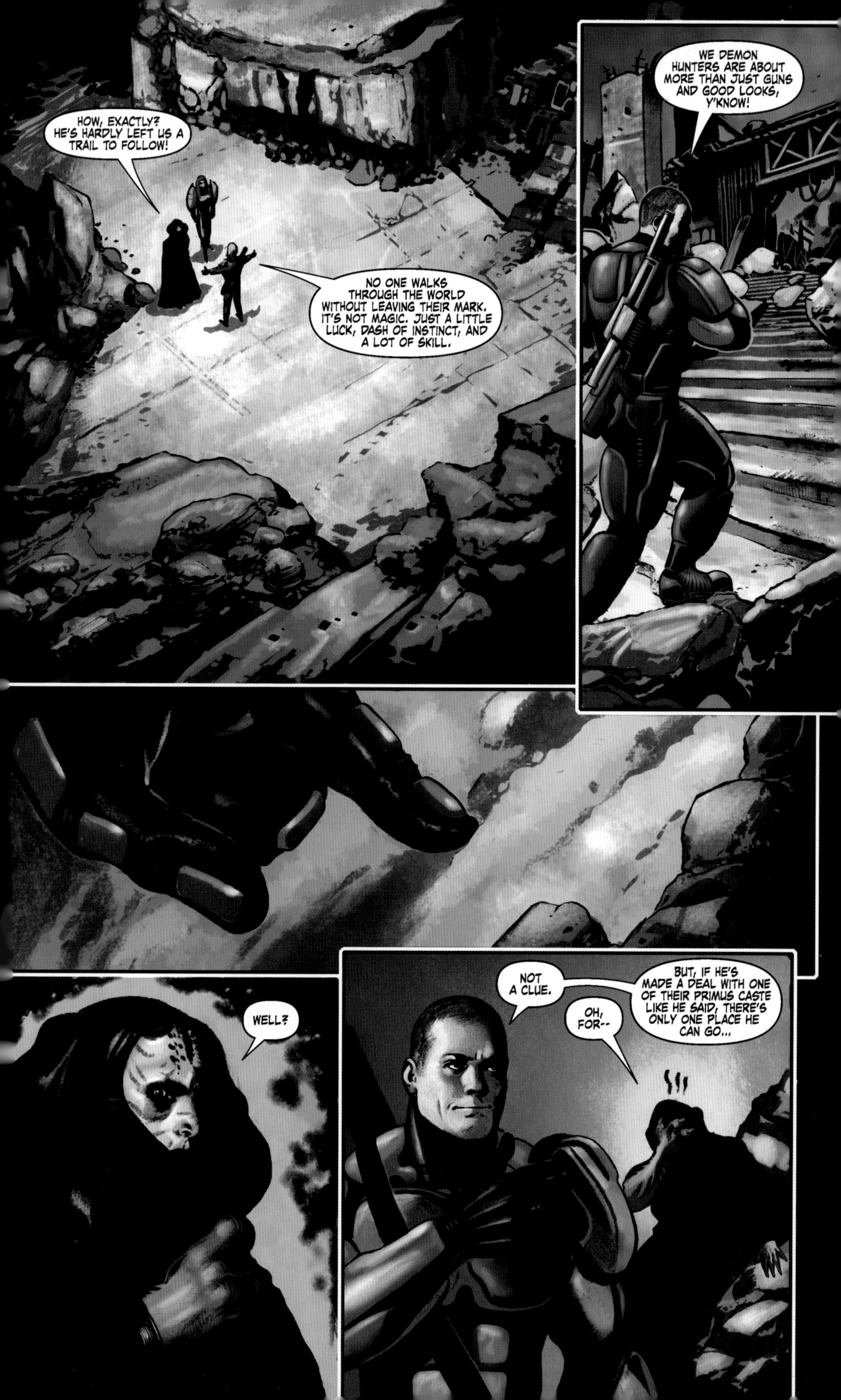
HOW, EXACTLY? HE'S HARDLY LEFT US A TRAIL TO FOLLOW!
NO ONE WALKS THROUGH THE WORLD WITHOUT LEAVING THEIR MARK. IT'S NOT MAGIC. JUST A LITTLE LUCK, DASH OF INSTINCT, AND A LOT OF SKILL.
WE DEMON HUNTERS ARE ABOUT MORE THAN JUST GUNS AND GOOD LOOKS, Y'KNOW!
WELL?
NOT A CLUE.
OH, FOR--
BUT, IF HE'S MADE A DEAL WITH ONE OF THEIR PRIMUS CASTE LIKE HE SAID, THERE'S ONLY ONE PLACE HE CAN GO...

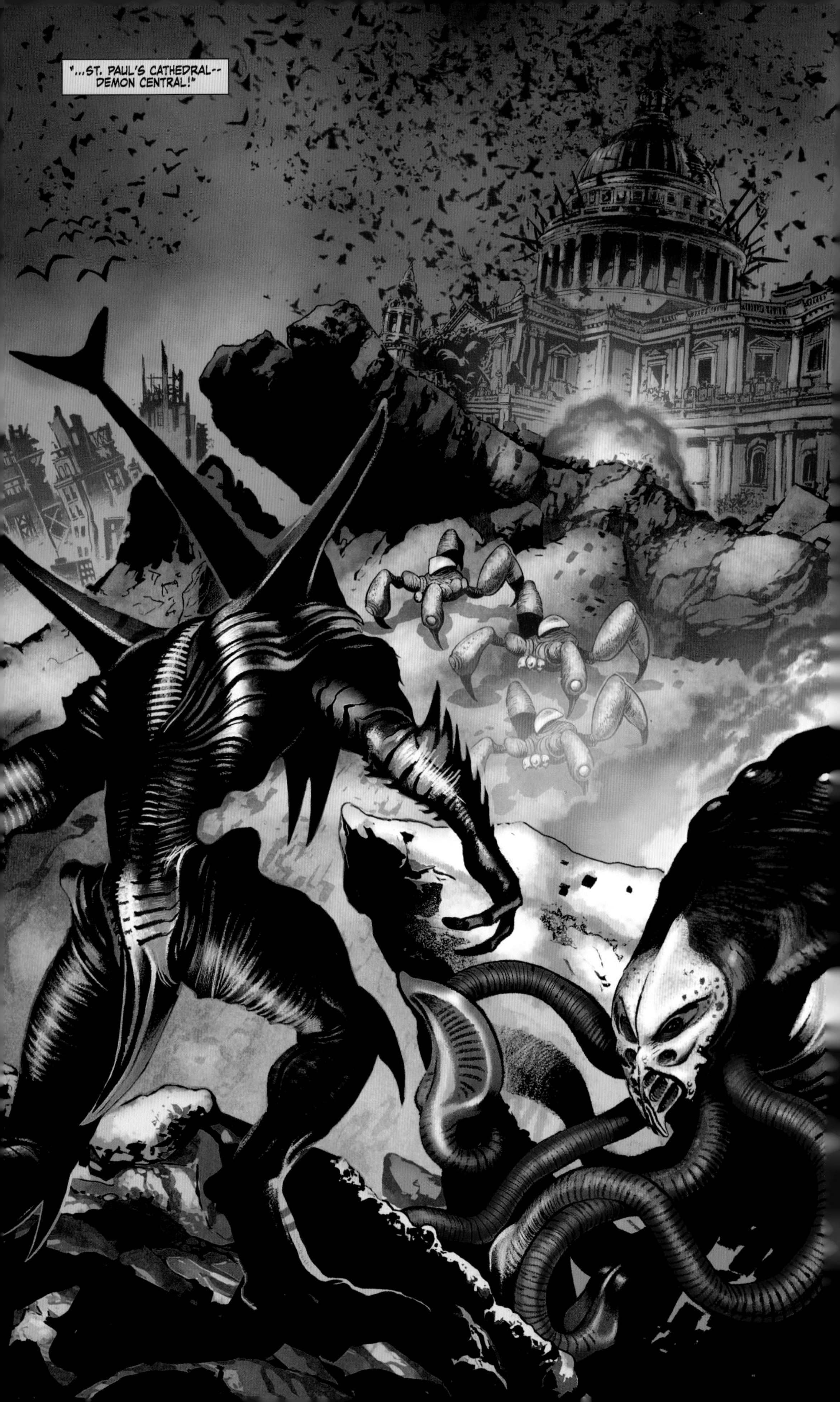
"...ST. PAUL'S CATHEDRAL--
DEMON CENTRAL!"

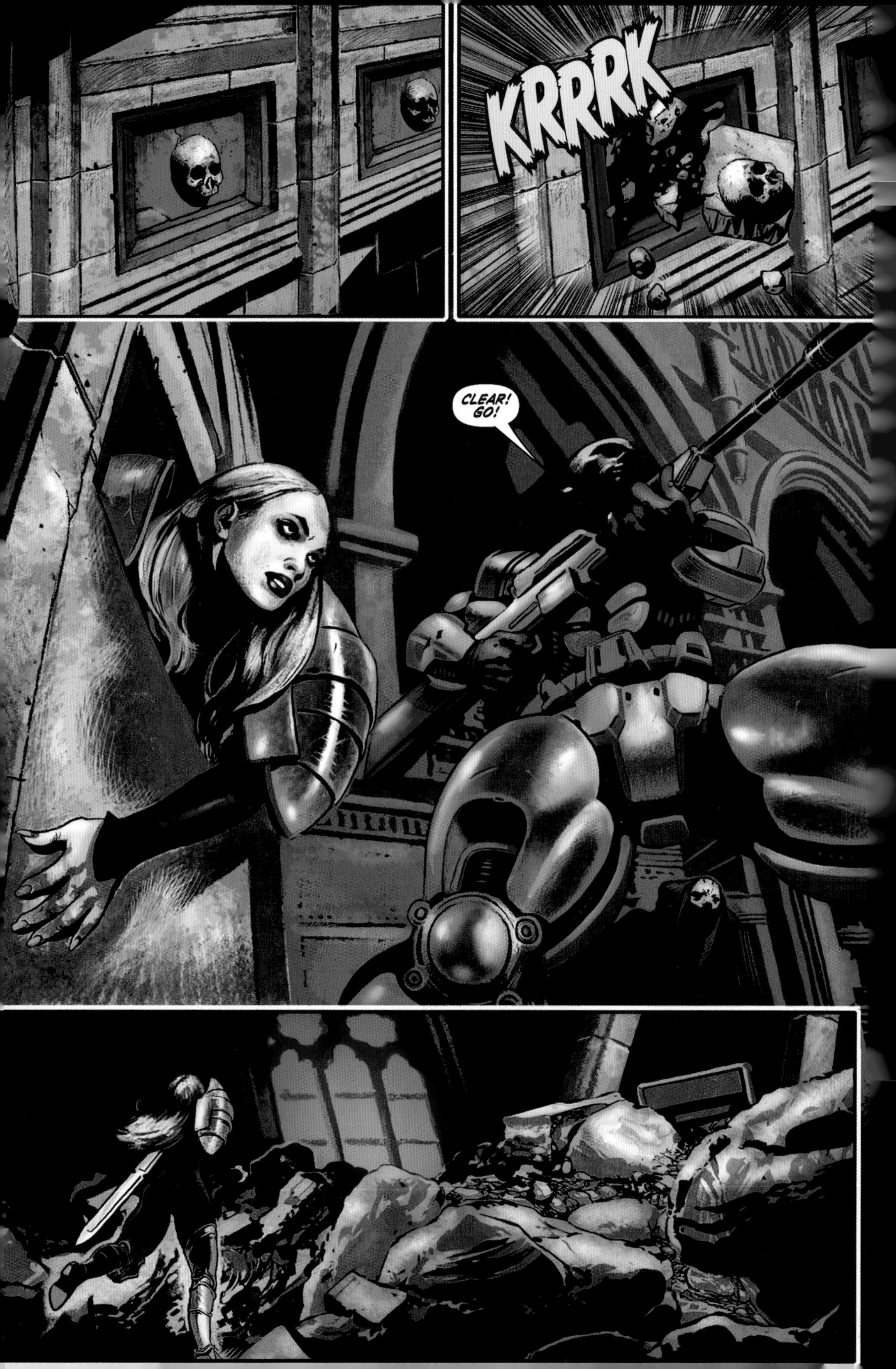
KRRRK
CLEAR! GO!

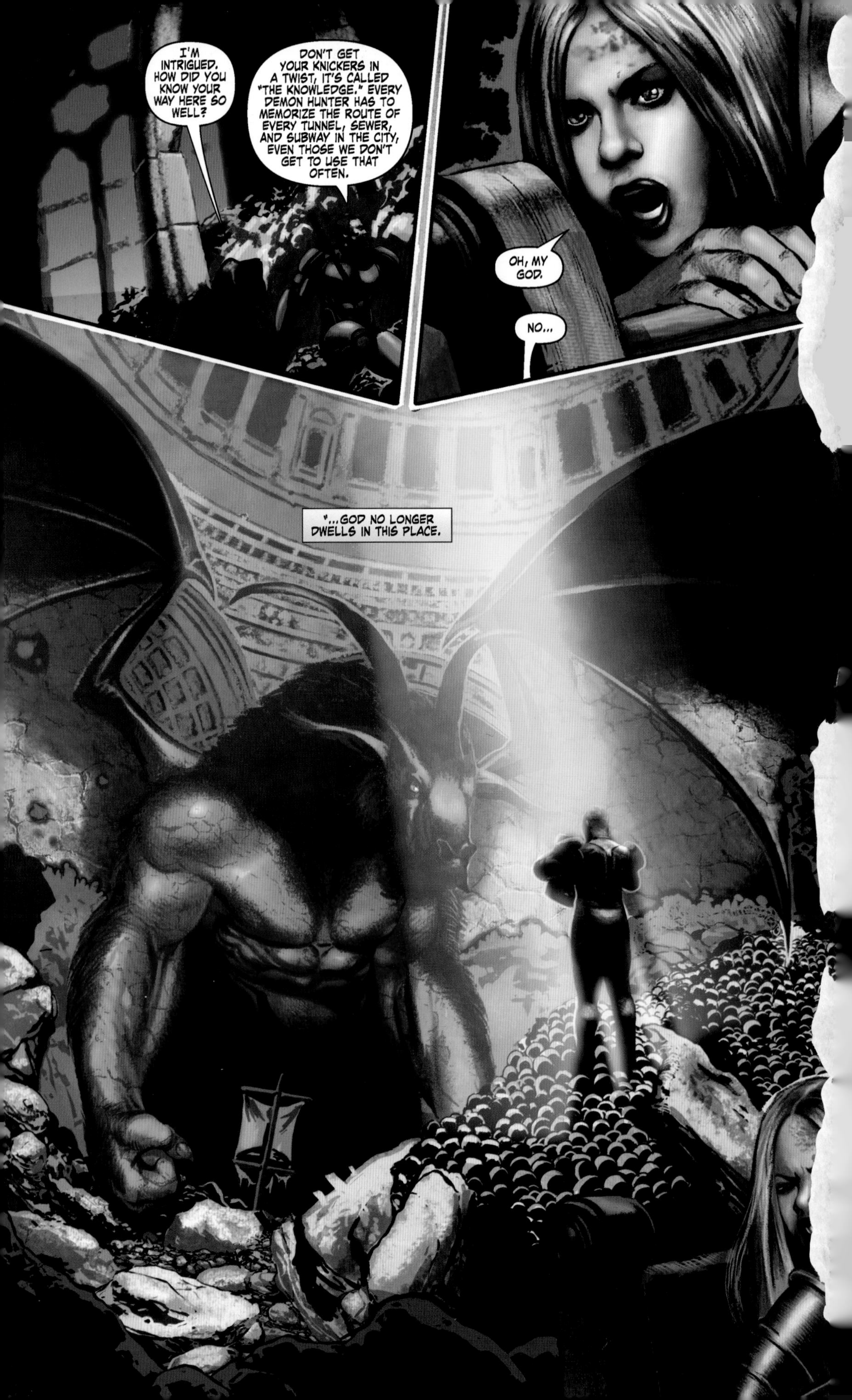
I'M INTRIGUED. HOW DID YOU KNOW YOUR WAY HERE SO WELL?
DON'T GET YOUR KNICKERS IN A TWIST, IT'S CALLED "THE KNOWLEDGE." EVERY DEMON HUNTER HAS TO MEMORIZE THE ROUTE OF EVERY TUNNEL, SEWER, AND SUBWAY IN THE CITY, EVEN THOSE WE DON'T GET TO USE THAT OFTEN.
OH, MY GOD.
NO...
"...GOD NO LONGER DWELLS IN THIS PLACE.

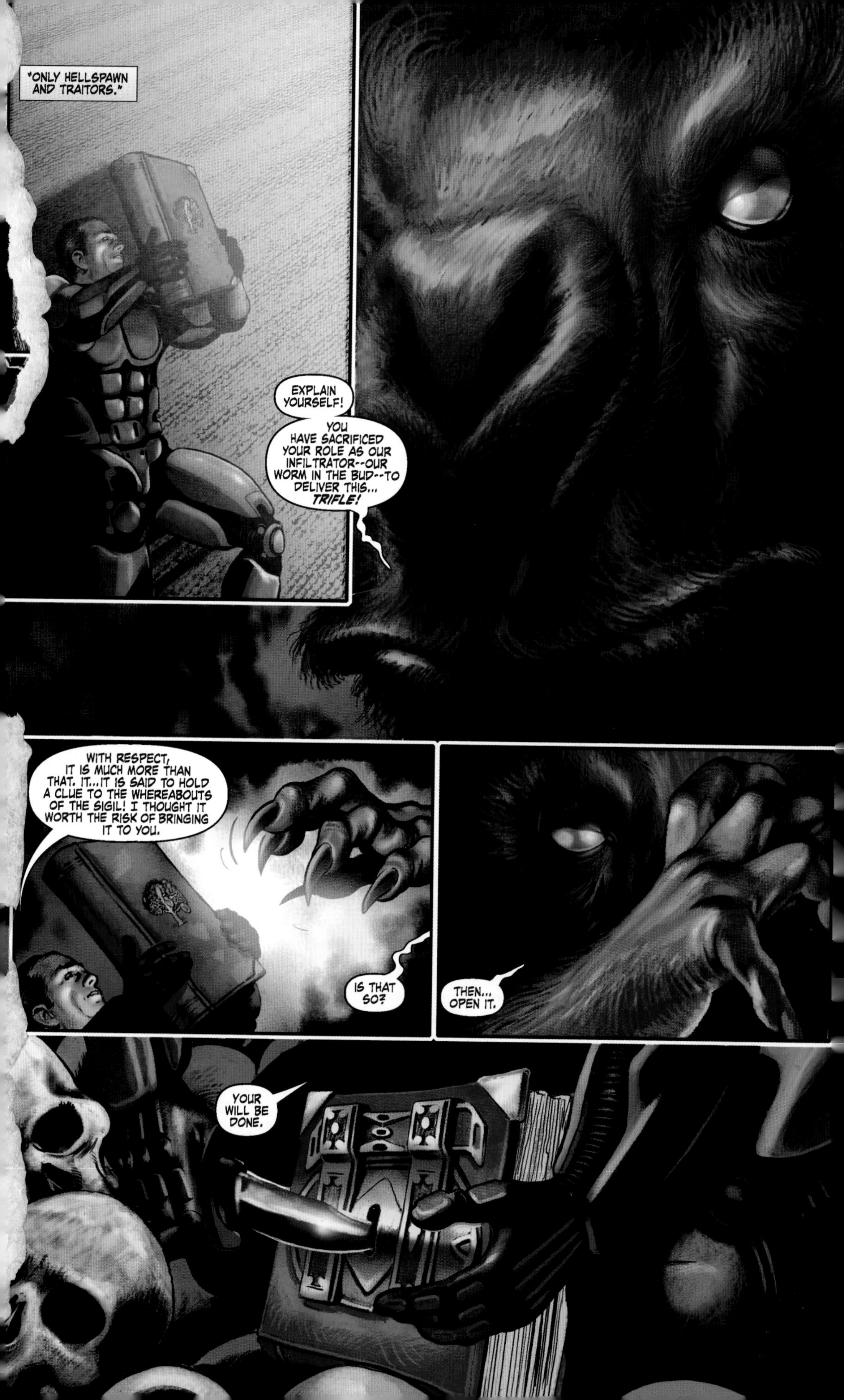
"ONLY HELLSPAWN AND TRAITORS."
EXPLAIN YOURSELF!
YOU HAVE SACRIFICED YOUR ROLE AS OUR INFILTRATOR--OUR WORM IN THE BUD--TO DELIVER THIS... TRIFLE!
WITH RESPECT, IT IS MUCH MORE THAN THAT. IT...IT IS SAID TO HOLD A CLUE TO THE WHEREABOUTS OF THE SIGIL! I THOUGHT IT WORTH THE RISK OF BRINGING IT TO YOU.
IS THAT SO?
THEN... OPEN IT.
YOUR WILL BE DONE.

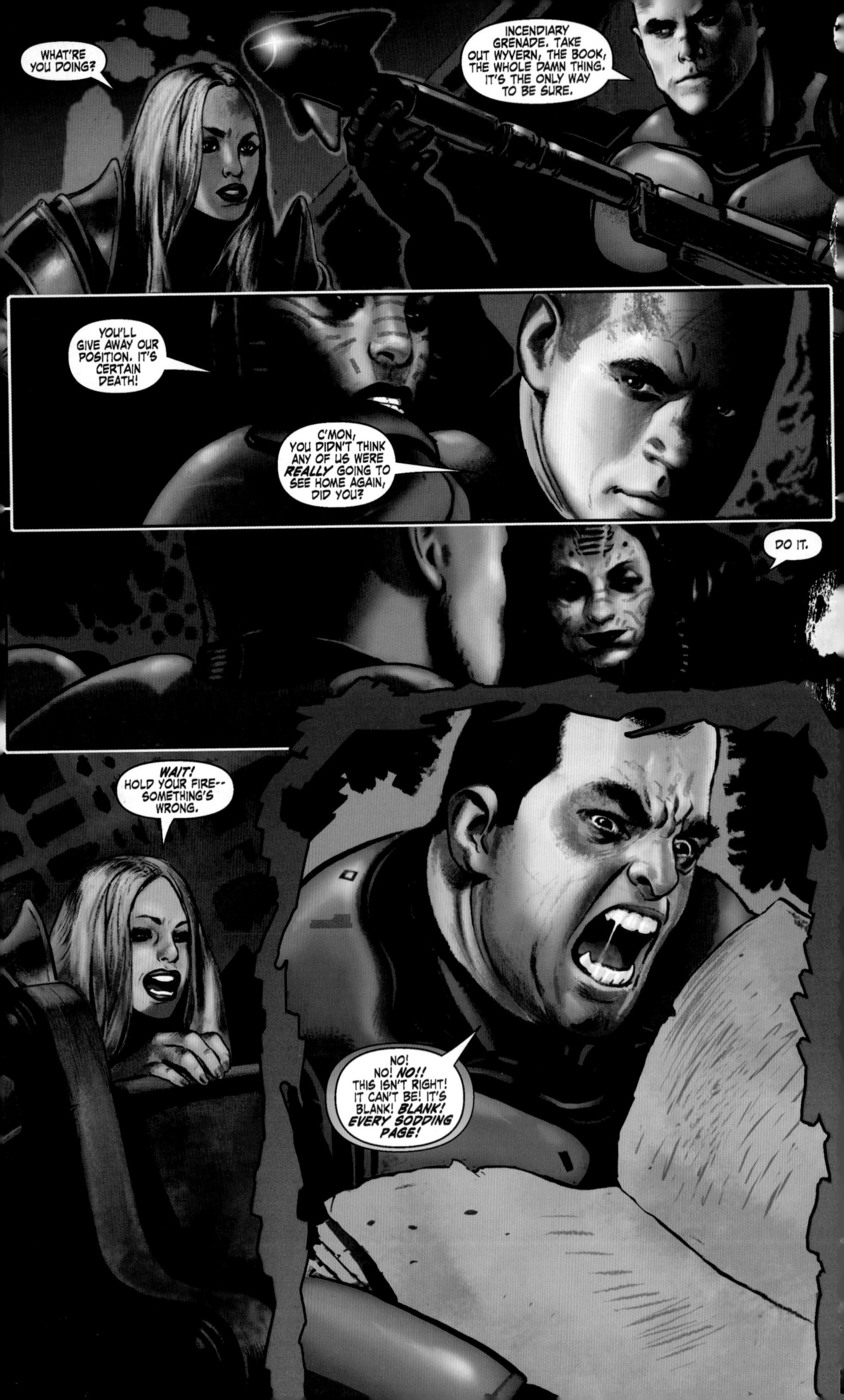
WHAT'RE YOU DOING?
INCENDIARY GRENADE. TAKE OUT WYVERN, THE BOOK, THE WHOLE DAMN THING. IT'S THE ONLY WAY TO BE SURE.
YOU'LL GIVE AWAY OUR POSITION. IT'S CERTAIN DEATH!
C'MON, YOU DIDN'T THINK ANY OF US WERE REALLY GOING TO SEE HOME AGAIN, DID YOU?
DO IT.
WAIT! HOLD YOUR FIRE-- SOMETHING'S WRONG.
NO! NO! NO!! THIS ISN'T RIGHT! IT CAN'T BE! IT'S BLANK! BLANK! EVERY SODDING PAGE!

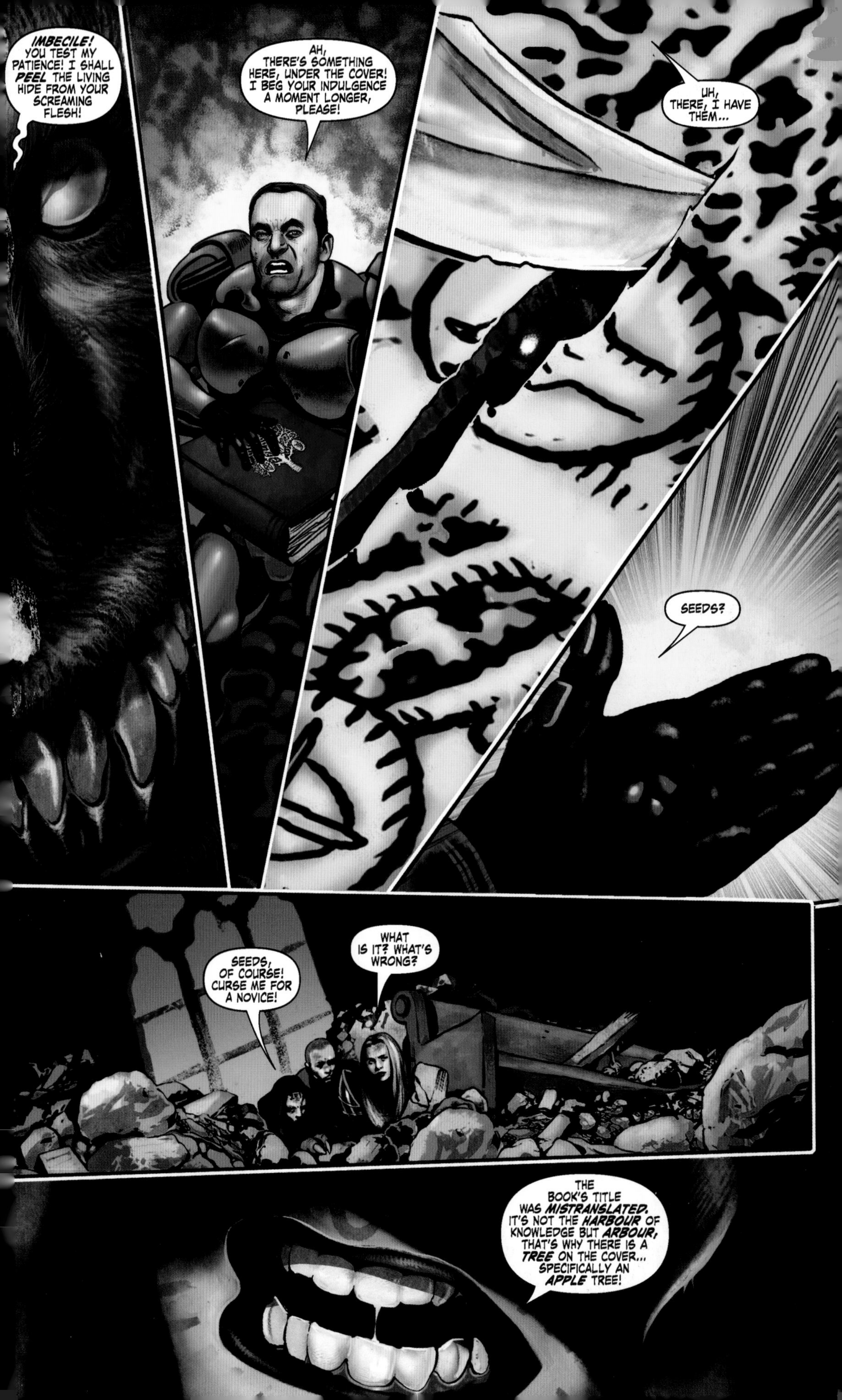
IMBECILE! YOU TEST MY PATIENCE! I SHALL PEEL THE LIVING HIDE FROM YOUR SCREAMING FLESH!
AH, THERE'S SOMETHING HERE, UNDER THE COVER! I BEG YOUR INDULGENCE A MOMENT LONGER, PLEASE!
UH, THERE, I HAVE THEM...
SEEDS?
SEEDS, OF COURSE! CURSE ME FOR A NOVICE!
WHAT IS IT? WHAT'S WRONG?
THE BOOK'S TITLE WAS MISTRANSLATED. IT'S NOT THE HARBOUR OF KNOWLEDGE BUT ARBOUR, THAT'S WHY THERE IS A TREE ON THE COVER... SPECIFICALLY AN APPLE TREE!

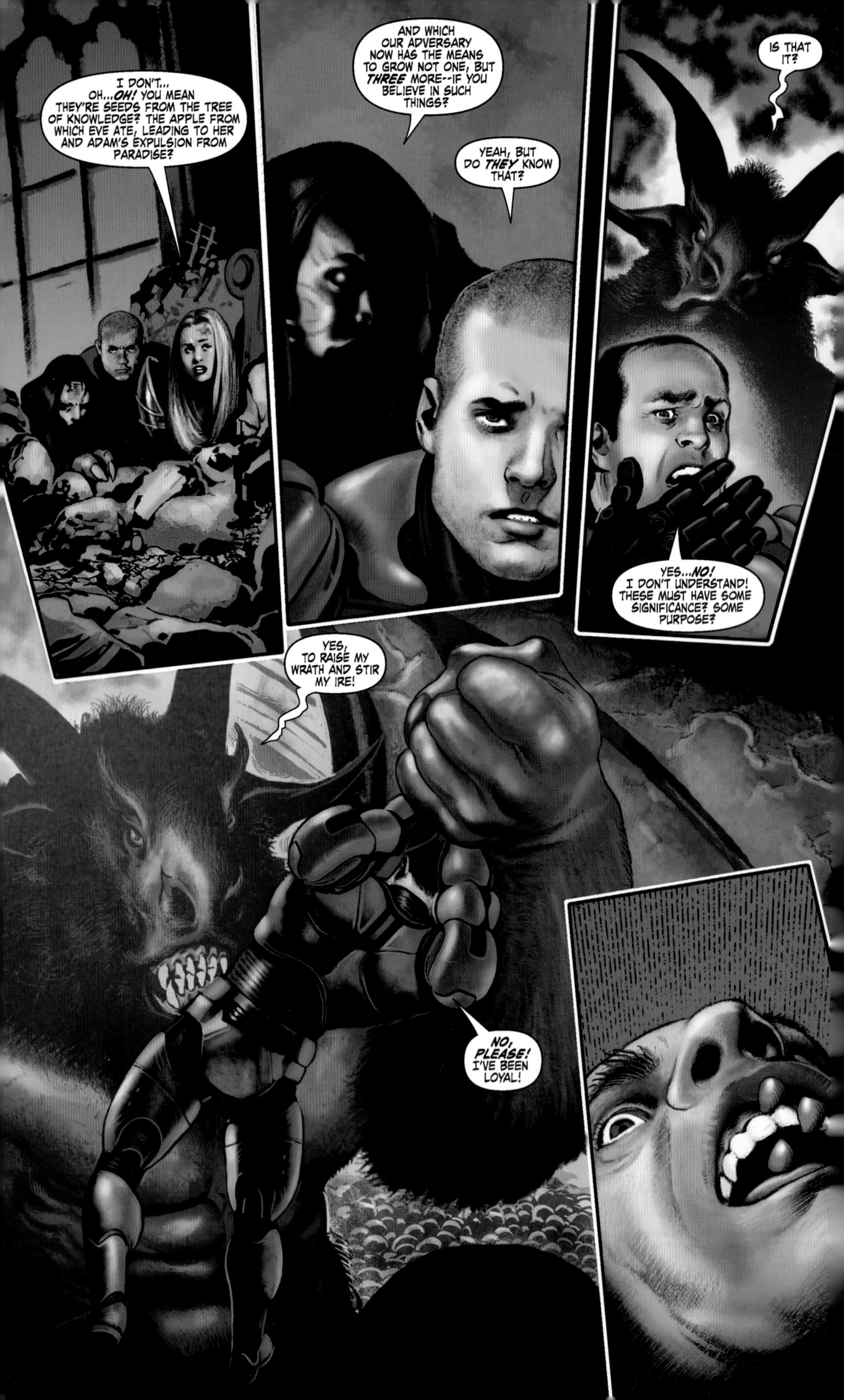
I DON'T... OH...OH! YOU MEAN THEY'RE SEEDS FROM THE TREE OF KNOWLEDGE? THE APPLE FROM WHICH EVE ATE, LEADING TO HER AND ADAM'S EXPULSION FROM PARADISE?
AND WHICH OUR ADVERSARY NOW HAS THE MEANS TO GROW NOT ONE, BUT THREE MORE--IF YOU BELIEVE IN SUCH THINGS?
YEAH, BUT DO THEY KNOW THAT?
IS THAT IT?
YES...NO! I DON'T UNDERSTAND! THESE MUST HAVE SOME SIGNIFICANCE? SOME PURPOSE?
YES, TO RAISE MY WRATH AND STIR MY IRE!
NO, PLEASE! I'VE BEEN LOYAL!

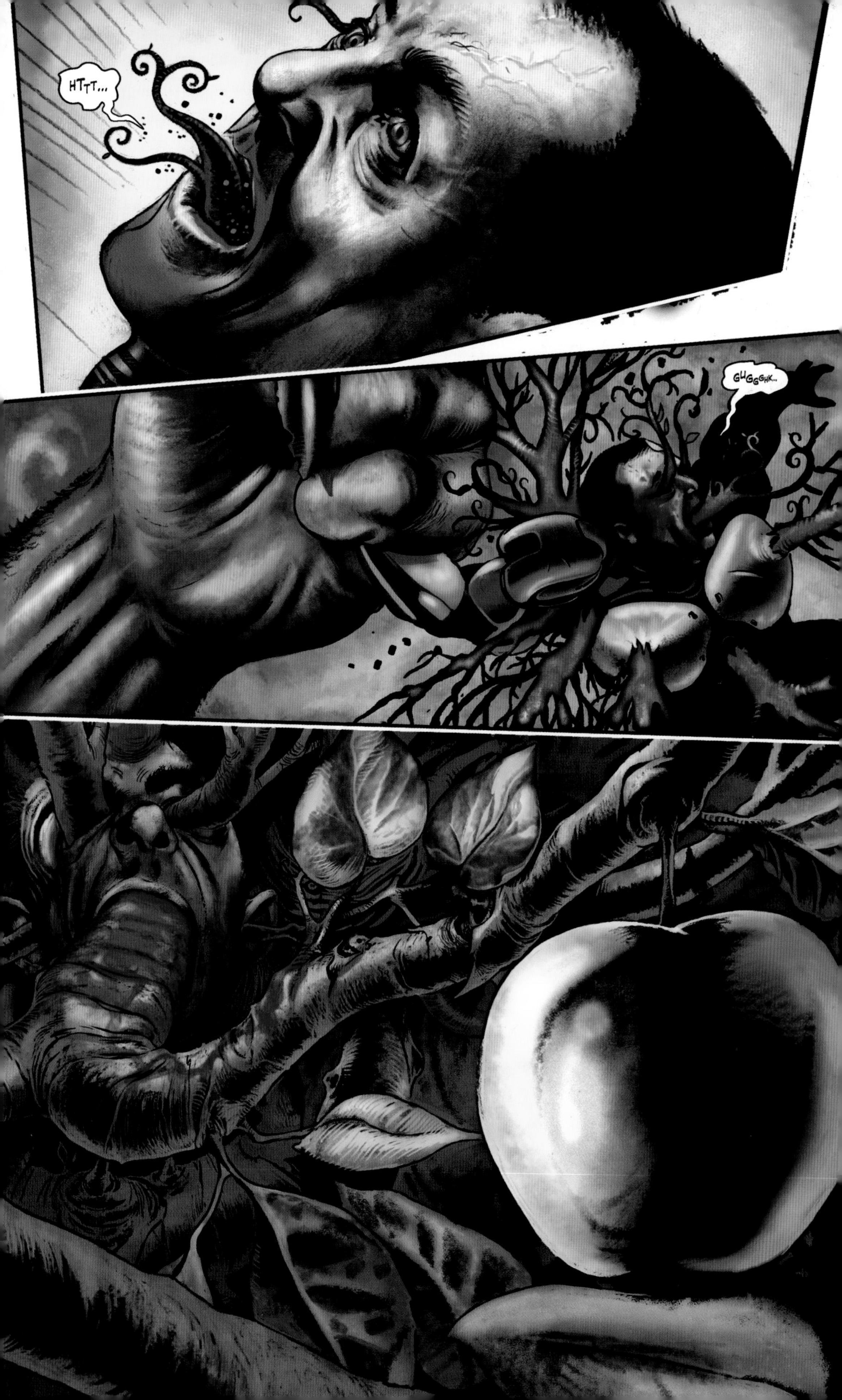
HTTT...
GUGGGHK...

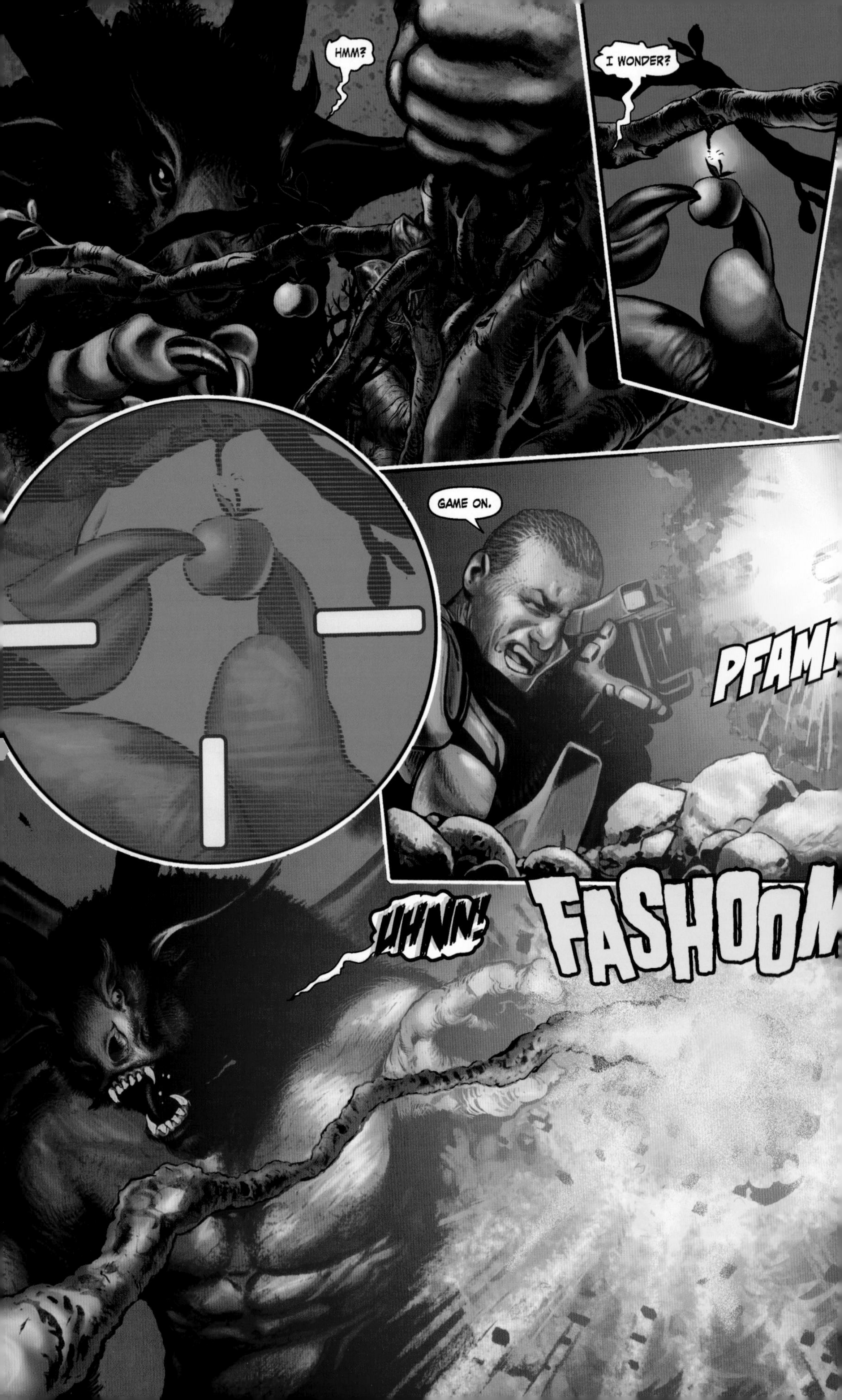
HMM?
I WONDER?
GAME ON.
PFAM!
UHNN!
FASHOOM

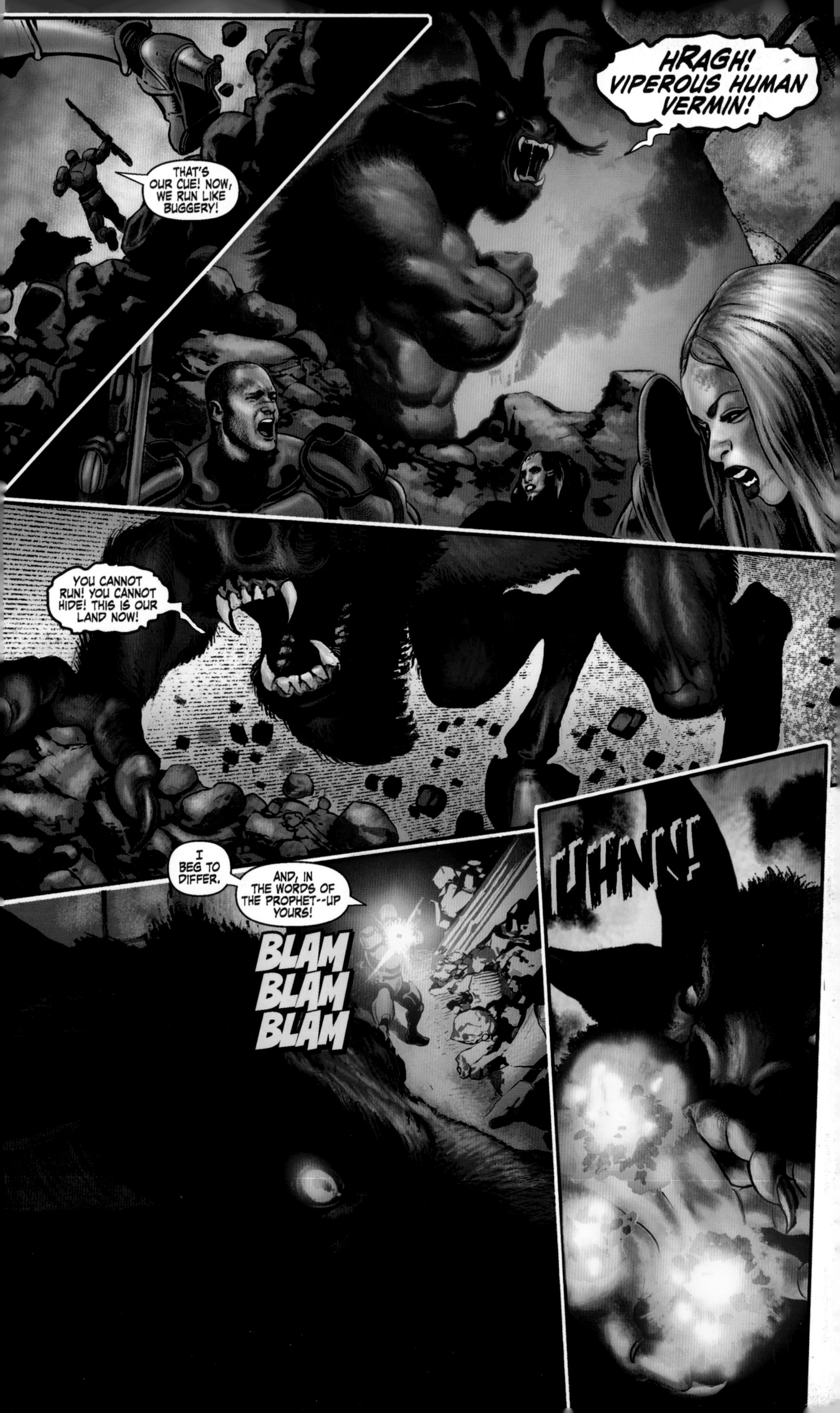
HRAGH! VIPEROUS HUMAN VERMIN!
THAT'S OUR CUE! NOW, WE RUN LIKE BUGGERY!
YOU CANNOT RUN! YOU CANNOT HIDE! THIS IS OUR LAND NOW!
I BEG TO DIFFER.
AND, IN THE WORDS OF THE PROPHET--UP YOURS!
BLAM BLAM BLAM
UHNN!

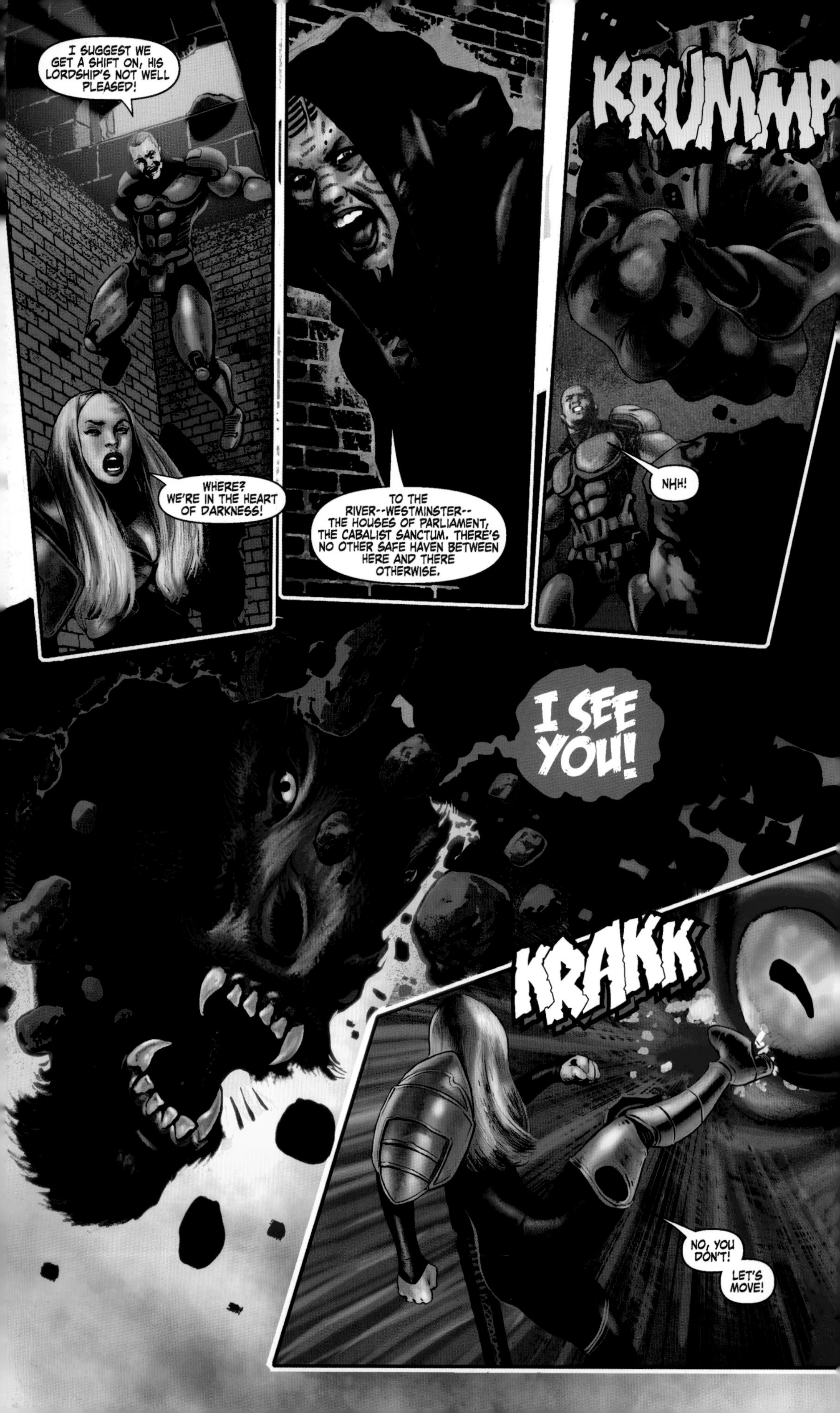
I SUGGEST WE GET A SHIFT ON, HIS LORDSHIP'S NOT WELL PLEASED!
WHERE? WE'RE IN THE HEART OF DARKNESS!
TO THE RIVER--WESTMINSTER--THE HOUSES OF PARLIAMENT, THE CABALIST SANCTUM. THERE'S NO OTHER SAFE HAVEN BETWEEN HERE AND THERE OTHERWISE.
KRUMMP
NHH!
I SEE YOU!
KRAKK
NO, YOU DON'T!
LET'S MOVE!

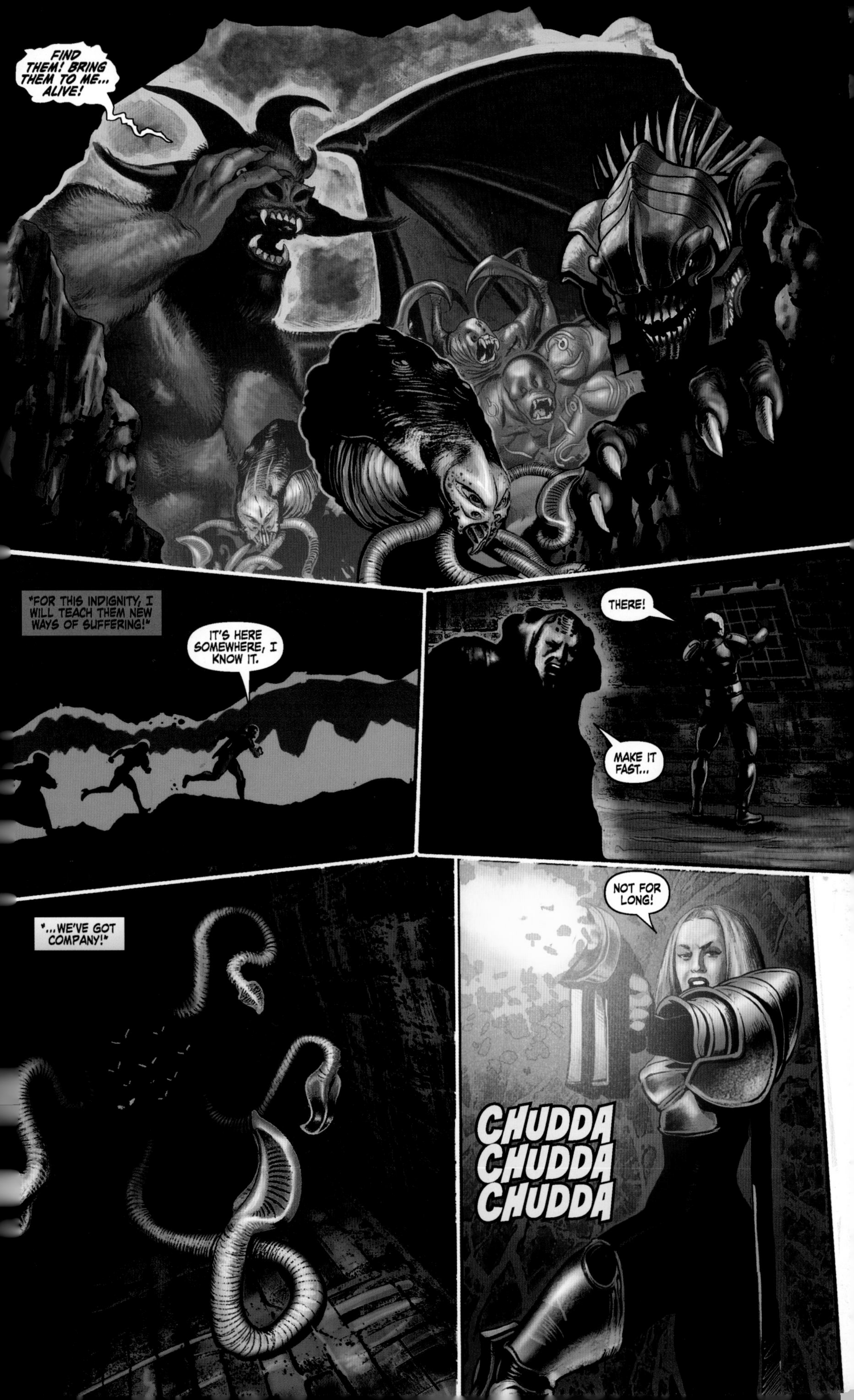
FIND THEM! BRING THEM TO ME... ALIVE!
"FOR THIS INDIGNITY, I WILL TEACH THEM NEW WAYS OF SUFFERING!"
IT'S HERE SOMEWHERE, I KNOW IT.
THERE!
MAKE IT FAST...
"...WE'VE GOT COMPANY!"
NOT FOR LONG!
CHUDDA
CHUDDA
CHUDDA

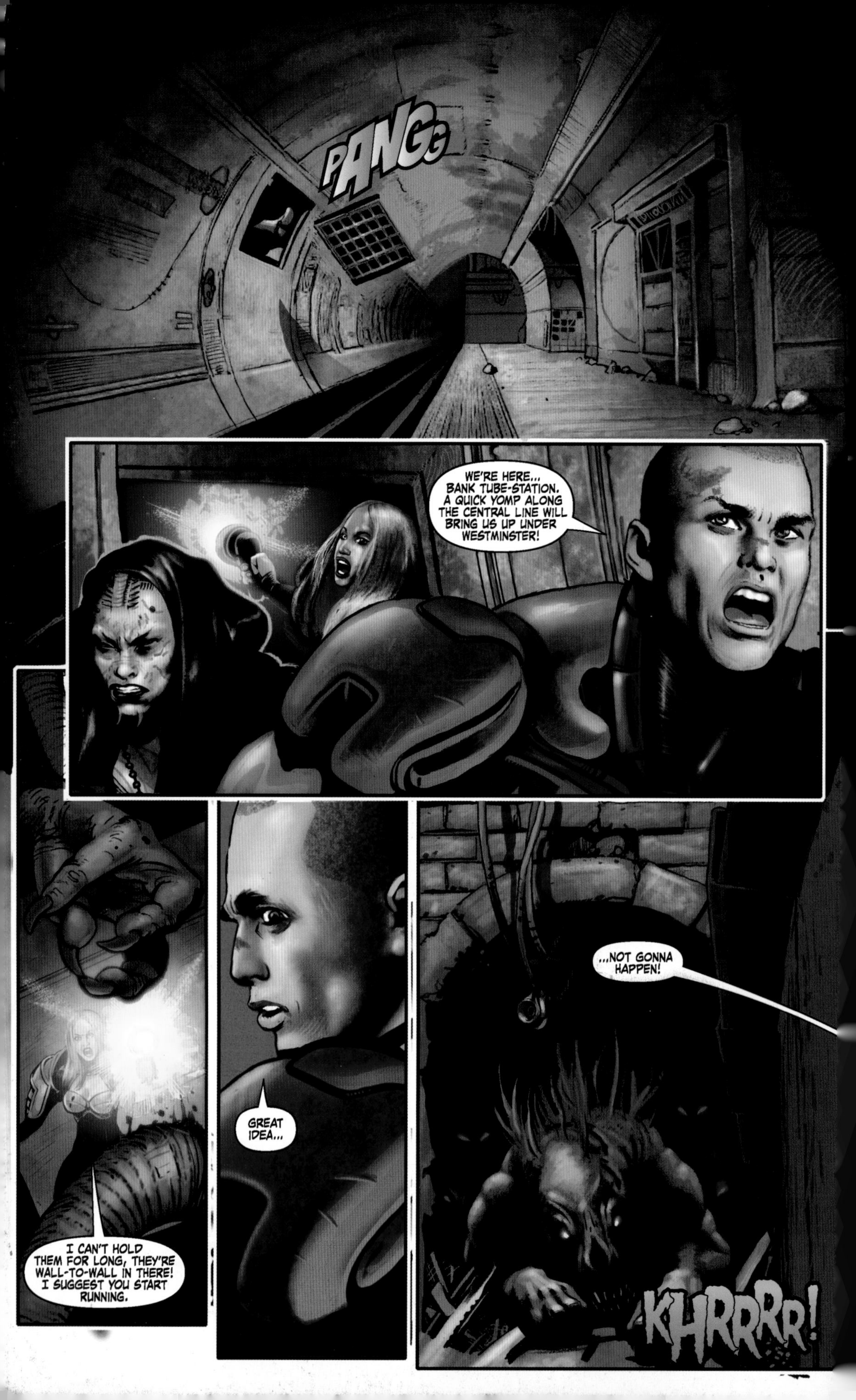
PANGG
WE'RE HERE... BANK TUBE-STATION. A QUICK YOMP ALONG THE CENTRAL LINE WILL BRING US UP UNDER WESTMINSTER!
I CAN'T HOLD THEM FOR LONG, THEY'RE WALL-TO-WALL IN THERE! I SUGGEST YOU START RUNNING.
GREAT IDEA...
...NOT GONNA HAPPEN!
KHRRRR!

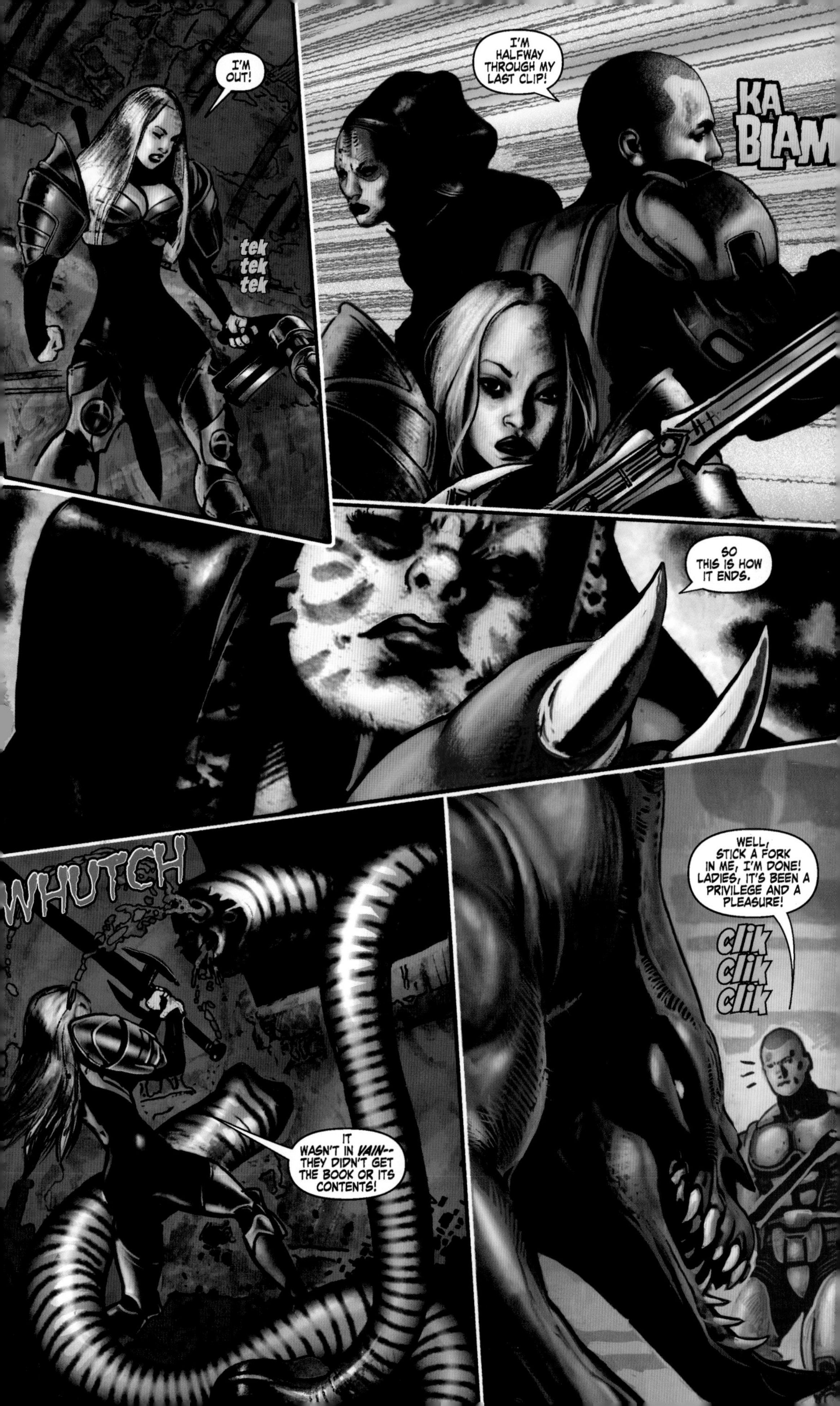

I'M OUT!
tek tek tek
I'M HALFWAY THROUGH MY LAST CLIP!
KA BLAM
SO THIS IS HOW IT ENDS.
WHUTCH
IT WASN'T IN *VAIN*-- THEY DIDN'T GET THE BOOK OR ITS CONTENTS!
WELL, STICK A FORK IN ME, I'M DONE! LADIES, IT'S BEEN A PRIVILEGE AND A PLEASURE!
clik clik clik

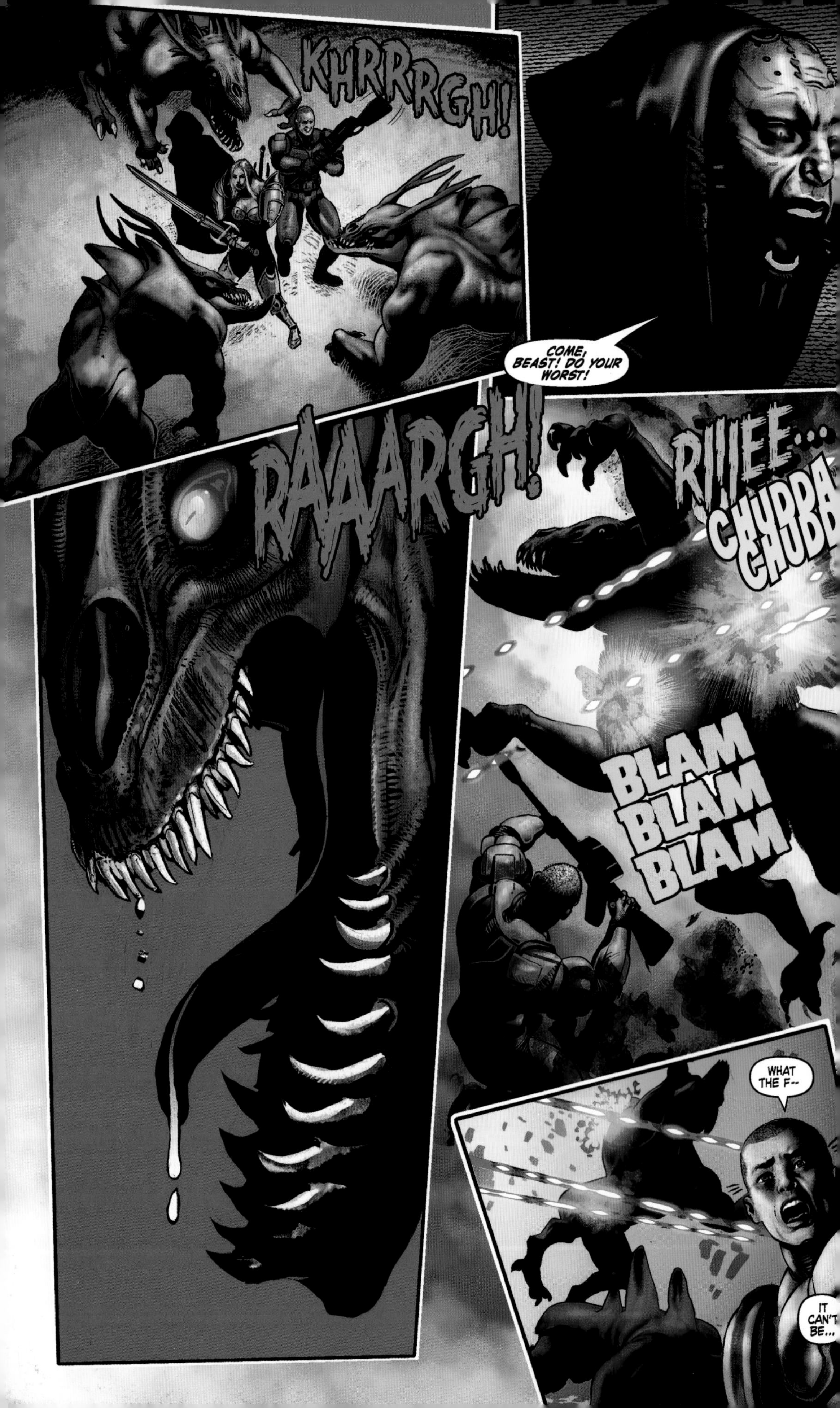

KHRRRRGH!
COME, BEAST! DO YOUR WORST!
RAAARGH!
RIIIEE...
CHUDDA CHUDD
BLAM BLAM BLAM
WHAT THE F--
IT CAN'T BE...

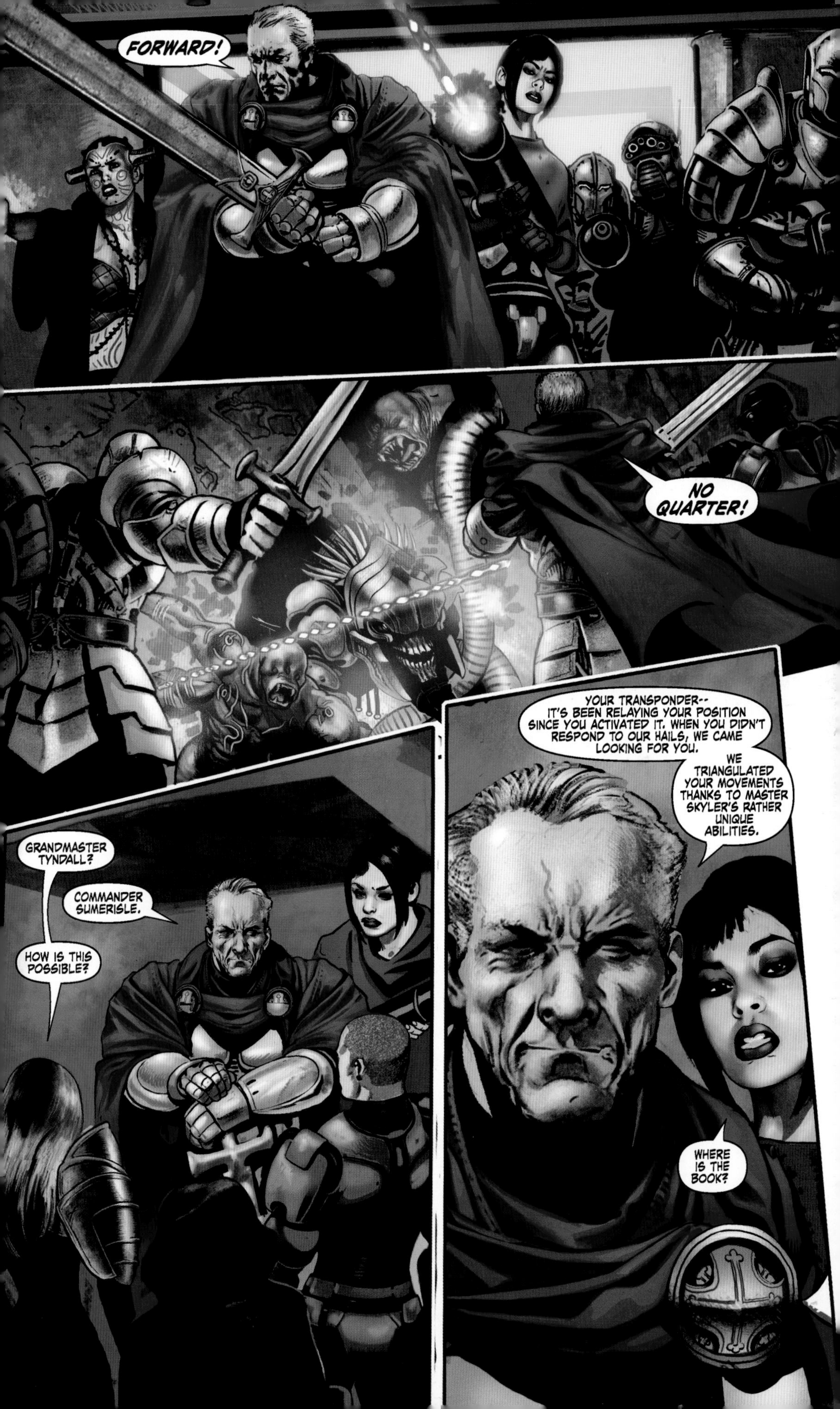
FORWARD!
NO QUARTER!
GRANDMASTER TYNDALL?
COMMANDER SUMERISLE.
HOW IS THIS POSSIBLE?
YOUR TRANSPONDER-- IT'S BEEN RELAYING YOUR POSITION SINCE YOU ACTIVATED IT. WHEN YOU DIDN'T RESPOND TO OUR HAILS, WE CAME LOOKING FOR YOU.
WE TRIANGULATED YOUR MOVEMENTS THANKS TO MASTER SKYLER'S RATHER UNIQUE ABILITIES.
WHERE IS THE BOOK?

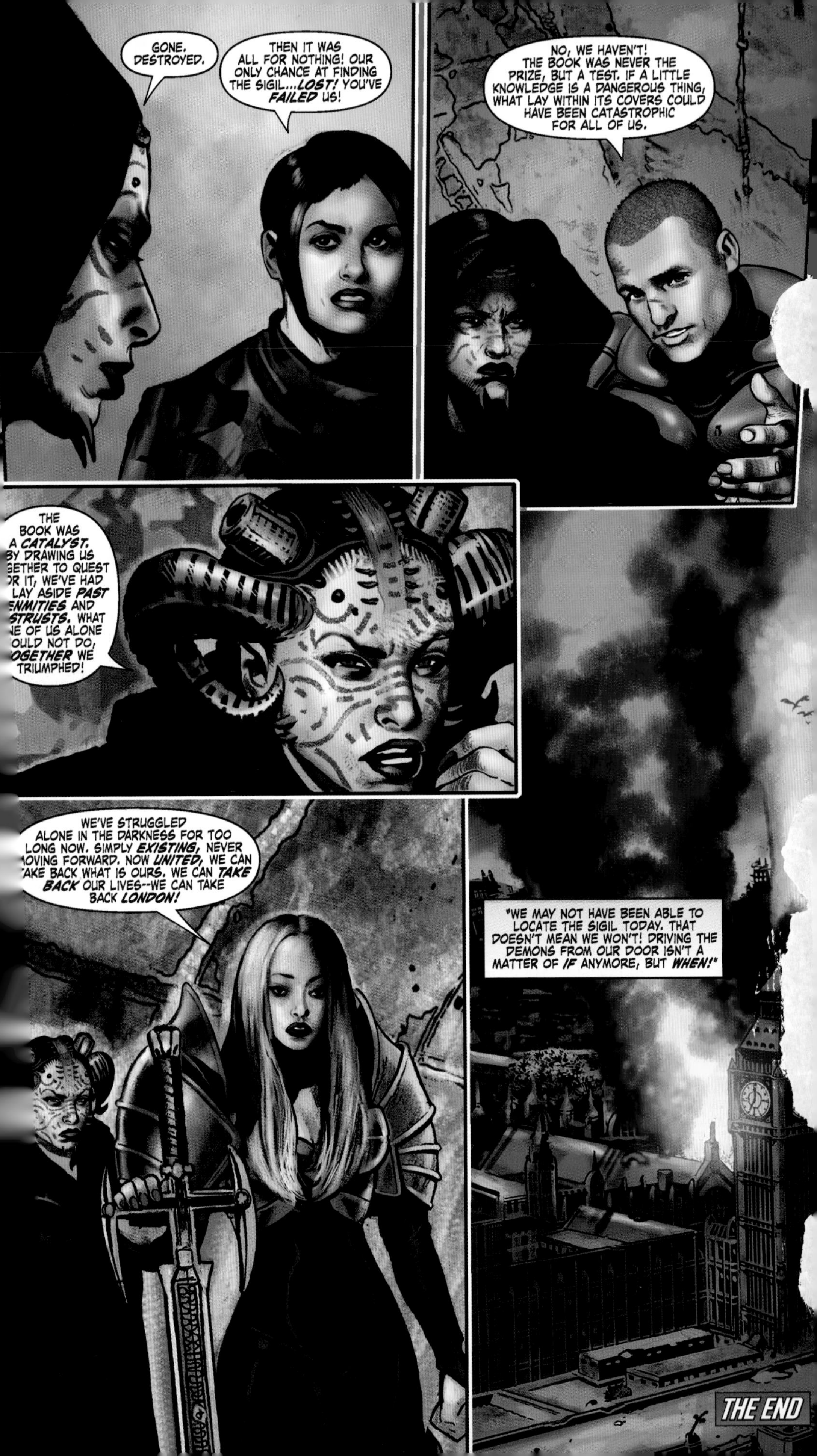
GONE. DESTROYED.
THEN IT WAS ALL FOR NOTHING! OUR ONLY CHANCE AT FINDING THE SIGIL...LOST! YOU'VE FAILED US!
NO, WE HAVEN'T! THE BOOK WAS NEVER THE PRIZE, BUT A TEST. IF A LITTLE KNOWLEDGE IS A DANGEROUS THING, WHAT LAY WITHIN ITS COVERS COULD HAVE BEEN CATASTROPHIC FOR ALL OF US.
THE BOOK WAS A CATALYST. BY DRAWING US GETHER TO QUEST OR IT, WE'VE HAD LAY ASIDE PAST ENMITIES AND STRUSTS. WHAT NE OF US ALONE OULD NOT DO, OGETHER WE TRIUMPHED!
WE'VE STRUGGLED ALONE IN THE DARKNESS FOR TOO LONG NOW. SIMPLY EXISTING, NEVER MOVING FORWARD. NOW UNITED, WE CAN TAKE BACK WHAT IS OURS. WE CAN TAKE BACK OUR LIVES--WE CAN TAKE BACK LONDON!
"WE MAY NOT HAVE BEEN ABLE TO LOCATE THE SIGIL TODAY. THAT DOESN'T MEAN WE WON'T! DRIVING THE DEMONS FROM OUR DOOR ISN'T A MATTER OF IF ANYMORE, BUT WHEN!"
THE END

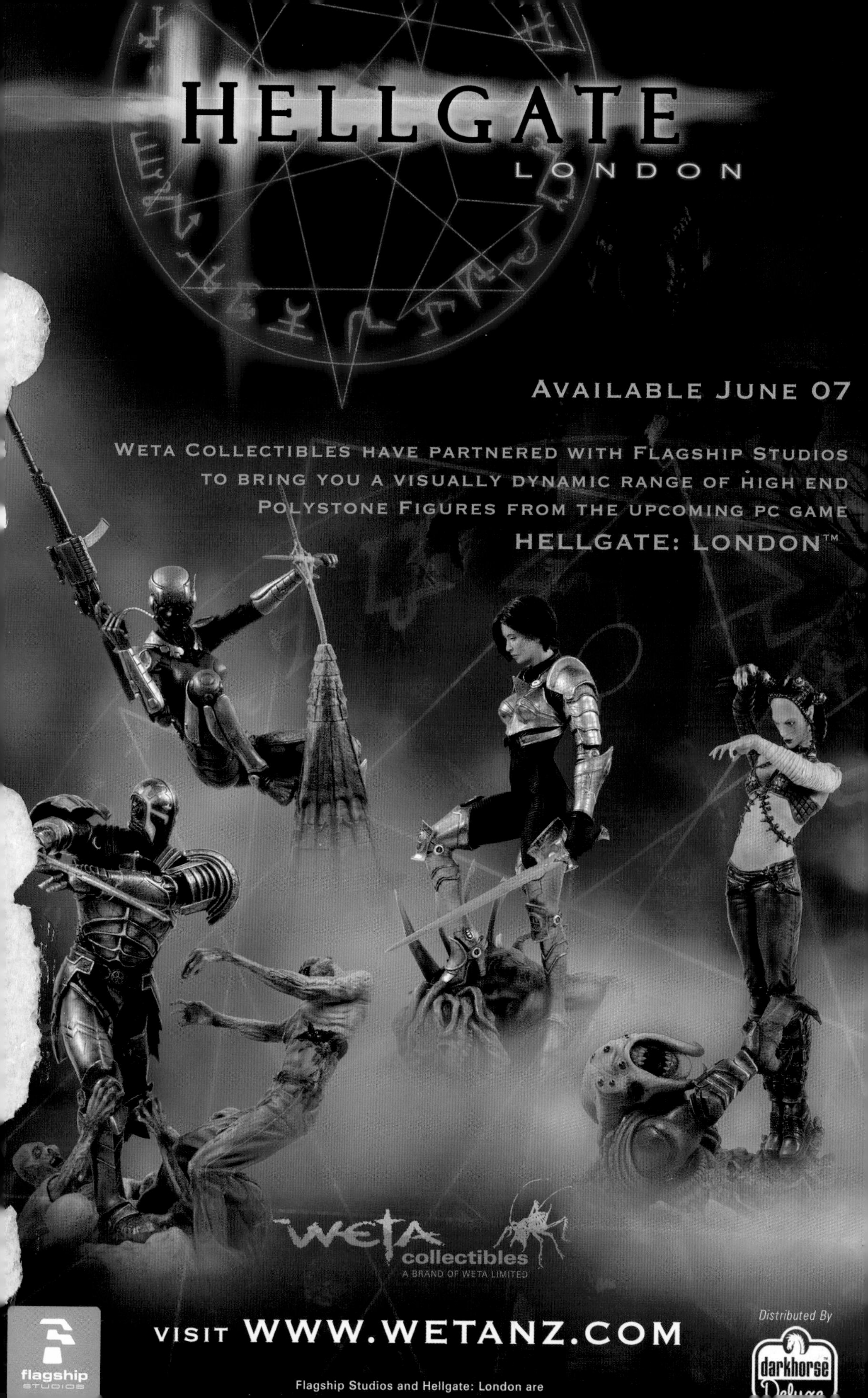
HELLGATE
LONDON
AVAILABLE JUNE 07
WETA COLLECTIBLES HAVE PARTNERED WITH FLAGSHIP STUDIOS TO BRING YOU A VISUALLY DYNAMIC RANGE OF HIGH END POLYSTONE FIGURES FROM THE UPCOMING PC GAME HELLGATE: LONDON™
WETA collectibles
A BRAND OF WETA LIMITED
flagship STUDIOS
VISIT WWW.WETANZ.COM
Distributed By
darkhorse
Flagship Studios and Hellgate: London are

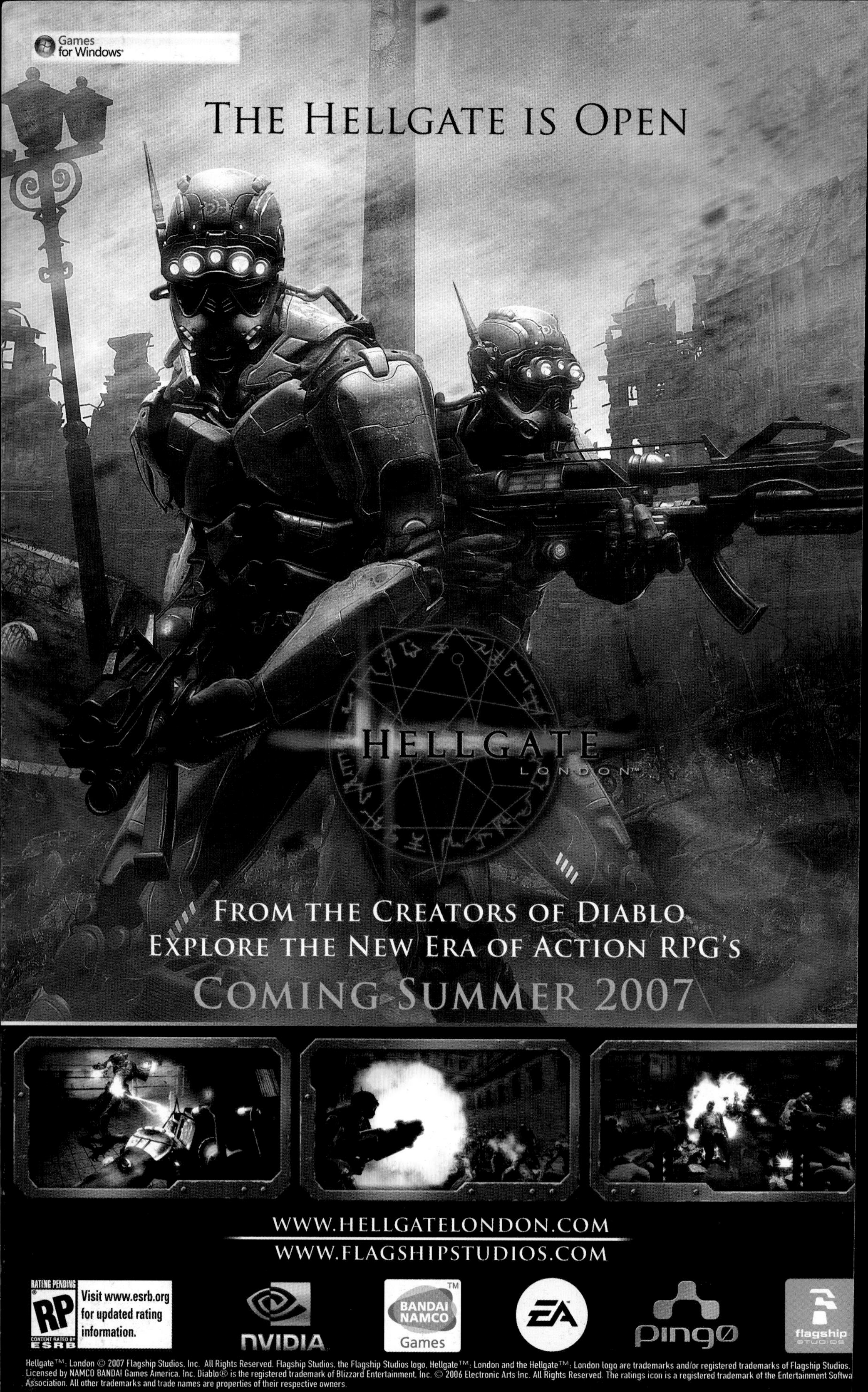
Games for Windows
THE HELLGATE IS OPEN
HELLGATE
LONDON™
FROM THE CREATORS OF DIABLO
EXPLORE THE NEW ERA OF ACTION RPG'S
COMING SUMMER 2007
WWW.HELLGATELONDON.COM
WWW.FLAGSHIPSTUDIOS.COM
RATING PENDING
RP
CONTENT RATED BY ESRB
Visit www.esrb.org for updated rating information.
NVIDIA
BANDAI NAMCO Games
EA
pingø
flagship STUDIOS
Hellgate™: London © 2007 Flagship Studios, Inc. All Rights Reserved. Flagship Studios, the Flagship Studios logo, Hellgate™: London and the Hellgate™: London logo are trademarks and/or registered trademarks of Flagship Studios. Licensed by NAMCO BANDAI Games America, Inc. Diablo® is the registered trademark of Blizzard Entertainment, Inc. © 2006 Electronic Arts Inc. All Rights Reserved. The ratings icon is a registered trademark of the Entertainment Softwa Association. All other trademarks and trade names are properties of their respective owners.